THE HABERMAS-RAWLS DEBATE

THE HABERMAS-RAWLS DEBATE

JAMES GORDON FINLAYSON

Columbia University Press
New York

Columbia University Press
Publishers Since 1893
New York Chichester, West Sussex
cup.columbia.edu

Library of Congress Cataloging-in-Publication Data
Names: Finlayson, James Gordon, author.
Title: The Habermas-Rawls debate / James Gordon Finlayson.
Description: New York : Columbia University Press, 2019. | Includes bibliographical references and index.
Identifiers: LCCN 2018043266 (print) | LCCN 2019011485 (e-book) | ISBN 9780231549011 (electronic) | ISBN 9780231164108 (cloth : alk. paper) | ISBN 9780231164115 (pbk.)
Subjects: LCSH: Habermas, Jèurgen. | Rawls, John, 1921–2002. | Political science—Philosophy.
Classification: LCC B3258.H324 (e-book) | LCC B3258.H324 F5835 2019 (print) | DDC 193—dc23
LC record available at https://lccn.loc.gov/2018043266

Columbia University Press books are printed on permanent and durable acid-free paper.

Printed in the United States of America

Cover design: Milenda Nan Ok Lee

CONTENTS

Acknowledgments vii
List of Abbreviations ix

INTRODUCTION: MUCH ADO ABOUT NOTHING 1

I. THE EARLY DEBATE

1. TWO NONRIVAL THEORIES OF JUSTICE 17

2. HABERMAS'S EARLY CRITICISMS OF RAWLS 51

II. HABERMAS'S AND RAWLS'S MATURE POLITICAL THEORIES

3. HABERMAS'S *BETWEEN FACTS AND NORMS* 79

4. RAWLS'S *POLITICAL LIBERALISM* 110

III. THE EXCHANGE

5. HABERMAS'S "RECONCILIATION THROUGH THE PUBLIC USE OF REASON" 145

6. RAWLS'S "REPLY TO HABERMAS" 174

7. "'REASONABLE' VERSUS 'TRUE'": HABERMAS'S REPLY TO RAWLS'S "REPLY" 199

IV. THE LEGACY OF THE HABERMAS-RAWLS DISPUTE

8. RELIGION WITHIN THE BOUNDS OF PUBLIC REASON ALONE 213

CONCLUSION 243

Notes 249
Bibliography 273
Index 287

ACKNOWLEDGMENTS

I would like to thank Tony Booth, Tim Carter, Andrew Chitty, James Gledhill, and Joseph Heath, whose perceptive comments and criticisms of drafts helped me greatly to improve the book. Thanks also to all my colleagues at the University of Sussex for providing a supportive and intellectually stimulating environment. The best way I can thank my wife, Blaire Bresnan, and my parents, Kathryn and Jon Finlayson, whose love and support has been unfailing, and to whom I owe more than I can say in words, is not to write another one for a while.

In the spirit of Bohumil Hrabal, I'd like to dedicate this book to all people who have not forgotten the fundamental house rules of human coexistence and who are still able to call things and events by their real names, and to recognize them for what they are.

ABBREVIATIONS

JÜRGEN HABERMAS

BFN	*Between Facts and Norms: Contributions to a Discourse Theory of Law and Democracy* (1996)
BNR	*Between Naturalism and Religion* (2008)
CES	*Communication and the Evolution of Society* (1979)
DEA	*Die Einbeziehung des Anderen* (1996)
DS	*The Dialectics of Secularization: On Reason and Religion* (2006)
EFP	*Europe: The Faltering Project* (2009)
FG	*Faktizität und Geltung* (1992)
FHN	*The Future of Human Nature* (2003)
JA	*Justification and Application: Remarks on Discourse Ethics* (1993)
JS	"Justice and Solidarity: On the Discussion Concerning 'Stage 6'" (1989)
MCCA	*Moral Consciousness and Communicative Action* (1990)
MW	"'Reasonable' Versus 'True,' or the Morality of Worldviews" (1998)
ND II	*Nachmetaphysiches Denken II: Aufsätze und Repliken* (1988)

PDM	*The Philosophical Discourse of Modernity: Twelve Lectures* (1987)
PF	*The Past as Future* (1994)
PMT	*Postmetaphysical Thinking: Philosophical Essays* (1992)
Reply 1	"Reply to Symposium Participants, Benjamin N. Cardozo School of Law" (1996)
Reply 2	"Reply to My Critics," in *Habermas and Rawls: Disputing the Political* (2011)
Reply 3	"Reply to My Critics," in *Habermas and Religion* (2013)
RPS	"Religion in the Public Sphere" (2006)
RPUR	"Reconciliation Through the Public Use of Reason: Remarks on John Rawls's Political Liberalism" (1995)
RR	*Religion and Rationality: Essays on Reason, God, and Modernity* (2002)
RW	"Richtigkeit vs. Wahrheit" (1998)
SE	"Sprechakttheoretische Erläuterungen zum Begriff der kommunikativen Rationalität" (1996)
TCA I	*The Theory of Communicative Action*, vol. 1 (1985)
TCA II	*The Theory of Communicative Action*, vol. 2 (1985)
TCC	"Towards a Communication-Concept of Rational Collective Will-Formation: A Thought-Experiment" (1989)
TIO	*The Inclusion of the Other: Studies in Political Theory* (1998)
TJ	*Truth and Justification* (2003)
VE	*Vorstudien und Ergänzungen zur Theorie des kommunikativen Handelns* (1984)
WR	*Wahrheit und Rechtfertigung* (1999)
ZNR	*Zwischen Naturalismus und Religion* (2005)

JOHN RAWLS

CP	*Collected Papers* (2001)
JFAR	*Justice as Fairness: A Restatement* (2001)
KC	"Kantian Constructivism in Moral Theory" (1980)
IPRR	"The Idea of Public Reason Revisited" (2005 [1993])
PL	*Political Liberalism* (2005)
RH	"Political Liberalism: Reply to Habermas" (1995)
TJ	*A Theory of Justice* (1972)

COLLECTIONS

HR	*Habermas and Religion* (2013)
HRDP	*Habermas and Rawls: Disputing the Political* (2011)
PRPS	*The Power of Religion in the Public Sphere* (2011)

THE HABERMAS-RAWLS DEBATE

INTRODUCTION

Much Ado About Nothing

A PHILOSOPHICAL EXCHANGE

From time to time, two great contemporary living philosophers engage each other in dispute. Sometimes when they do, their disputes become landmarks in the history of philosophy. One thinks of Leibniz's correspondence with Clarke, and his dispute with Newton over the nature of space and time, or more recently of Cassirer's debate with Heidegger at Davos on the somewhat less tractable question of what it is to be a human being. John Rawls and Jürgen Habermas are arguably the two most important, and undoubtedly the two most influential, figures in social and political philosophy of their era.

The debate between them took place in the mid-nineties shortly after both had completed monumental works of political philosophy. Habermas's *Faktizität und Geltung* was originally published in 1992 (and swiftly appeared in an excellent English translation in 1996 as *Between Facts and Norms*), while Rawls's *Political Liberalism* appeared in 1993, thirteen years later than Rawls had originally intended.[1]

According to Thomas McCarthy, the two philosophers knew each other personally, though it seems not well. In 1985, Rawls accepted an invitation to hold the Suhrkamp Lecture for the Social and Human Sciences, to take place the following year, but declined the offer of a visiting professorship in Frankfurt. They also met in Cambridge to discuss matters of common concern. In the summer of 1992, a conference on Rawls took place in Bad Homburg at which Habermas was to give a paper and Rawls to hold a plenary lecture. As it happened, Habermas had to limit his participation because he was struggling to finish the final chapter of *Faktizität und Geltung*. Sidney Morgenbesser of Columbia University, the special projects editor of the *Journal of Philosophy*, learned of the conference and wrote to Rawls, proposing a special issue of the journal "wherein you and Professor Habermas publish articles on each other's work as it relates to questions of justice."[2]

Rawls generally avoided getting involved in such disputes, finding them unfruitful, but embraced this opportunity and replied that he would talk to Habermas personally about the format. The eventual arrangement was that Habermas would make some comments about Rawls's new book to which Rawls would reply. This is an important fact if we are to properly understand the eventual shape of the dispute. Habermas approached his task as a reviewer of a new book of which he had seen an early, unpublished manuscript. Not that there was no existing literature to orient Habermas's reception: Rawls had been working on the idea of political liberalism in a series of articles from the mid- to the late 1980s, and, like everything Rawls wrote, this work had attracted much critical attention.

For his part, Rawls seems to have been fairly familiar with Habermas's work on discourse ethics. In the autumn of 1986, after returning from Frankfurt, he held a graduate seminar on Habermas's discourse ethics in which he paid close critical attention to Habermas's *Moral Consciousness and Communicative Action*. As he usually did, Rawls wrote up his notes from those seminars, including the various questions posed by students and his answers to them. A marginal comment in his written notes in which he asks of Habermas's principle (U), "Analogue or substitute for OP?" shows that he was wondering whether discourse ethics posed challenges to his own theory of justice.[3] It also shows that Rawls considered Habermas's discourse ethics to be the appropriate point of comparison with his own idea of public reason as set out in lecture VI of *Political Liberalism*.[4]

In the ensuing chapters I challenge this assumption, and I argue that it had the unfortunate consequence of derailing much of the subsequent dispute, even having a distorting effect on the work of the two disputants. It was only later, in the course of preparing his long response to Habermas's "Reconciliation Through the Public Use of Reason," that Rawls engaged with Habermas's political and democratic theory as set out in *Faktizität und Geltung*.

By the time the long-heralded Habermas–Rawls exchange appeared in the *Journal of Philosophy* in 1995, expectations were running high. Sadly, but maybe predictably given the circumstances, these initial high expectations were soon followed by a sense of disappointment in the aftermath of the exchange, which subsided into the received opinion that the exchange was a failure. Rather than providing an intellectual beacon for practical philosophers in the twentieth century, the dispute was widely judged to have been much ado about nothing.

An indicative example of such an appraisal comes from Andrew Kuper, who, in a discussion among political philosophers at Cambridge addressing the somewhat curiously framed question "How real is the Habermas–Rawls accord?" claimed that the "rapprochement" between them was "largely a failure" because of the "very different aims and limitations" of their theories (Skinner et al. 2002, 8). Six years later, Jonathan Wolff referred to it as an "exchange which other readers have felt to be a somewhat embarrassing failure of two of the greatest contemporary minds to meet" (Wolff 2008).[5]

What were the reasons for this presumed failure? The general assumption is that Habermas and Rawls failed to engage each other on the same ground. Onora O'Neill notes that their respective theories took shape in response to very different political realities—for Habermas, "the German legacy and the construction of a constitutional order" in the aftermath of nationalism, whereas "for Rawls it was the civil rights movement, and a few other struggles." She concludes that Rawls's and Habermas's respective works contain "too many premises heading in too many different directions" for there to be any deep or interesting points of agreement or disagreement between them (Skinner et al. 2002, 9).

It is often pointed out, as a kind of explanation for the exchange's failure to live up to its billing, that Rawls and Habermas worked in different traditions. Rawls's liberalism has its origins in Anglophone analytic philosophy and was inspired by his tutors at Oxford, Isaiah Berlin and H. L. A. Hart. And the method of philosophizing he developed, "constructivism," which proceeds from slender normative premises to richer normative conclusions, has its origins in his critical engagement with Kant on the one hand, and his rejection of the intuitionism of Prichard and Ross and the utilitarianism of Mill and Sidgwick on the other. Habermas's discourse theory by contrast represents a radical rethinking of the German tradition of critical social theory of Horkheimer and Adorno, a transformation he initiated in tandem with his colleague at Frankfurt, Karl-Otto Apel, and that drew on a wide variety of sources, including the "pragmaticism" of Charles Sanders Peirce and the speech-act theory of Austin and Searle. Habermas's thinking about politics and law is shaped by his critical engagement with the sociology of law, from Weber and Durkheim through to Talcott Parsons and Niklas Luhmann, and his close engagement with the German legal and political theorists Hans Kelsen and Bernhard Peters. Habermas, too, piloted political philosophy in Germany in a new direction and developed a novel approach, one he dubbed "rational reconstruction," which is supposed to reconstruct the rules and principles underlying the competences and practices of practitioners.[6]

All this may be true, but in my view, these appraisals throw little light on the dispute itself and on the alleged mutual failure to engage with each other's work. Each had a good enough grasp of the other's intellectual background to have engaged with his counterpart's project. The following two points are much more germane to what actually occurred.

First, the eventual proposal to which Habermas agreed was nothing like the idea that Morgenbesser first envisaged, namely that Rawls and Habermas would "publish articles" on "each other's work as it relates to questions of justice." It was merely for Habermas to comment on Rawls's new book, *Political Liberalism*, and for Rawls to reply. This is evident from their respective titles: Habermas's "Reconciliation Through the Public Use of Reason: Remarks on John Rawls's *Political Liberalism*" and Rawls's "*Political Liberalism*: Reply to Habermas." As Habermas would later reflect, "I saw myself at the time in the role of a reviewer who could expect a response from the author" (Reply 2, 284). And that is what happened: Habermas wrote a review of *Political Liberalism*, and Rawls replied. They did not directly debate the nature of democratic legitimacy or the role of political theory from the perspective of their own work. Had more commentators noted that fact, they may not have been so sorely disappointed.

Second, as we have just seen, neither had detailed first-hand knowledge of the other's recent work. Habermas's remit was not to bring his own newly minted theory of democratic legitimacy into play, although, as he later admitted, the fact that his own theory was in his head "may have been an obstacle" to his fully understanding *Political Liberalism*. Indeed, the full significance of that book and its salient differences from *A Theory of Justice* dawned on Habermas "only gradually" (Reply 2, 284). It is partly for this reason that Habermas later wrote a second critical article on *Political Liberalism* and a response to Rawls's "Reply": "'Reasonable' Versus 'True,' or the Morality of Worldviews." This was worked up from the text of a lecture on public reason given at a conference in October 1995, attended by Rawls, at the University of California, Santa Cruz, to celebrate the twenty-fifth anniversary of the publication of *A Theory of Justice* (TIO, 75–101). By the time he wrote this second article, Habermas believed he better understood Rawls's innovations in *Political Liberalism*. (It is for this reason Habermas now insists on having "'Reasonable' Versus 'True'" published alongside his initial article "Reconciliation Through the Public Use of Reason.") Rawls, by contrast, had invested his time in a critical reception of discourse ethics in the early 1990s, but he had had little time to digest Habermas's *Faktizität und Geltung* prior to the exchange, although he was always assiduous in such matters.

As one might expect given that I'm writing a book on the topic, I disagree with the view that the Habermas–Rawls dispute was a "failure," if that implies that it does not broach any deep and important issues and that their respective theories do not engage each other. This precipitate judgment is far too sweeping and superficial. When the exchange is examined carefully, as we will do in chapter 4, it becomes clear that, while it is the widespread and oft-repeated first word on the topic of "Habermas and Rawls," it should certainly not be the last, either on the 1995 exchange or on the broader dispute.

HABERMAS AND RAWLS: PHILOSOPHICAL COMMONALITIES

Of course, I'm not denying that Rawls and Habermas are of different intellectual formations and persuasions. It is just that such differences do not justify the precipitate judgment and anyway are much exaggerated. Indeed, they tend to conceal significant underlying affinities between the two thinkers. Both Habermas and Rawls, as we will see later, think of themselves, and are rightly thought of by others, as broadly post-Kantian, in the sense that they start from Kantian assumptions and that they welcome a Kantian interpretation of their enterprise, while rejecting the metaphysical assumptions behind Kant's project, such as his two-worlds metaphysics and the strict transcendental–empirical distinction.[7]

Furthermore, both Rawls and Habermas can be thought of as bearing the stamp of pragmatism. This is more obvious in Habermas's case, since he draws explicitly and extensively from C. S. Peirce (the pragmatic theory of truth) and G. H. Mead (the social conception of the self). And while he rejects Richard Rorty's conclusions, he engages closely with his work, as he does with Robert Brandom's, to which he is more sympathetic. The pragmatist influence on Rawls is more subterranean, for two reasons. For one thing, pragmatism is often taken to be opposed to Rawlsian "ideal theory," and, for another, W. v. O. Quine, Nelson Goodman (and Hilary Putnam) are often taken as analytic philosophers who opposed classical pragmatism. However, this standard view of pragmatism is a caricature, as Robert Talisse has shown. Pragmatism is better understood as a tangle of philosophies united by no particular doctrine but all to some degree attracted to naturalism and Darwinism (Talisse 2018).

Rawls's philosophy is clearly deeply marked by the ideas of his Harvard colleagues Goodman and Quine. His conception of "reflective equilibrium" is borrowed from Goodman's work on induction and is closely related to Quine's notion of the web of belief (Talisse 2018). Moreover, both Habermas and Rawls exhibit some of the characteristic philosophical traits of pragmatism thus understood. Both philosophers reject the assumption that philosophy or reason can play some kind of foundational role in political theory. Consequently, both *Between Facts and Norms* and *Political Liberalism* begin "in mediis rebus" (Dreben 2003, 322). Habermas's rational reconstruction is an attempt to raise instances of reflection and existing reason in everyday practices, such as communication and discourse, to the level of a systematic theory. And Rawls's quietism about metaphysical and philosophical doctrines in *Political Liberalism* is an answer to the problem of how citizens of a political community profoundly divided by the fact of reasonable pluralism can respect legitimate laws. Doubtless they appeal to different representatives of the somewhat loose and unruly group of pragmatist philosophers, and they exhibit this influence in different ways. For example, Habermas, as Rawls is quick to point out, is certainly no quietist. But the influence of pragmatism on him is at least as deep, and as important, as that of Kantianism.

In fact, the term that Habermas began to apply to his own work because of these formative philosophical influences—"Kantian pragmatism"—which is deployed as the guiding theme in a recent interpretation of his work by a leading scholar in the field, could equally be applied to Rawls (Baynes 2016, 2; see also TJ, 8, 30). So, as it happens, the fact that they worked in different philosophical traditions is not the whole truth, nor is it the decisive one. And it does not warrant the precipitate judgment. There are deep philosophical commitments both above and below the surface, which draw their distinct projects closer together and which invite interesting and fruitful comparison. This is just one reason, and not the only one, that Habermas claims his initial remarks on *Political Liberalism* "remain within the bounds of a familial dispute" (RPUR, 110).[8]

Further, it is of course true that their respective theories were developed under different political circumstances and responded to different sets of problems. Rawls's theory of distributive justice addresses the problem of how to divide the social surplus of the postwar boom, whereas Habermas was always more focused on the question of how to understand (and to protect and preserve) the moral and political basis of social integration in modern welfare-state capitalist society, particularly after the collapse of the Weimar Republic and the catastrophe of the Third Reich. But this observation must be tempered by the more obvious fact that both thinkers are liberal democrats interested in how the rights and liberties of individuals both structure and nourish democratic politics. In Rawls's case, this needs no comment. But Habermas argues in *Between Facts and Norms* (as Rawls notes in their exchange) that democratic politics "depends for its enduring life upon a liberal background culture that sustains it" (RH, 169/81).[9] Indeed, Habermas has been much criticized by Marxists and communitarians for the fact that his work turned from Marxism and critical theory in the 1960s toward liberalism in the late 1980s. Interestingly, Habermas denies this interpretation, claiming that there has been no "liberal turn" since he has been a "left-liberal, left of social democracy" with a concern for constitutional democracy since the 1960s.[10]

Not only do both Rawls and Habermas focus on, and give parallel accounts of, constitutional liberal democracy, but they both address the question of how such a political order confers legitimacy on its laws.

This is easy to see in Habermas's case since he uses the term "legitimacy" throughout his work from *Legitimation Crisis* onward, and legitimacy is a—if not *the*—key concept in *Between Facts and Norms*. Habermas inquires into the moral and political basis of legitimate law and its functional role in facilitating political will formation and social integration. By contrast, Rawls comes to the realization fairly late that the fundamental question of *Political Liberalism* is that of legitimacy. He deploys the term in that book remarkably seldom in comparison with the terms "justice" and "liberty," but the passages in which he does are among the most important (PL, 133–44). Burton Dreben sees the point clearly. Rawls is chiefly interested in how a just constitution can provide "stability for the right reasons" in a democratic society of free and equal citizens. When Rawls says that the problem of *Political Liberalism* is "how can a just society of free and equal citizens" remain stable for the right reasons under conditions of reasonable pluralism, he is assuming justice and explaining legitimacy.[11]

If this is so, then there is good reason to question the judgment that Rawls and Habermas had nothing interesting to say to each other about the very issues that were so central to their respective inquiries, issues on which they had written at such length. It would be very surprising if they really had nothing interesting to say about each other's theories. The real surprise, and what needs explaining, if anything, is why the precipitate judgment became the standard view.[12]

WHY THERE ARE ISSUES BETWEEN HABERMAS AND RAWLS

So far, I have suggested that the strategy of merely listing significant differences between the projects and approaches of Habermas and Rawls and then concluding that the two don't engage on the same terrain is not very convincing. By the same token, the argument would be no more convincing if I merely listed all the similarities between the two and countered that they do after all engage on the same terrain. At best, I could by that means call the precipitate judgment into question. What I propose to do instead is to cut through the differences in style and vocabulary between the two, to examine the questions they both raise, and to identify and bring into focus the significant claims that one of them affirms (and has to affirm) and the other denies (and has to deny). By "significant claim," I mean one that is a central organizing idea of a theory, and thus one that cannot easily be modified or dropped. And, in this way, I will bring to light the significant issues that are in dispute.

But before I go on to do that, I want to look at another line of criticism that goes in the same direction as the precipitate judgment. Two influential commentators have made arguments to the effect that even if Habermas and Rawls are engaging on the same terrain, and even if they are interested in the same questions, they nonetheless fail to engage closely, and in a philosophically interesting way, with each other's theories.

The first of these is Christopher McMahon, who has written three important articles on the dispute. One of these, the trenchantly entitled "Why There Is No Issue Between Habermas and Rawls," appeared in 2001 in the *Journal of Philosophy*, the same journal in which the original exchange took place in 1995. I call this the trenchant thesis. We will examine all McMahon's arguments in more detail in chapter 5. My rejoinder to McMahon is that, even if his argument is successful, as some of his objections against Habermas are, he shows only that one particular issue that figured in the 1995 exchange is a nonissue. That issue concerns the alleged differences between their respective devices of representation, principle (U) and the original position. McMahon does not show that these are the only issues that divide the two, nor that they are the most important ones. In my view, as I argue in chapter 5, they are not.

In a not dissimilar vein, Joseph Heath maintains that the most unsatisfying feature of the 1995 exchange between Habermas and Rawls "was the relatively low level of philosophical engagement between the two thinkers" (Heath 2011a, 115). Where McMahon directs his argument broadly against one of Habermas's criticisms of Rawls, Heath contests Rawls's interpretation of Habermas. Roughly, Rawls judged Habermas's theory to be Hegelian in a bad way, namely a comprehensive philosophical doctrine that takes all kinds of theoretical hostages to fortune; he did not consider it to be a serious rival to his own "political conception." Heath proposes his own more parsimonious interpretation of Habermas's theory of democracy as "transcendental, not metaphysical" in order to correct what he considers to be Rawls's misinterpretation.

In my interpretation, Rawls's charge that Habermas's theory is a comprehensive doctrine, while his own is not, lies at the heart of their dispute about what democratic legitimacy is and how morality relates to legitimate law. I don't see this as a misinterpretation that prevents the dispute from getting going. But I think a lot more needs to be said about which doctrines are comprehensive and why, and which are not and why. And such questions need to be directed not just to Habermas but also to Rawls. So, to that extent, I take Rawls's criticism as a fruitful point of departure for understanding what is at issue between the two philosophers.

But Heath's general point cuts the other way, too. It is true that Habermas initially had a relatively loose grasp of what Rawls was up to in *Political Liberalism* and how that book's conception of justice as fairness differed from the one set out in *A Theory of Justice*. On this matter, Habermas has been candid, as we have seen: He viewed "Reconciliation Through the Public Use of Reason," his first sally against *Political Liberalism*, simply as a book review to which he expected a reply from the author.

In my view, Habermas is not to be faulted for not immediately grasping Rawls's new intent in *Political Liberalism*, because Rawls's own ideas were nascent, to the point that, as Dreben claims, even Rawls himself did not fully grasp their implications until the paperback version of the book was published in 1996 (Dreben 2003, 331–32). As evidence, he adduces the three final chapters, in which Rawls does not distinguish between a "political conception" and a "comprehensive doctrine." Only after his exchange with Habermas, in the second introduction to the paperback version (which Dreben rightly thinks should really have been published as a second *edition* of the book), does Rawls grasp the distinction and manage to set out a clear and consistent view. So if this interpretation is right (and I think it is), Habermas, who had only the first version to go on, is not entirely to blame for not fully grasping the defining features of *Political Liberalism*.

My view of Heath's complaint is that the low level of philosophical engagement that so dissatisfies him is, in a way, only to be expected. However well formed philosophical theories aim to be, and sometimes end up being, they come into the world unfinished in one way or another. This is certainly true both of Habermas's *Between Facts and Norms* and Rawls's *Political Liberalism*. Having finished their own long books, each had to review a difficult and lengthy work that he did not fully comprehend.

In that it involved a degree of mutual misunderstanding, the Habermas–Rawls dispute is thus not peculiar. And it is no less interesting for being hard to keep score, for having no clear winner, and because it did not result in "accord." To think that the exchange should have had a clear winner, or have resulted in agreement, sets the bar too high. Virtually no philosophical dispute would conform to such a standard.

The Habermas–Rawls exchange is of interest not least because it reveals the steps and missteps by way of which two important philosophers came to understand each other's work and their own ideas better. It is of interest because it was what gave initial impetus to the effective histories of two great works of political theory. But it was also of philosophical moment, because although the debate was to an extent hit-and-miss, there were some important hits: Each philosopher makes insightful and well-placed criticisms of the other's theory, and each makes important revisions and qualifications to his own theory after reflecting on and responding to those objections.

THE OUTLINE OF THIS BOOK

Before we begin, I want to say a little about the structure of this book and the rationale for it. The Habermas–Rawls debate is not confined to the 1995 exchange and its immediate aftermath. Its roots go back much earlier, and it branches out beyond the event. Habermas was already engaging critically with Rawls's *A Theory of Justice* in his article "Legitimation Problems in the Modern State" from 1974 (CES, 178–205), and he continued to engage with Rawls's work throughout the late 1970s and into the 1980s in the series of essays in which he developed his moral theory of discourse ethics. Although Rawls does not write about Habermas's work until the exchange, we know he had read it. His library contains an annotated 1975 first English edition of *Legitimation Crisis*. Furthermore, in the 1980s and 1990s, a number of commentators and critics conducted a critical comparison of the works of Habermas and Rawls.

I call this the "early debate," though that label oversimplifies what is in fact a polyphony of voices and arguments hailing from various disciplines directed toward various targets. Rawls did not actively participate in this, though one can tell from his course outlines, his library, and his annotations and notes that he read almost every contribution to it.

Part I of this book examines the early debate. Chapter 1 adumbrates the basic concepts and arguments of Rawls's *A Theory of Justice* and Habermas's discourse ethics. Chapter 2 lays out and critically examines the following:

- Specific arguments that Habermas levels at Rawls's *A Theory of Justice* in *Moral Consciousness and Communicative Action* and elsewhere,
- Assessments of those arguments by various critics of and commentators on Habermas, and
- Arguments leveled at both Habermas's discourse ethics and Rawls's justice as fairness by communitarian and feminist critics of both.

Part I exists neither for the sake of chronology nor for the sake of completeness only, though my account is chronologically ordered and does aim to be more or less complete. The early debate is, as we will see, interesting in its own right. It is also important because it impinges on the exchange and the dispute and colors their effective history. In particular, the early debate gives impetus to interpretations and misinterpretations of both Rawls and Habermas that make the precipitate judgment appear more plausible than it is.

Part II is given over to critical expositions of Habermas's 1992 work, *Between Facts and Norms*, and Rawls's 1993 work, *Political Liberalism*. The rationale for this is plain. These works together form the indispensable backdrop to the 1995 exchange and the broader dispute between the two theorists.

These chapters are mainly expository and interpretative, though they are so with a purpose. The goal of chapter 3 is to make salient Habermas's criticisms of Rawls's *Political Liberalism*, their basis in Habermas's own discourse theory, and the features of Rawls's theory that they target.[13] The rationale for chapter 4 is slightly different, for *Political Liberalism* does not contain any specific criticisms of Habermas but is the basis for the criticisms that Rawls eventually makes. My exposition is also designed to help draw attention to Habermas's misinterpretations of *Political Liberalism*, which may cloud the issues later in the day.

Experts and advanced students already knowledgeable about Habermas's and Rawls's philosophies might want to skip lightly over chapters 3 and 4, although they may need to refer back to them when the occasion arises. (Of course, I hope that even the experts, and there are many out there, will find something of interest here, if only points of interpretation and analysis with which they disagree.) At the risk to them of going over familiar ground, however, I need to briefly summarize, in chapter 1, the argument of Rawls's *A Theory of Justice* and Habermas's discourse ethics and, in chapters 3 and 4, to set out in more detail the arguments of *Between Facts and Norms* and *Political Liberalism*. For the book is also designed to serve as a self-standing introduction to students of the philosophies of Habermas and Rawls. So parts I and II serve the dual purpose of setting the stage for the Habermas–Rawls exchange and of introducing readers to their respective philosophies. If I succeed in that, the book can also serve as an advanced introduction to two stalwart representatives of the major traditions of contemporary political philosophy.

Part III, the heart of the book, comprises chapters 5, 6, and 7, which are given over to the analysis and evaluation of two articles, Habermas's "Reconciliation Through the Public Use of Reason: Remarks on John Rawls's *Political Liberalism*" and Rawls's "*Political Liberalism*: Reply to Habermas," which appeared alongside each other in the *Journal of Philosophy* in 1995, and to Habermas's second article, "'Reasonable' Versus 'True,' or the Morality of Worldviews," which appeared in 1996 in the first edition of Habermas's *The Inclusion of the Other* (TIO, 75–105). I dedicate chapter 7 to a discussion of this article, which forms Habermas's extended response to *Political Liberalism*, and to Rawls's "Reply," and thus thematically and temporally speaking belongs to the exchange. In each chapter, I aim to identify, separate, and set aside all those criticisms that are in my view based on misinterpretations and to confine my assessment to the surviving criticisms.

Part IV deals with the legacy of the dispute. This consists in a debate about the role of religion in the political public sphere and the idea of public reason that arose in response to Rawls's view as set out in *Political Liberalism* and his 1997 article, "The Idea of Public Reason Revisited." This is a debate prosecuted by various parties, to which Habermas contributes late in the day, responding directly to Rawls.

Throughout the book, I distinguish the "exchange" from what I call the "dispute." By "dispute," I refer to theoretical differences between Habermas's theory as laid out in *Between Facts and Norms* and Rawls's theory as laid out in *Political Liberalism*—and not only the differences but also the points of contention in which the ideas of the one thinker conflict with or contradict the ideas of the other. Like the early debate, the "dispute" can be carried out not only by Habermas and Rawls but also by critics and supporters commenting on their work.

By "exchange," I refer specifically to the arguments made by Habermas and Rawls in the *Journal of Philosophy*. So the dispute is an argument with a wider frame of reference, staged between Habermas's theory as set out in *Between Facts and Norms* and Rawls's theory as set out in *Political Liberalism*. By comparison, the exchange consists largely of internal criticisms of Rawls's *Political Liberalism* by Habermas and Rawls's defense of his own position. No doubt the dispute and the exchange overlap somewhat. Habermas initiates the dispute, since some of his criticisms clearly presuppose the truth of discourse ethics or his own discourse theory of law, whereas Rawls contributes to the dispute in his "Reply" insofar as he not only defends *Political Liberalism* but also makes important criticisms of Habermas's political theory in *Between Facts and Norms*.

It is worth noting that much of the literature on the Habermas–Rawls debate, and the judgments that arose from it, including the precipitate judgment (which I reject), are judgments about the exchange, sometimes referring only to the two articles in the *Journal of Philosophy*. The evidence base of many of the conclusions drawn is slim and may have encouraged certain misapprehensions. As Thomas McCarthy rightly notes, the fact that Habermas's "Reconciliation Through the Public Use of Reason" is essentially a critical review that remains within the terms of reference of Rawls's *Political Liberalism* (and is in that sense an "internal criticism") has led some people to infer wrongly that the Habermas–Rawls debate (both the dispute and the exchange) is a contest between two rival "ideal theories." Arguably the term "ideal theory" fits what Rawls is doing in *Political Liberalism*, but to apply it to Habermas's political theory is, as we will see, an egregious mistake. There is a wider lesson here: Not everything that can be justifiably said about the exchange also applies to the dispute, and much that is does not.

I

THE EARLY DEBATE

1

TWO NONRIVAL THEORIES OF JUSTICE

1.1 RAWLS'S *A THEORY OF JUSTICE* IN A NUTSHELL

We begin with Rawls's conception of justice as fairness as set out in *A Theory of Justice* in the early 1970s. This landmark book is enormous, particularly in its reach and influence, and I cannot hope to do justice to it here. I also want to avoid repeating summaries that have been set out much more ably elsewhere.[1] This exposition will be highly stylized and abbreviated. Its purpose is to bring into focus certain salient features of justice as fairness, as set out in Rawls's early book, that arise in the exchange, play a role in the dispute, and, in one way or another, shape Habermas's interpretation and understanding of Rawls's philosophy.

1.1.1 THE ARGUMENT FROM THE ORIGINAL POSITION AND THE VEIL OF IGNORANCE

The chief aim of *A Theory of Justice* is to lay out and justify the most appropriate conception of justice for a democratic society comprising free and equal citizens (TJ, viii, xviii). One of the main ways Rawls does this is through the device of the original position. The original position is a hypothetical-choice situation that models the ideal perspective of persons who regard themselves as free and equal and who have the two moral powers: a capacity for an effective sense of justice and a capacity for a conception of the good. The parties in the original position are thus assumed to be economically rational in the sense that, other things being equal, they prefer a greater share of primary social goods to a lesser one. They are also reasonable in the sense that they are disposed to act according to their moral powers provided others do so. Their rationality and reasonability connect with their pursuit of three higher- or highest-order interests, which follow from their two moral powers. They aim to advance their conception of the good, whatever it is. And they seek conditions under which they can exercise and develop their two moral powers. These are the interests in the light of which they choose principles of justice.

Higher-order interests they may be, but they are the chooser's own interests. Rawls stipulates that the choosers in the original position are "mutually disinterested," in the sense that they take no interest in other people's interests (provided those other people's interests do not affect their own) (TJ, 13). Consequently, they will strive to ensure the best share of primary social goods for themselves, whatever their conception of the good life may be. They are not motivated by envy and so will not forgo the enjoyment of a good in order to deny it to others.

Rawls's argument is that the principles of justice that would be chosen by rational persons thus construed are thereby "explained and justified" on the basis of slender, rational premises: "The theory of justice is a part, perhaps the most significant part, of the theory of rational choice" (TJ, 16).

These moral persons or choosers stand in for flesh-and-blood citizens and are charged with the task of agreeing on principles of justice that are to regulate their social and political institutions. The original position is not an actual contract, the results of which are binding on those who enter into it, so much as a thought experiment designed to clarify our considered convictions about justice. Though the description of the situation contains idealizations, Rawls nonetheless insists that the "conditions . . . in the description of the situation are ones we do in fact accept" (TJ, 587). Thus, the real citizens for whom the persons in the original position are delegates ought, insofar as they are reasonable and rational, to accept the decision on the principles reached by those delegates, Rawls argues.

The parties to the original position, tasked with deciding upon principles of justice, stand under what Rawls calls a "veil of ignorance," meaning they are deprived of information about their future status and standing in the society to be regulated by the principles they choose. For example, they do not know their gender, physical attributes, race, class, talents, or degree of wealth. They are deprived of any information that might prompt them to tailor their choice of principles to benefit themselves (TJ, 12). This is important because the choosers in the original position are assumed to be rational in the economic sense described earlier: They can rank their final ends consistently, select the most effective means to their ends, and, all things considered, prefer more of their ends to be satisfied than less. They are not so deprived of information that they cannot make rational decisions. They know general, uncontroversial facts about human beings and political associations that have been established by psychology and the social and natural sciences. They understand basic economic concepts, and they know about what Rawls calls the "circumstances of justice," namely that conditions of moderate scarcity and limited altruism obtain. They also know what "primary social goods" are, and they know that these are essential to anyone who wants to live a good life. All told, in Rawls's view, they have sufficient information to make an informed and rational choice of principles of justice but not enough to rig the decision in their favor.

The veil of ignorance introduces the idea of formal equality into the model in the sense that equal persons are to be treated equally and that everyone is "situated symmetrically" in the original position (TJ, 4). At the same time, Rawls thinks, it filters out reasons that are irrelevant to the goal of determining principles of justice for a society of free and equal citizens and constrains them in their deliberation as rational choosers only to adduce reasons germane to the task at hand. Thus, with the veil of ignorance in place, the original position first models fairness, namely what "we," here and now, consider to be fair conditions under which the choosers are to agree to the principles that are to regulate the basic structure and, second, models good reasons, namely what "we" consider to be acceptable constraints on the reasons that can properly be put forward for the said purpose.

For our purposes, we do not have to go into the details of Rawls's argument for why he thinks that choosers in the original position behind the veil of ignorance would and should opt for the two principles of justice set out below, rather than any of the existing alternative conceptions of justice, such as utilitarianism, rational intuitionism, or perfectionism. Suffice it to say that the argument aspires to do just that. The point of the original-position thought experiment is to establish the superiority of Rawls's two principles over existing alternative conceptions. The fact that rational and reasonable persons, so conceived, would choose the two principles under such conditions is not itself supposed to be a logical deduction of the two principles of justice but an argument in their favor.

1.1.2 THE PRINCIPLES OF JUSTICE

A Theory of Justice centers on two principles of what Rawls later calls "domestic justice" for a liberal constitutional democratic polity:

- First principle: "Each person is to have an equal right to the most extensive total system of equal basic liberties compatible with a similar system of liberty for all" (TJ, 60, 302).
- Second principle: "Social and economic inequalities are to be arranged so that they are both (a) to the greatest benefit of the least advantaged . . . , [and] (b) attached to offices and positions open to all" (TJ, 60, 302).

These two principles are, Rawls holds, to be lexically ordered such that the first principle must be satisfied before the second comes into play. This is because liberty can be constrained only by liberty (TJ, 266). That is, liberty has ultimate value in that it cannot be traded off against any other good or value.

Later Rawls reformulates the first principle to make clear that he does not presuppose that there is one preeminent value, "liberty," toward which a constitutional democracy must aim, but rather a list of basic rights and liberties that we have historically come to have and that are adequate for the development and full exercise of the two moral powers possessed by every free and equal person. The two moral powers are not ranked but stand alongside each other (JFAR, 18–19, 45).

The second principle is a version of the republican ideal that dates back at least to Aristotle: that in a good polis, laws should operate in and be made to serve the common interest. It includes the "difference principle": that inequalities are to be arranged so that they benefit the least advantaged most.

Although they are to be taken together, broadly speaking, the first principle regulates constitutional essentials, whereas the second is a distributive principle regulating social and economic institutions under given actual conditions, or what Rawls calls "matters of basic justice," which allow for the best approximation to perfect justice.

Since Rawls's is a theory of social justice, he takes the subject of justice to be the basic structure of society, namely "the way in which the major social institutions . . . determine the division of advantages from social cooperation" (TJ, 6). That is, in the first instance, justice as fairness applies to domestic policy in liberal constitutional democracies and not to the sphere of global justice (the lawful and legitimate relations between states). It is supposed to apply generally to the basic political, social, and economic institutions of a liberal democratic polity. Just what these are is a matter of controversy. For example, in *A Theory of Justice*, Rawls says that the monogamous family is part of the basic structure, but he later, to the consternation of some feminist critics, appears to deny that the principles of justice apply directly to it (Munoz-Dardé 1998, 335–36).[2] Still, it is clear that the principles are meant to impose just constraints on the constitutional and institutional design of a society understood as a cooperative endeavor between free and equal citizens. The importance of this point, which we will come to later, is that that, although *A Theory of Justice* sets out universal principles of domestic justice for a liberal constitutional democratic state, it is not supposed to be what Rawls will later call "a moral doctrine of justice general in scope," that is, a moral doctrine to regulate all actions of individuals within a democratic state (PL, xvii).

Connected to the idea of the basic structure is the notion of "primary social goods," which are what Rawls takes to be the basis of interpersonal comparison. Primary social goods are defined as those goods that citizens require for the realization of their final ends, whatever those ends are, or, to put it another way, the goods that any rational person will want, whatever else they want. Rawls describes the primary social goods in broad terms as "rights and liberties, opportunities and powers, income and wealth" and later adds freedom of movement, choice of occupation against a background of opportunities, and the social bases of self-respect (JFAR, 58–59; TJ, 7–10). These are the essential conditions and the basic building blocks of the development of a sense of justice, as well as a conception of the good and its full exercise by free and equal citizens, and it is the citizens' shares of primary social goods over the course of their complete lives that the two principles are to regulate.

1.1.3 THE FOUR-STAGE SEQUENCE

The four-stage sequence is a framework that Rawls devises to elaborate on the original position and simplify the various complications that arise in the application of the principles of justice (TJ, 195–96). Each stage introduces a perspective whereby the veil of ignorance is partly lifted so that new information can be fed in. The stages interlock, with each inheriting the constraints adopted at preceding stages (TJ, 200). The first stage is "constitutional convention," in which the parties are assumed to be delegates charged with choosing a constitution. At the second stage, the parties become legislators enacting laws according to the constitution and the principles of justice. At the third stage, the parties with more refined knowledge of society are able to endorse specific laws that realize the two principles in the agreed constitutional framework. At the final stage, the parties assume the role of judges, interpreting the constitution and laws as members of the judiciary. Rawls writes, "The flow of information is determined at each stage by what is required to apply these principles intelligently to the kind of question of justice at hand" (TJ, 200). At no stage, however, is the veil lifted so much that the parties gain information about themselves, their social standing, or their interests that would enable them to bias their decisions in their own favor.

1.1.4 THE KANTIAN INTERPRETATION

As Samuel Freeman points out, Rawls's original position is an "account of the moral point of view with regard to matters of justice" (Freeman 2016).[3] There are various accounts of the moral point of view in the history of philosophy, but the one that is uppermost in Rawls's mind in *A Theory of Justice* is that represented by Kant's categorical imperative. Indeed, Rawls deliberately invites the comparison between Kant's moral theory and justice as fairness. He claims that his principles of justice are categorical imperatives in Kant's sense, not because they are general and universal, but because they are the expression of the interests of free and equal moral persons (TJ, 253). He points out that the veil of ignorance deprives the choosers of information about themselves that would "enable them to choose heteronomous principles," because parties in the original position lack any "particular desires" and have only a "preference for primary goods . . . derived from only the most general assumptions about rationality and the conditions of human life" (TJ, 253). He notes that his assumption of the "mutual disinterest" of the choosers' motivations links his conception to the "Kantian idea of autonomy," and he concludes as follows:

> The original position may be viewed, then, as a procedural interpretation of Kant's conception of autonomy and the categorical imperative. The principles regulative of the kingdom of ends are those that would be chosen in this position, and the description of this situation enables us to explain the sense in which acting from these principles expresses our nature as free and equal rational persons. (TJ, 256)

Rawls acknowledges in passing that justice as fairness adds to Kant's theory in important respects; for example, the principles chosen in the original position are "to apply to the basic structure" and facts about the basic structure enter into the derivation of the principles.

In his later lectures on "Kantian Constructivism in Moral Theory," Rawls makes some detailed remarks about his method of political philosophy and the task of political philosophy. There he argues that there is an analogy between justice as fairness and Kant's philosophy as a whole in certain fundamental respects, though he puts far less emphasis on the analogy between Kant's categorical imperative and the original position. In broad terms, Rawls uses the term "constructivist" to describe a philosophical theory in ethics that justifies substantive principles on the basis of slender and supposedly uncontroversial claims about reason, action, and a certain conception of the person. In these lectures, however, Rawls is generally—though perhaps not so much in his title—more cautious about the putative analogy between justice as fairness and Kant's moral theory. In particular, he observes that justice as fairness "assigns primacy to the social," since, in his theory, a conception of justice is arrived at collectively, by "fellow citizens," such that the hypothesis of the parties reaching agreement in the original position is merely a way of interpreting this prior understanding (KC, 552). By contrast, Kant's account of the categorical imperative is a procedure "undertaken singly by each individual for the purpose of judging . . . personal maxims of . . . individuals in everyday life" (KC, 552). In other words, justice as fairness involves a different kind of procedure, and has a different sphere of application, from Kant's categorical imperative (see O'Neill 2015, 74–75).[4]

1.1.5 REFLECTIVE EQUILIBRIUM

Rawls imposes a further condition of adequacy on the principles that would be chosen by rational parties behind the veil of ignorance. The chosen principles must fit with the parties' considered judgments about justice in a state of reflective equilibrium. Reflective equilibrium is a state of maximal coherence among one's beliefs on a matter—here, on the appropriate principles of justice for the basic institutions of society.

Reflective equilibrium is not just a state but also a method. As Norman Daniels describes it,

> The method of reflective equilibrium consists in working back and forth among our considered judgments . . . about particular instances or cases, the principles or rules that we believe govern them, and the theoretical considerations that we believe bear on accepting these considered judgments, principles, or rules, revising any of these elements wherever necessary in order to achieve an acceptable coherence among them. (Daniels 2003)

The considered judgments are comparatively fixed points in our belief system, the credibility of which depends on grounds distinct from their coherence with our other beliefs.[5] Scanlon argues that the method consists in first finding "principles that account for those judgments in which we feel most confidence" and that have been decided upon under favorable epistemic conditions (Scanlon 2003, 144).[6] The method can be carried out by persons acting individually or jointly. It may be more effective when carried out jointly, but, in principle, collective reasoning is not required for the method to achieve its aim of establishing coherence among a set of beliefs.

Reflective equilibrium can be both narrow and wide.[7] Narrow reflective equilibrium strives to achieve coherence among "general convictions, first principles, and considered judgments" and does so with the fewest possible revisions. By contrast, wide reflective equilibrium considers alternative conceptions of justice and the relevant arguments for them: "In a wide reflective equilibrium, for example, we broaden the field of relevant moral and non-moral beliefs (including general social theory)" (Daniels 2003). The broader the set of beliefs, the harder it is to achieve the state of reflective equilibrium, but the better justified are the beliefs in such a state.

What this means for the argument from the original position is that the principles of justice, together with the arguments for them, complete with all the normative ideas and assumptions contained in the device of the veil of ignorance, the ideas of free and equal persons and of society as a fair, cooperative venture, should be in reflective equilibrium with each other and with considered particular judgments. Furthermore, the principles of justice should also cohere with arguments for other elements of justice as fairness, such as the argument for autonomy, which demonstrates the congruence of justice and the good. And the whole conception of justice as fairness should be tested against rival conceptions and the arguments for them. The justificatory role of establishing reflective equilibrium need not, however, be seen as a separate test, carried out on the principles decided upon in the original position, for the original position itself can be construed as a component of a broader process of seeking reflective equilibrium, such that reflective equilibrium "works through the original position" (Freeman 2007, 39).

1.1.6 THE STANDARD BLUEPRINT

Before we turn to Habermas's discourse ethics, which provides the context for the early debate, I need to say a word here about what A. S. Laden has called the "standard blueprint" for interpreting *A Theory of Justice*, not just because it was widespread at the time, but rather because, as I will argue, it shows the way in which Habermas interprets Rawls's first work. As Laden puts it, according to the standard blueprint,

1. Rawls is engaged in a grand philosophical project,
2. he advances a philosophical theory in the traditional sense of that word,
3. this theory starts from an account of human rationality and proceeds from slender normative premises, and
4. the theory aims to show the rationality of justice via its centerpiece, the argument from the original position for the two principles of justice (Laden 2003, 384).

Whether this approach to Rawls's early work is justified, all things considered, is a moot point. The approach is motivated by some of Rawls's remarks, for example, about the relation between Rawls's theory of justice and the social contract tradition (TJ, 11) and its being the most important part of the theory of rational choice (TJ, 16).[8] For the moment, it suffices to point out that this way of reading Rawls was widespread in the literature and is endorsed by Habermas's interpretation, which, as we will see, entirely colors his criticisms of Rawls.

1.2 HABERMAS'S DISCOURSE ETHICS

We now turn to Habermas's discourse ethics. Discourse ethics is a moral theory that developed out of Habermas's first work, *The Theory of Communicative Action*, published in the early 1980s. In what follows, I shall not offer a critical analysis or evaluation of Habermas's background theory of communication. I note only that it is extensive, comprising a theory of social action, a pragmatic theory of the meaning of assertoric and moral statements, a theory of truth, a moral phenomenology, a reconstruction and defense of the moral point of view, and a sociological account of the social function of morality. As any such theory would, it contains a lot of controversial claims. My primary purpose is to lay it out in as much detail as is necessary for us to understand the context in which, and the vantage point from which, the early debate with Rawls is prosecuted.

Unlike Habermas's later theory of democratic legitimacy, and unlike Rawls's *A Theory of Justice*, no single complete work sets out Habermas's discourse ethics. Rather, it is an evolving research project sketched out in incomplete fashion in a series of essays. The most important of these are contained in two collections: *Moral Consciousness and Communicative Action*, first published in 1983, and *Justification and Application*, most of which originally appeared in 1991. In these books, Habermas outlines and defends a quite different conception of justice from that of Rawls.[9]

To call discourse ethics a moral theory is not really to do justice to its peculiarities. It is by no means a standard normative moral theory of what one ought to do and why. Rather, it is a broadly Durkheimian social theory of morality, reinterpreted in the light of Habermas's theory of communication.

1.2.1 DISCOURSE ETHICS AND *THE THEORY OF COMMUNICATIVE ACTION*

When I say that Habermas approaches morality from the perspective of social theory, I mean that he sees morality, and its basis in communication and discourse, as the solution to a social problem that afflicts citizens and social agents in modern societies. We can call this the problem of social order for short, though it is really a number of related problems of how to establish social order, to bring about social integration, and to continue the process of social and cultural reproduction in a stable and predictable manner. The problem arises, Habermas argues, because modernization processes, including, but not limited to, industrialization, urbanization, the increasing movement of people, the effects of education and technology, the capitalist economy, and the system of modern law, have resulted in the erosion of settled habits and customs, the dismantling of traditions, and the fragmentation of the shared basis of meaning and understanding that hitherto provided the basis of social order and sociocultural reproduction. As Marx and Engels wrote in *The Communist Manifesto*, "All that is solid melts into air. All that is holy is profaned" (McLellan 2000, 248).

To cope with the resulting fluidity of modern life, social agents have to renew the basis of social order and sociocultural reproduction. The trouble, as Habermas puts it in *The Philosophical Discourse of Modernity*, is that modernity cannot borrow sources of normativity from the past, but henceforth "has to create its normativity out of itself" (PDM, 7). There is no shared ethos, no overarching religious doctrine, no underlying universal moral order on which members of modern societies can rely to fix their beliefs, to coordinate their attitudes and interactions, and to ensure their peaceful and conflict-free coexistence. Rather, modern social agents have continually to thematize, to negotiate, and to rationally agree on the terms of their interaction and the basis of their common life. And all this has to be done, as it were, on the fly, in a way that keeps pace with the various processes of modernization that continually dissolve and set aflow the normative substance of society, such as shared religious traditions. The only medium through which this ongoing task can be accomplished, according to Habermas, is that of communication and its reflexive counterpart, discourse. It is through communication and discourse that subjects can reach reasoned agreement with one another, for, as Habermas puts it in *The Theory of Communicative Action*, "reaching understanding is the inherent telos of human speech" (TCA I, 287). However, this is a very demanding process that places enormous cognitive, motivational, and organizational burdens on individual agents and that faces the ever-present danger of disagreement leading to social conflict.

1.2.2 DISCOURSE ETHICS AND THE PRAGMATIC THEORY OF MEANING

To understand how communication and discourse can solve these problems, we have to delve into Habermas's idea of communicative action in a little more detail. The key point here is that Habermas is able to show how the procedure of moral argumentation (discourse) and the moral principle (U) are embedded in and derived from the social structure of communicative action.

Habermas's pragmatic theory of understanding in *The Theory of Communicative Action* states that there are three basic kinds of speech act, characterized by three different validity claims: to truth, to rightness, and to truthfulness (TCA I, 75). A validity claim, according to Habermas, is a pragmatic guarantee to justify one's utterance (or action), if called upon to do so, which each speaker cannot but provide if they speak or act sincerely.

The central idea is that the meaning (and understanding) of an utterance or speech act depends on its validity claim, which means that it depends on the reasons that the speaker could adduce to support it and their acceptance by the hearer. Habermas refers to this as the "validity basis of meaning." The pragmatic and social-ontological consequences of speech issue from the validity basis of meaning, that is, from the reasons that implicitly underlie speech act offers. The meanings established by speech rest in part on reasons, and these reasons constitute the rationality of the social world and ensure its stability. On the everyday plane of communication, the appeal to reasons, which the speaker or actor cannot but make, remains largely implicit, as does the acceptance of the reasons by the speaker. But whenever a validity claim is not accepted but challenged by a hearer, the interlocutors switch from the plane of action to the plane of discourse or argumentation. Discourses are, Habermas contends, a reflective form of communication or "understanding-oriented action that, so to speak, sit on top of the latter" (JS, 245). Discourse is a reflective medium in which a problematized or disrupted consensus can be renewed or replaced whenever first-order communication breaks down and the shared meanings and understandings that normally coordinate interactions and secure social integration are disrupted (JS, 245–46). So discourse is argumentation—*not* a verbal free-for-all but a disciplined practice governed by rules.

Habermas identifies three levels of rules. On the first level are the basic rules of logic, such as the principle of contradiction, and the basic semantic rules of universalizability and consistency: "(1.1) No speaker may contradict himself. (1.2) Every speaker who applies predicate F to object A must be prepared to apply F to all other objects resembling A in all relevant respects. (1.3) Different speakers may not use the same expression with different meanings" (MCCA, 86).

On the second level are procedural norms, such as the principles of sincerity and accountability, namely that all participants must undertake, if only implicitly, to assert only what they genuinely believe and always either to justify upon request what they assert or to provide reasons for not offering a justification. These are, Habermas contends, preconditions for all genuine argumentation, that is, argumentation conceived as a "search for truth" (MCCA, 87–88).

On the third level are the processual preconditions that immunize discourse against coercion, repression, and inequality, and against all persuasive forces except the "unforced force of the better argument," and these must be followed if a rationally motivated consensus is to be reached.

Habermas concludes from this that certain basic norms or rules of discourse can be reconstructed from the idealizing pragmatic preconditions to which participants in discourse are always already committed:

1. Every subject with the competence to speak and act is allowed to take part in the discourse.
2. Everyone is allowed to question any assertion whatsoever.
   a. Everyone is allowed to introduce any assertion whatsoever into the discourse.
   b. Everyone is allowed to express his attitudes, desires and needs.
3. No speaker may be prevented, by internal or external coercion, from exercising his rights as laid down in (1) and (2) above. (ED, 161; MCCA, 89).[10]

This is not a complete set of rules, but rather examples of rules for the third level, which Habermas culls from the work of the German legal theorist Robert Alexy (MCCA, 89).[11] That said, they are the only rules that he discusses in detail and the ones that seem to do most of the work for him. Habermas does not give a justification for them. Indeed he thinks that such rules cannot be justified by argument, because they are pragmatic preconditions of argumentation. But it can be shown that these rules are in fact such preconditions, because one cannot deny them without falling prey to a "performative contradiction" (MCCA, 95). In other words, the rules of discourse can be shown to have no alternatives, since one invokes them by dint of beginning to argue.[12]

1.2.3 THE PRINCIPLES OF DISCOURSE ETHICS

The key idea of Habermas's discourse ethics is principle (U). The "U" stands for "universalization":

> (U) A norm is valid if and only if the foreseeable consequences and side effects of its general observance for the interests and value-orientations of each individual could be freely accepted jointly by all concerned. (TIO, 42)[13]

I will investigate the principle in more detail later on. But first I want to briefly state how Habermas proposes to justify it theoretically. For unlike the rules of discourse, principle (U) is in need of justification; indeed, as the subtitle of his major essay indicates, Habermas conceives discourse ethics as a "program of philosophical justification" (MCCA, 43).[14] Of course, (U) is justified insofar as it is a correct reconstruction of the practice of moral discourse. But in addition to (U) capturing our intuitions about moral argument, Habermas contends that it can be derived "philosophically." Occasionally, he makes statements that imply that (U) can be derived directly from the rules of discourse. For example, he claims that "Discourse ethics . . . derives the contents of a universalistic morality from the general presuppositions of argumentation" (JS, 245).[15] And indeed his proposed derivation went through several versions, but the version he settled on is that (U) is derived via some kind of inference from the conjunction of the rules of discourse set out earlier and a weaker, less frequently formulated principle (D) (see Rehg 1991; Ott 1996; Lumer 1997)[16]:

> (D) Only those norms can claim to be valid that meet (or could meet) with the approval of all affected in their capacity as *participants in a practical discourse*. (MCCA, 66)

(D) states that it is a necessary condition of the validity of practical norms that it meet with the reasoned agreement of all affected. Unlike (U), then, it is not a biconditional, which also states what it is for a moral norm to be valid. Habermas takes (D) to be relatively uncontroversial. It is just what moral justification is assumed to be by mature, modern moral agents in modern, fully rationalized societies.[17] According to the view in question, principle (U) is adequately justified if it can be "derived" from two premises:

1. The normative (but nonmoral) preconditions of argumentation in general (MCCA, 92).
2. A "weak [that is, nonmoral] idea of normative justification" or "the conception of normative justification in general as expressed in (D)" (MCCA, 92, 97, 198).[18]

I have argued elsewhere that premise 2 presupposes Habermas's modernization theory, which conceals rich normative assumptions (Finlayson 2000a, 335). The same claim, namely that it is heavily moralized, has also been made about premise 1. Together, these suspicions undermine the idea that Habermas's argument is a form of constructivism that argues from slender premises about rationality to richer normative conclusions. In itself, that might not be an objection to Habermas (although it renders the argument somewhat less powerful and thwarts one of his original intentions, which was to refute moral skepticism).[19] For it safeguards the argument from the suspicion that it violates Hume's law by deriving a moral ought from premises that do not contain any. The main problem with the argument construed as a formal derivation is that it is formally invalid, since principle (U)—as a biconditional—does not follow from the conjunction of the two premises.[20]

However, Habermas hedges his bets by also maintaining that (U) can be given a weaker defense as an "abduction" or as what might more accurately be called an inference to the best explanation. Habermas contends that by one of these routes we can *philosophically* justify principle (U) as the single underlying moral principle, the social function of which is to coordinate moral actions and hence provide the underlying moral basis of social order.

1.2.4 PRINCIPLE (U) AS A TEST OF UNIVERSALIZABILITY

Habermas conceives the moral point of view as one accessible to subjects who, as participants in discourse, encounter one another on the first and second person axis. In his view, impartiality is attained by each person's actively exploring their own interests while allowing their own assessment of a norm to be shaped by their equally active exploration of the interests of everyone else:

> This impartial standpoint overcomes the subjectivity of the individual participant's perspective without becoming disconnected from the performative attitude of the participants. (JA, 13)

In Habermas's model, all participants must project themselves into the positions of every other *seriatim* and imaginatively identify and empathize with their interests, desires, and so forth in order that each person's partiality acts as a corrective to everyone else's partiality. The result is a kind of self-correcting mechanism by which biases of individual perspective are knocked out and participants are able to forge "the social bond that unites humanity as a whole" (JA, 130). The social bond of which Habermas speaks consists in part in morality, and its internal structure is articulated by the rules of discourse (especially 2 [a] and [b] iii, above).[21]

The key notion in (U) is thus that of a universalizable or generalizable interest. (U) states that only those norms that embody the interests of each participant are justified in discourse and as such can be freely accepted by all in an ideally prosecuted discourse. The discursive consensus to which all valid norms must be amenable will give "equal consideration" to the interests of each person concerned (BFN, 108).[22] This means that a norm will be justified if, and only if, it satisfies the interests of all concerned and is adopted by everyone because they can see that it does. This is what Habermas has in mind when he uses more compressed descriptions of valid moral norms such as "equally good for all," "equally in everyone's interest," and embodying "universally shared," "common," "general," or "universalizable" interests.

Among contemporary theorists who investigate the moral significance of the idea of the common interest, G. H. Mead has the most direct impact on Habermas's work. For Mead, the idea of the common interest captures the social significance of the institution of morality:

> When we reach the question of what is right . . . the only test we can set up is whether we have taken into account every interest involved. (Mead 1967, 386)[23]

In Habermas's discourse theoretical model, then, morality is the standpoint we take when we accept only those norms that have been discursively tested and demonstrated to be in the equal interest of everyone, that is, not only *all* participants in discourse, but also *all* those affected by the norm in question.

Without going into the details, we can see from this that, to misquote Rawls, for Habermas, justice is the first principle of the domain of social interaction, as truth is of systems of thought, or, as Ciaran Cronin nicely puts it, "Habermas treats the sphere of the moral as coextensive with questions of justice" (JA, xviii). In other words, Habermas claims that the central moral intuition of modern morality (and moral theories), which discourse ethics sets out to rationally reconstruct, is that "only such norms as embody generalizable interests correspond to our conception of justice" (MCCA, 78). Since justice, as Habermas conceives it here, is equivalent with moral rightness, I refer to this conception henceforth as justice-qua-morality.

1.2.5 HABERMAS'S MORAL COGNITIVISM: THE ANALOGY BETWEEN TRUTH AND RIGHTNESS

Habermas denies that normative sentences can be true (or false) "in the same sense in which descriptive sentences can be true or false" (MCCA, 56; TCA I, 297). Rather, he contends, moral utterances make validity claims to rightness but do not make validity claims to truth. In this respect, he shares an assumption common to many who describe themselves as "non-cognitivists," because he holds that, strictly speaking, no moral utterance or statement is true, or even aspires to truth. Habermas makes this assumption because he assumes that to deny it would commit him to moral realism, and he rejects moral realism. Moral realism, as Habermas understands it, involves the positing of mind-independent (or language-independent) moral values and properties and thus threatens to burden moral theory with an outlandish ontology.[24] But Habermas endorses moral cognitivism, though by this he means just that moral norms and statements are reason sensitive and apt to be justified in similar ways to assertive statements or fact-stating discourse.[25] So Habermas's conception of moral cognitivism rests on the thesis that there is an analogy between truth and rightness, but that it is an *only* analogy (DEA, 50ff.; JA, 39–40; MCCA, 56, 65, 196; VE, 144): "The rightness [*Richtigkeit*] of moral norms (or of general normative statements) and of particular normative injunctions based on them can then be understood as analogous to the truth of descriptive statements" (TIO, 38).[26]

This raises the question of what the analogy consists in. Habermas's view seems to be that moral discourse has a surface similarity with theoretical discourse in that it behaves in syntactically and grammatically similar ways to propositional logic. Habermas claims, for example, that he "has never doubted that valid moral statements behave logically just like true descriptive statements."[27] If we ask what the ground of this underlying isomorphism is, Habermas's answer is that both normative rightness and truth are specifications of a generic underlying conception of validity.[28] To grasp Habermas's position here, we need to know what the analogs are. Now, Habermas himself does not do this, so the following exposition is mine. I have done it in a way that makes as plain as possible what his view of the analogy between truth and rightness consists in.

Truth as a Validity Claim

Habermas's conception of truth as a validity claim is roughly this: Whenever a speaker asserts *p*, he or she unavoidably (if only implicitly) claims that *p* is true. The truth of what is asserted has a necessary pragmatic connection with the rationally motivated consensus (*Verständigung*) of participants in an ideally prosecuted discourse. This view can be captured with the following formula:

> (T) For any assertion *p*: If *p* is true, then *p* is amenable to rationally motivated consensus.

The speaker is pragmatically committed to the truth of what is asserted. The speaker shows this commitment by undertaking to "redeem" or to "make good" his or her validity claim to truth, that is, to justify the assertion (what is asserted, namely *p*) when challenged, questioned, or just not understood by the hearer. And by the very act of making an assertion, the speaker must suppose that every participant in discourse can assent to *p* on the basis of the reasons that can be adduced in support of it in an ideally prosecuted discourse of all concerned. A discourse is ideally prosecuted and the resultant consensus rationally motivated when the rules of discourse are adequately followed. In this way, Habermas contends, truth can be understood pragmatically as a specification of an underlying generic notion of validity (*Gültigkeit*); that is, it is a construct of a single underlying pragmatic norm of correctness.

Unfortunately, Habermas does not say nearly enough about what the underlying generic concept of validity is, but at the heart of it lies the connection between reasons and ideal justifiability in discourse:

(V) For any *x*: If *x* is valid, then *x* is amenable to rationally motivated consensus.

It is this basic notion of "validity," rather than the concepts of truth and truth-conditions, which is the underlying explanatory idea in Habermas's pragmatic theory of meaning: "Not 'truth' but an epistemically understood generalized concept of validity [*Geltung*] in the sense of 'rational acceptability' is the master concept of the pragmatic theory of meaning" (SE, 91).

Rightness as a Validity Claim

According to Habermas, moral utterances make validity claims to rightness, not validity claims to truth. The thought is that in making a moral utterance, I tacitly endorse the underlying norm of action. Just as in the act of asserting *p*, I unavoidably commit myself to the truth of *p*, so when I utter the sentence "Theft is wrong," I implicitly endorse the underlying norm "do not steal." In short, theoretical utterances (such as assertions) and moral utterances have a similar underlying structure and exhibit a similar pragmatic function, namely that of eliciting consensus on the plane of communicative action and in discourse.

Habermas's pragmatic conception of rightness (or justice-qua-morality) can thus be represented with a slightly different formula:

(R) For any norm *n*: If *n* is valid, then *n* is amenable to rationally motivated consensus.[29]

I've put this in the barest form possible to bring to light the internal connection between the validity of norms and their amenability to rationally motivated consensus. This same underlying connection between reasons and consensus is present in Habermas's discourse principle (D) and the richer moral principle (U).[30]

This, then, is the analogy between truth and rightness (when the two are understood as validity claims) that underwrites Habermas's conception of moral cognitivism. It is this position that affords him the opportunity to embrace moral universalism, and moral cognitivism, without paying the ontological price of moral realism. Habermas offers it as an explanation of the isomorphism between the syntactical discipline (or rational structure) of theoretical and moral discourse. It allows him to claim that moral discourse and moral action involve, and so are characterized by, the ability to be right and wrong, and the ability to learn.

The Validity Requirement

One more essential feature of the analogy has not yet been spelled out. It is a feature of what Habermas calls "rationally motivated consensus": agreement in an ideally prosecuted discourse. As Habermas puts it, "Valid statements deserve the acceptance of everyone for the same reasons" (MW, 178–79, 191). I shall call this "the validity requirement," since, according to Habermas, it flows from the underlying generic conception of validity, of which both truth and normative rightness are, in his eyes, specifications. The validity requirement that everyone can accept a norm (or proposition) for the same reason is a very strong requirement indeed. It raises the question of what it is to accept something for the same reasons. Obviously, it rules out that a principle such as "one should not eat pork" is justified because every member of a community accepts it if some members of that community accept it only because they are vegetarians, and others who are not vegetarians accept it only on religious grounds. Validity does not consist in mere consensus or convergence, but rather in deep consensus that extends to the rational ground of the consensus. Still, this leaves important questions unanswered. For example, is the harm principle justified merely by virtue of every individual's having an agent-relative reason to avoid being harmed themselves? That is, does each person's selfish reason to avoid harm to themselves count as a "shared" reason or the "same" reason? On various occasions, Habermas has implied that it does not, because he thinks morally justifying reasons must be agent neutral, not merely agent relative (DEA, 15; SE, 78).[31] The trouble with the validity requirement is that it is a very strong condition that few moral principles will in fact meet.

1.2.6 DISCOURSE ETHICS AND KANT

Principle (U) is Kantian in various respects. It reformulates what Habermas calls "the basic intuition contained in Kant's categorical imperative . . . to ensure that only those norms are accepted as valid which express a general will" (MCCA, 68). Habermas has in mind the first formulation of Kant's categorical imperative, the "formula of the universal law" (FUL): "Act only according to that maxim which you can at the same time will that it should become a universal law" (Kant 2011, 31/AA 421).

Like Kantian ethics, discourse ethics is supposed to be a universalist, cognitivist, formalist, deontological theory that reconstructs the moral standpoint in a single principle of universalization (MCCA, 33–37). That said, (U) is a reformulation of FUL, and so the differences are important:

1. To begin with, Kant does not call the moral law a principle of "justice" [*Gerechtigkeit*]. Unlike the terms "virtue" [*Tugend*] and "ethics" [*Sitte*], "justice" does not figure in Kant's moral philosophy.
2. Unlike FUL, (U) is not itself a basic norm and hence is not formulated as an imperative; rather, it is a procedure for the selection of norms.
3. Discourse ethics remains strictly procedural in that it confines itself to reconstructing the procedure of moral discourse while refraining from making any substantial moral claims or generating any first-order moral norms. Habermas's discourse ethics leaves it up to participants to determine which norms are valid. In virtue of being strictly procedural, Habermas claims, discourse ethics is "post-metaphysical."
4. The fourth main difference from FUL is that (U) reconstructs a procedure of argumentation that is essentially "dialogical" (a plurality of subjects reasoning jointly), not "monological" (one subject reasoning alone). On this point, Habermas quotes Thomas McCarthy: "The emphasis shifts from what each can will without contradiction to be a universal law, to what all can will in agreement to be a universal norm" (MCCA, 67).[32]
5. Finally, in contrast to Kant's FUL, (U) establishes the validity of a moral norm by assessing whether it would, when applied, meet the interests of every individual, whereas, according to Kant, genuine moral action must abstract from all interests save the pure or a priori interest in conforming to the moral law. Habermas's contention that

valid moral norms embody universalizable interests makes (U) look more like a principle of justice traditionally conceived, that is, a rule oriented toward the common good, although further difficult questions arise about what counts as a universalizable interest.

1.2.7 DISCOURSE ETHICS AND G. H. MEAD

Habermas's conception of universalization is influenced by the pragmatist social philosopher George Herbert Mead. In *Mind, Self, and Society* (1967), Mead argued that the perspective of the individual is given by his or her particular desires and interests: Individual selves are "constituted out of" their interests. However, through education and socialization, "the social process of community enters as a determining factor into the individual's thinking" (Mead 1967, 154). Moral behavior is a matter of modifying one's own interests in the light of one's understanding and recognition of the interests of everyone else, a process that leads to the development of a "larger self," a self that identifies with the interests of others and is wont to adopt "the attitude of the whole community" (Mead 1967, 154, 167). Mead uses the phrase "the generalized other" to denote this social conception of the self (Mead 1967, 154, 156).

In *The Theory of Communicative Action*, Habermas follows Mead in insisting on the social nature of morality: "We are what we are through our relationship to others. Inevitably then our end must be a social end, both from the standpoint of its content . . . and from the point of view of form" (TCA II, 93). Moral agents become fully individualized in discourse by learning how to integrate themselves into society by fulfilling different social roles. They do this by a process of "ideal role taking" (MCCA, 65, 121, 163–67). In discussing whether a norm is valid, they have to exchange perspectives with every other person affected by the norm in order to ascertain whether a norm serves everyone's interests. This is a demanding undertaking, one that decenters the self (MCCA, 132–39), but it protects social bonds on which the integrity of moral agents and their individuality depend. Just as for Mead, what is morally right is in the interests of all, similarly, for Habermas, justice-qua-morality requires that we determine "what lies in the equal interest of everyone, and what is equally good for all" (MCCA, 66–68, 121).[33]

1.2.8 DISCOURSE ETHICS AND LAWRENCE KOHLBERG

The other major influence on Habermas's discourse ethics is the developmental psychologist Lawrence Kohlberg, who was a colleague of Rawls's at Harvard.[34] One can say that the combined influences of Mead and Kohlberg lie at the root of Habermas's Kantian pragmatism. Kohlberg claims that the moral competence of subjects develops through three temporally invariant levels, each subdivided into two stages. These structures are supposed to be "natural" in the sense that they are universal—they exist across cultures—and that their presence can be empirically demonstrated. It is the third level that concerns us here, so I will omit details of the other two:

1. Preconventional level (stages 1 and 2)
   At this level, the child responds to the labels of "good" and "bad" and "right" and "wrong" but interprets these labels in terms of the physical or hedonistic consequences of action, that is, punishment and reward.
2. Conventional level (stages 3 and 4)
   At this level, maintaining the expectations of one's family is valued in its own right, regardless of the consequences. The characteristic attitudes are conformity to expectations and loyalty to social order.
3. Post-conventional level
   At this level, there is a clear effort to define moral values and principles that have validity and application apart from the authority of the groups or persons holding these principles and apart from the individual's own identification with these groups. Moral decisions are generated from rights, values, or principles that are (or could be) agreeable to all individuals composing or creating a society designed to have fair and beneficial practices.
4. Social-contract, legalistic orientation (stage 5)
   What is right is upholding the basic rights, values, and legal contracts of a society even when they conflict with the concrete rules and laws of a group. At this stage, one can recognize among the values and rules that are relative to one's group some nonrelative values and rights, such as life and liberty, which must be protected regardless of majority

opinion. The reasons one has for doing right are feelings of obligation to abide by the social contract, to foster the good of all, and to protect one's own rights and those of others. The commitments one has to family, friends, and colleagues are freely entered into and entail obligations and respect for the rights of others. Laws and duties are based on rational calculations of overall utility.

5. Universal ethical principle orientation (stage 6)
What is right is what is in accord with universal, self-chosen ethical principles. Validity is conferred on particular laws or social agreements by the underlying principles. When laws conflict with the principles, one acts in accordance with the principles. Such principles are universal principles of justice, equality, and respect for the dignity of all other human beings. At this stage, the reason one has for doing right is that, as a rational person, one has an insight into the validity of the underlying principles and has committed oneself to them.

According to Kohlberg, each level, and each stage within each level, is a phase in a continuous learning process and is superior to the previous ones. At each new stage, subjects manage to resolve moral problems more satisfactorily and with a greater level of reflectiveness and complexity. Each new level preserves the moral problem-solving capacities of the previous level and at the same time improves upon them, such that at each new level, solutions can be found to moral problems that remained unsolved at the previous level. A solution to a problem at a new level will typically bring about an "equilibrium" by providing an appropriate principle that can be recognized as fair by all parties and by bringing the moral intuitions of each person into reflective harmony. Thus, generally speaking, moral subjects will prefer higher levels of moral consciousness to previous levels once they have made the transition to them.

Kohlberg presents these findings as a complex, and in part empirically testable, hypothesis. He argues that there is an isomorphism between moral psychology and normative ethical theory. The moral psychological side of the theory, such as agents' preference for higher-level over lower-level solutions to moral problems, is supported by empirical data.

The other side of the theory, the normative ethical theory—for example, claims about the alleged theoretical superiority of stage 6 over stage 5 solutions, and so the superiority of Kantian approaches to morality over, say, utilitarian approaches—must, Kohlberg claims, be established within moral philosophy by philosophical argument. The argument he gives for this is that a stage 6 morality, a principled morality of rights and duties, must satisfy certain internal formal criteria of adequacy, namely, *universalizability*, *reversibility*, *prescriptivity*, and *primacy*, and that Rawls's idea of choosing principles of justice behind a veil of ignorance in the original position satisfies these criteria better not only than welfarist, contractual, and utilitarian theories (which he locates, to the consternation of their proponents, at stage 5), but also than Kant's categorical imperative. Therefore, Rawls's theory, which provides the model for Kohlberg's own device of "moral musical chairs, represents the most cognitively and philosophically adequate form of moral reasoning."[35]

The relevance of Kohlberg to Habermas's discourse ethics is fourfold. First, Kohlberg's approach is a working example of the method of rational reconstruction that Habermas deploys in his own work. Second, Kohlberg's sequence of developmental stages provides a model of a learning process that Habermas borrows, fine tunes, and deploys on both the individual and social levels. Third, with his critical engagement with Kohlberg, Habermas wants to demonstrate that his action theory has the necessary resources to reconstruct the sequence of developmental stages. Fourth, Habermas's conception of moral consciousness in mature adults—that is, agents at stage 6—is essentially Kohlbergian (MCCA, 125).

It is the fourth point that concerns us here. Habermas made significant objections and refinements to Kohlberg's stage 6, which eventually convinced Kohlberg to modify his view (Kohlberg 1986). The most important of these objections for our purposes are that Habermas denies that stages 5 and 6 are "hard" or "natural" stages. At level 3, he claims, the superiority of one stage over another can be established only by philosophical argument and consists solely in that stage's degree of reflexivity and cognitive complexity. Second, according to Habermas, stage 6 moral consciousness consists in the disposition to participate in a dialogical procedure with others rather than to apply reason monologically (MCCA, 170). As a consequence, Habermas argues, principle (U), which is a dialogical conception of the moral standpoint, is a more adequate reconstruction of moral consciousness than that of Rawls's original position or Kohlberg's stage 6.

1.2.9 THE METHOD OF DISCOURSE ETHICS: RATIONAL RECONSTRUCTION

The final feature of discourse ethics that deserves mention is Habermas's method of "rational reconstruction." In an early work, he describes the approach of reconstruction as "taking a theory apart and putting it back together again in a new form in order to attain more fully the goal it has set itself" (CES, 95). He initially developed this method in the late 1960s and early 1970s, and it later became central to his understanding of post-metaphysical philosophy, which was influenced in turn by Habermas's engagement with the sociology of understanding [*Verstehen*] and cultural hermeneutics (PMT, 28–56). What the method of rational reconstruction takes from the latter is the idea of engaging with its object in the first and second person rather than from the perspective of the observer, as in the natural sciences. Essentially, rational reconstruction makes explicit general structures or universal (culturally invariant) capacities and capabilities that are implicitly possessed and performed by participants in practices (MCCA, 37). It lays out these structures theoretically as rules and shows how these structures develop over time. Although a philosophical task of analysis and explication, the results of rational reconstruction should be open to empirical testing, Habermas claims. He cites Chomsky's theory of universal grammar as a paradigm example (CES, 14). In some ways, though, his other examples—Piaget's theory of cognitive development and Kohlberg's work on the moral development of children—are more pertinent. In particular, Habermas highlights the way the empirical data Kohlberg took from his experiments and the philosophical arguments for the superiority of the higher stages support each other. Their mutual coherence is taken to be further evidence for the correctness of the theory: "On the meta- or inter-theoretical level, the only governing principle is that of coherence. We want to find out what elements fit together, which is a bit like doing a jigsaw puzzle" (MCCA, 118).

Philosophy in its post-metaphysical role is a reflective meta-theoretical discipline that works alongside the social sciences and natural sciences.

Which is not to say that philosophy does not have a distinct role. Unlike those who think philosophy can be "naturalized"—that is, supplanted by natural (and social) science—Habermas thinks that because philosophy is more closely linked to common sense, the public realm, and everyday culture, it lives on as a reflective discipline that acts as a "stand-in" and "interpreter" that makes the results of specialized science fruitful for everyday life (MCCA, 1–20). This means that not only does philosophy rely on the sciences for its content—it does not have its own object domain—but it also shares their findings and inherits the defeasibility of those findings (PMT, 36). Accordingly, Habermas conceives his overall theory as an interdisciplinary research program, the individual pieces of which "fit together as it were like those of a jigsaw puzzle" (VE, 506).

Another feature of Habermas's approach of rational reconstruction is that, in explicit contrast to "foundationalism" or "first philosophy," it denies to philosophy any foundational or substantial role. This is in part because its guiding idea is that, owing to the structure of speech acts, validity claims, and communicative action, there are *already normative claims* implicit in our practices and institutions, and it is the task of the post-metaphysical philosopher merely to make these explicit. They require neither to be worked up by the moral philosopher nor to be justified by philosophical arguments. Indeed, he claims that people's everyday moral intuitions "are not in need of clarification by the philosopher" (MCCA, 98). This view is at first blush in tension with the idea of discourse ethics as a program of philosophical justification, at the center of which lies the derivation of (U). However, the supposed "derivation" is just a way of showing that the principle of universalization is indeed implicit in our everyday practice of moral discourse, and the justification is philosophical only in the attenuated sense of post-metaphysical philosophy. Weak "transcendental-pragmatic justification," as Habermas calls it, is not an "ultimate justification" (MCCA, 98). Indeed, the philosopher contributes nothing substantial to moral debate. The philosopher does not address people in the first or second person or tell them what they ought to do and why. Insofar as the philosopher engages in first-order moral debate, the philosopher is just one participant in moral discourse among others, with no special status or knowledge. This brings us to another distinguishing feature of Habermas's conception of morality sketched out in discourse ethics. Principle (U) is supposed to capture the underlying structure of the practice of moral discourse. It is thus fundamentally different from Kant's FUL or Rawls's device of the original position, with which the philosopher, and in fact any rational person, *can figure out for themselves what is morally required of them*. In Habermas's view, no individual moral agent can do that on his or her own. To do so, one needs to participate in an actual discourse with other participants, which, if successful, will enable one to identify or establish the valid moral norm that is to inform his or her conduct.

1.3 DISCOURSE ETHICS AND ETHICAL DISCOURSE

There are two distinct phases in the development of discourse ethics, which correspond roughly to Habermas's works of the 1980s and 1990s. The second phase is more appropriately named the discourse theory of morality, as distinct from discourse ethics. This is because in this phase, from about 1991, Habermas introduces a systematic distinction between "morality" and "ethics," or rather between moral discourse and ethical discourse. On the basis of that distinction, it becomes clear that discourse ethics was and remains chiefly a theory of morality.[36] In the early 1990s, Habermas made some significant amendments and additions to discourse ethics in response to communitarian and feminist objections to Kant and Rawls. These amendments have important ramifications for his conception of the political and his dispute with Rawls.

1.3.1 MORALITY AND ETHICAL DISCOURSE

Phase two of the development of Habermas's conception of justice begins with the publication in German of *Erläuterungen zur Diskursethik* (most of which appears in English translation in *Justification and Application*). The crucial innovation here consists in a threefold division of practical reason into moral, ethical, and pragmatic employments (JA, 1–19).

Habermas already had a conception of "ethics" in phase one. But, according to his original Kohlbergian model, ethical questions—that is, questions of the good life—are sloughed off at stage 6 and relegated to an ancillary role. As a consequence of this separating out of ethics and morality, at stage 6, Habermas argues, solutions to moral problems "retain only the rationally motivating force of insights" (MCCA, 178). And since the motivating force of justice-qua-morality is weak, problems of "application" and "motivational anchoring" have to be solved through "hermeneutic effort and the internalization of authority" (MCCA, 179).

The crucial development here is that the category of "ethical discourse" is introduced alongside that of "moral discourse." So now both ethics and morality enjoy the status of "discourse." Ethical discourse concerns questions of what is good for the individual or for the group and is accordingly divided into ethical–existential and ethical–political discourses. When successful, it issues in "clinical advice" about self-realization and how to achieve an authentic or good life (JA, 9, 12). Ethical discourse has its own validity claim, which Habermas calls a claim to authenticity (JA, 9). This seems to be a practical analogue to the validity claim to truthfulness (TCA I, 75). There is an important difference, though. In Habermas's work up to and including *The Theory of Communicative Action*, he asserts that the three validity claims are universal features of discourse. Truth claims and rightness claims are universal in the sense that, if an assertion is true, it is true for everyone, and if a norm is right, it is right for everyone. There are no exceptions. Ethical discourse, by contrast, is limited in scope to cultural groups with a shared ethos or repertoire of values, and that must apply also to the validity claim to authenticity. It is limited both in the constituency of participants—those who share cultural values—and in the application of the agreements or decisions in which it results, which apply only to the relevant cultural group and not to people who do not share the participants' values.

In phase two, ethical and moral discourses operate in tandem. Some issues, Habermas claims, can be taken up and answered within both ethical and moral discourse (JA, 1–17). That said, Habermas attempts to draw a strict distinction between morality and ethics. He claims that the moral principle "acts like a knife that makes razor-sharp cuts between evaluative statements and strictly normative ones, between the good and the just" (MCCA, 104). Indeed, Habermas makes two separate but related claims. The first is that in modern, rationalized, post-conventional societies—that is, societies inhabited by post-conventional moral agents—morality requires that agents distinguish strictly "between the good and the right"

(JA, 122). For Habermas, this distinction is equivalent to, indeed identical to, the distinction between ethics and morality.[37] The second is that the latter has priority over the former. Habermas insists on the priority of the right, which in his case normally means the priority of valid moral norms. Moral discourse is cognitively superior to ethical discourse, since validity claims to rightness, he contends, are analogous to validity claims to truth. The practical upshot is that ethical discourses must always already operate within the bounds of moral permissibility set by valid moral norms (JA, 71; TIO, 12, 25).

Both Habermas's strict distinction between morality and ethics and his doctrine of the priority of moral rightness have come under heavy criticism (see, for example, Benhabib 1986, 304–309; McCarthy 1993, 181–200; Putnam 2002, 112–14). Some have seen this alteration in his theory as a retrograde step (McCarthy 1993; Kettner 2002; Heath 2014). Whether or not they are correct, it is important to note the consequences of this alteration for Habermas's conception of justice-qua-morality. The chief one is that, henceforth, instead of conceiving justice as the master concept in a broad and uniform domain of the moral-practical, Habermas conceives the moral point of view as a narrow core of highly general norms at the center of a broad and variform domain of practical reason. "The sphere of questions that can be answered rationally from the moral point of view," he claims, "shrinks in the course of the development toward multiculturalism within particular societies" (JA, 91). The fact that (U) contains such a demanding necessary and sufficient condition of the validity of any moral norm, so that very few moral norms survive the test of universalizability, Habermas argues, is not so much a function of his theory but a reflection of the historical and social reality of modern society. He points out that, although the number of moral norms diminishes in the course of modernization, their importance increases, citing as evidence "the growing consensus concerning human rights" (JA, 91). But if justice-qua-morality becomes an increasingly scarce resource in modern societies, then moral discourse can no longer fulfill unaided the task of social integration that Habermas originally assigned to it. That task falls increasingly to ethical–political discourses. However, as we have seen, such discourses are by their nature limited in scope to members of particular cultural groups with shared repertoires of values, and they lack the universal scope of morality. Eventually, Habermas claims, under these conditions, it is modern law that comes to fill the vacuum, working with whatever moral and ethical resources it can find to coordinate the actions of social agents and secure social integration (JA, 88).

1.3.2 JUSTICE AND SOLIDARITY

The other major innovation in phase two of discourse ethics is the introduction of a moral concept of solidarity. In addition to the criticisms outlined earlier, Habermas believed that Kantian moral theories are open to the objection that they presuppose social atomism "insofar as they begin with isolated, private, autonomous, self-possessing subjects, who treat themselves like property" (JS, 241). He also believed them to be unable to explain why moral subjects would be disposed to prioritize justice to strangers over stronger loyalties and attachments to friends and neighbors (TIO, 24). Habermas argues that the way to meet these objections is not to introduce a principle of benevolence at stage 6 alongside the principle of "justice," as Kohlberg attempted to do, but instead to recognize that "justice conceived deontologically requires solidarity as its reverse side" (JS, 244). Importantly, "solidarity" is not a counterpart or complement to "justice." Rather, insofar as justice is not only a principle but a disposition to act fairly deeply engrained in fully socialized moral selves, solidarity is essential to it." "It is a question not so much of two moments that supplement each other as of two aspects of the same thing" (JS, 244). So to properly understand justice-qua-morality, we need to know what solidarity is.

Solidarity, for Habermas, is a device that compensates for the extreme vulnerability of individuals: not the physical vulnerability of fragile, needy, and chronically under-adapted beings, but rather the psychosocial vulnerability of beings whose individuality and integrity are constituted by their membership of a community of communication and discourse.[38] Where justice safeguards the inviolability of each individual, solidarity "protects the web of intersubjective relations" on which each individual depends (MCCA, 200). Solidarity is a stance held by each individual toward everyone that consists in the willingness of each person to stand in for the other (JS, 10). This stance has its origins in the "primary group loyalties" of a community with a shared ethos, that is, ethics (TIO, 14).

In the course of history, Habermas maintains, these group loyalties were taken up by the great world religions and extended into relations of universal fellowship and, subsequently, owing to modernization and rationalization processes, further transformed into a general secular "sense of humanity" that demands that "each must be able to recognize himself or herself in all that wears a human face" (PMT, 14). In other words, under modern conditions, the demands of solidarity are universal in scope, as are those of justice. Universal solidarity is related to the capacity for ideal role-taking. It is an affective disposition to take an interest in the interests of all other human beings affected by a norm, a disposition inscribed in the social nature of the self. Habermas introduces the idea for several reasons, the main one being that it is a putative explanation for how morality, as rational insight, can motivate action (MCCA, 179). Habermas is adamant that universal solidarity no longer depends on the existence of a shared substantial ethos, repository of values, or fellowship in a common way of life. Indeed, Habermas insists, universal solidarity is not an affect. For "feelings," Habermas argues, "offer too narrow a basis for the solidarity between members of an impersonal community of moral beings" (TIO, 14). Rather, like justice, it is a socio-cognitive achievement and as such will only have the weak motivational force of rational insight.

In this chapter, I have merely laid out Rawls's conception of justice as fairness as set out in *A Theory of Justice* and Habermas's moral theory as set out in his theory of discourse ethics. I examined discourse ethics in more detail, in part because it has more background theory, which one must know if one is to properly understand and appraise Habermas's early criticisms of Rawls. It is clear that the two theories are very different in composition. Rawls's theory is a more traditional self-contained philosophical theory, drawing selectively on sources from economic theory and moral philosophy. Discourse ethics is more of a vast interdisciplinary jigsaw puzzle assembled from components of moral psychology, social theory, moral philosophy, speech-act theory, and the pragmatic theories of meaning and truth developed in *The Theory of Communicative Action*. However, the most important differences between these theories are not matters of style or approach but of subject matter, or, to put it differently, object domain.

In the introduction to the first edition of *Political Liberalism* (1993), Rawls admits that in *A Theory of Justice* he was unclear about whether justice as fairness was intended as a theory of institutional design or as a "moral doctrine of justice general in scope" (JFAR, 186; PL, xv). This suggests that *A Theory of Justice* was not intended as the kind of general moral theory of human action that Kohlberg takes it to be. Now the point here is not whether Rawls's own interpretation of his earlier conception of justice is warranted. (Kohlberg's theory is not meant as an interpretation of Rawls, or even as an application of Rawls's theory; it is a theory of moral development inspired by elements of Rawls's argument in *A Theory of Justice*). The point is that Kohlberg and, more importantly, Habermas, under Kohlberg's influence, take Rawls's theory and put it to work in a different domain, namely the domain of general moral theory. Consequently, Kohlberg and Habermas mean something rather different by "justice" than does Rawls. Habermas, whose conception of stage 6 morality takes its point of departure from Kohlberg, depoliticizes and moralizes Rawls's theory of justice and proposes instead justice-qua-morality as the central idea of a general moral theory; that is, he proposes a "moral doctrine of justice general in scope" exactly contrary to what Rawls later claimed he intended. This is why I claimed that Rawls's justice as fairness in *A Theory of Justice* and Habermas's justice-qua-morality in discourse ethics are not, in spite of some appearances, rival conceptions of justice. Rawls's justice as fairness and Habermas's discourse ethics are not in competition with each other, so there are no real points of contestation. One is a general theory of morality, albeit viewed from the perspective of the social theorist; the other is a substantive theory of justice for a liberal constitutional democratic society.

One should not infer from the fact that they both focus on notions of justice that they are rival theories.

2

HABERMAS'S EARLY CRITICISMS OF RAWLS

2.1 HABERMAS'S FIRST CRITICISMS OF RAWLS

Back in 1974, Habermas engaged with Rawls's *A Theory of Justice* in a paper entitled "Legitimation Problems in the Modern State," when his idea of discourse ethics was still only incipient and lacking in detail.[1] In *Communication and the Evolution of Society*, Habermas situates Rawls squarely in the tradition of contract theorists such as Hobbes and Locke, who use the fictional idea of a state of nature to specify the "conditions under which an agreement expressed the common interest" (CES, 184). To the extent that it does express the common interest, agreement is rational and can be used to legitimate the modern state without any appeal to the ultimate grounds of nature or God. That said, Habermas is critical of the implicit social ontology of social contract theories, which presupposes an ideology of "possessive individualism" that treats happiness merely as "accumulating material objects of which one disposes privately," rather than, say, a "social relation in which mutuality predominates" (CES, 199). Habermas clearly thinks this criticism applies to Rawls's two principles of justice, the point of which is to regulate the distribution of "primary social goods" (CES, 198).

Habermas's earliest criticisms are not developed in any detail and are directed at Rawls's theory understood in the contract tradition as a legitimation of the modern state. In the 1980s when Habermas was developing his theory of discourse ethics, his interest in Rawls was renewed. Indeed, it was renewed twice. First, he was driven by his interest in Kohlberg's theory of moral consciousness to engage with Rawls's argument from the original position as a way of operationalizing the moral point of view. Later in the 1980s, along with several other commentators and critics working in critical social theory, his interest was piqued again by the communitarian critique of Rawls's social ontology. His early criticism of Rawls thus consisted in two broad phases, which mirror the two phases of the development of discourse ethics discussed in chapter 1. I shall now analyze each in turn.

In phase one, roughly covering Habermas's work of the 1970s and 1980s, his relation to Rawls's work is complex and indirect. In *A Theory of Justice*, Rawls emphasizes the Kantian and constructivist credentials of justice as fairness primarily to distinguish it from utilitarianism and rational intuitionism. Kohlberg takes the Kantian interpretation even further. As we saw, Kohlberg concludes that Rawls's idea of choosing principles of justice behind a veil of ignorance in the original position satisfies the criteria of stage 6 moral consciousness better than welfarist and utilitarian theories, and even better than Kant's categorical imperative. Stage 6 is an orientation toward universal, and thus post-conventional, moral principles: "Principles are universal principles of justice, equality, and respect for the dignity of human beings as individuals" (MCCA, 124). So, whereas Rawls had used the term "justice" in a specific sense, in which the application of his two principles of justice is tailored in the first instance to the basic structure of society, Kohlberg sees in the original position and the veil of ignorance a model for the highest stage of moral judgment of an actually existing morality in the sense of right conduct. In his essay "The Claim to Moral Adequacy of a Highest Stage of Moral Judgment," Kohlberg writes,

> A decision reached by playing moral musical chairs corresponds to a decision as to what is ultimately "just" or "fair." Ideal role taking is the decision procedure ultimately required by the attitudes of respect for persons and of justice as equity recognized at higher stages. This is suggested by Rawls's derivation of principles of justice as equity from the original position. (Kohlberg 1973, 644)

Effectively, as we saw earlier, Kohlberg generalizes and moralizes Rawls's notion of justice. The debate concerning stage 6 is consequently one between Habermas and Kohlberg about the best way of construing the moral point of view, and it only indirectly concerns Rawls.

Now, Habermas's engagement with Kohlberg also forms part of his wide-ranging critique of Frankfurt School critical theory and his subsequent transformation of critical social theory. In section IV of his *Theory of Communicative Action*, Habermas famously claims, "From the beginning, critical theory labored over the difficulty of giving an account of its own normative foundations" (TCA I, 374).

Habermas confronts the critical theory of Adorno and Horkheimer with a serious problem and is not content to find fault with it while offering nothing in its place. Instead, he develops critical social theory, which does not suffer from the same problem, since, he claims, it contains within it an "account of its own normative foundations" (TCA I, 374, 377). To cut a long and complex story short, discourse ethics is that account of the normative foundations of critical theory, or is at very least central to that account.[2] Yet Habermas's critical social theory construed so as to include discourse ethics as the hitherto lacking but indispensible account of its own normative foundations is a better candidate for a rival theory to Rawls's justice as fairness than is discourse ethics construed separately. One could say that in phase one of discourse ethics two debates with Rawls are nested within each other: one that bears on his work indirectly through the lens of Kohlberg, and one that engages with it directly as a rival social theory. Neither Habermas, nor any of his many commentators, distinguishes these carefully enough.

2.2 HABERMAS'S CRITICISMS OF RAWLS IN *MORAL CONSCIOUSNESS AND COMMUNICATIVE ACTION*

I've mentioned that Habermas makes some detailed and eventually winning criticisms of Kohlberg's stage 6. We can interpret these as indirect criticisms of Rawls. One of the criticisms Habermas makes is that Rawls, like many contemporary moral theorists, does not actually offer a "justification of the moral principle" (MCCA, 79).

This is a confusing claim for a number of reasons. Given that Rawls is not defending a general moral theory, it is unclear what he is supposed to have failed to justify: the original position and its assumptions or the two principles of justice. The standard way of reading *A Theory of Justice* is to see the principles of justice as justified to the extent that they would be agreed on by mutually disinterested parties in an original position in which they are ignorant of their personal traits, social roles, and positions (Estlund 1992, 695; Laden 2003). The context of Habermas's criticism here, though, shows that it is directed toward Rawls's notion of reflective equilibrium. But reflective equilibrium is a method of justifying the principles of justice by showing that they can be made to cohere with our "firmest" and most "considered convictions" (TJ, 20, 40).[3] What Habermas is actually objecting to is Rawls's appeal to considered moral intuitions as "provisional fixed points which we presume any conception of justice must fit" (TJ, 20). But this is an odd thing for him to criticize, since Habermas makes virtually the same move when he claims that no "ultimate justification" of the moral principle is needed because "the moral intuitions of everyday life are not in need of clarification by the philosopher" (MCCA, 98).

Since Habermas's "Notes" on discourse ethics (MCCA, 43–116) are designed to sketch out his own theory rather than to interpret Rawls's, the dialectic of his critique of Rawls is hard to gauge. Still, there is an implied contrast between discourse ethics, which does provide some kind of philosophical justification of the moral principle (U), and Rawls's theory, which allegedly does not. The passage in which Habermas offers this criticism of Rawls occurs in the context of his argument that, although no "ultimate" justification, and certainly no "foundationalist" justification, of the moral principle is necessary or possible, *some* kind of justification of it is both necessary and possible. Habermas concludes, "The necessary justification of the proposed moral principle could take the following form: Every argumentation . . . rests on pragmatic presuppositions from whose propositional content the principle of universalization (U) can be derived" (MCCA, 82). Habermas refers to his proposed formal "derivation" of principle (U), discussed earlier, and appears optimistic about the prospects for deriving (U) from the pragmatic presuppositions of argument in general. However, he does not actually provide such a derivation in *Moral Consciousness and Communicative Action*, and to date, neither he nor any of his followers has done so. Instead, Habermas has outlined a much more indirect "program of philosophical justification" that itself is fraught with difficulties (TIO, 41, 43; see also Ott 1996; Lumer 1997; Finlayson 2000a; Steinhoff 2009). Habermas's assertion that a derivation of (U) is possible does not demonstrate the possibility and is no substitution for the derivation itself. And there is reason to think that whatever argument for (U) can be given will be as reliant on moral intuitions as Rawls's own argument for justice as fairness is (according to Habermas), and so there is little reason for him to claim discourse ethics as superior in that respect.

The second criticism Habermas makes is that Rawls conceives the original position as a rational procedure for selecting principles of justice that can be applied *monologically* by moral agents, that is, by individuals reasoning on their own (MCCA, 66, 74, 122). This is an objection we saw Habermas aiming at Kant and that he frequently brings to bear on Rawls. Since this forms part of the 1995 exchange, I will postpone a more detailed discussion of it until chapter 5.

The third of Habermas's early criticisms is that Rawls meddles in matters of substance; that is, he determines what the principles of justice actually are and does this from the point of view of a philosophical expert. By contrast, discourse ethics is procedural in the sense that it leaves the determination of valid moral norms up to the participants in moral discourse themselves. The moral content percolates up into discourse from the lifeworld, the repository of sedimented meanings and reasons, whenever the behavioral expectations of agents are thwarted. A philosopher can participate in moral discourse but only as one of the many and various participants in discourse.

There are two closely related points of dispute here. The first concerns the way in which, in Habermas's eyes, discourse ethics remains procedural while Rawls's theory is substantial. The second is methodological, namely that discourse ethics distinguishes more stringently between the perspective of the expert theorist and the perspective of the participant. Again, both points come up in the 1995 exchange, and I will discuss them again in that context in chapter 5. But the contrast Habermas draws is relevant here. He claims that the task of philosophy begins and ends with the theoretical task of constructing (or reconstructing) the moral point of view. This is done from the perspective of the theorist, with the theorist's expertise. The practical task of determining which norms are valid, by contrast, is performed by participants in discourse with no particular philosophical expertise but with the everyday competence of stage 6 moral agents. This is why Habermas thinks that Rawls as a philosopher should stick to his task of constructing the original position and the veil of ignorance and not attempt to justify substantive normative principles by dint of these devices. Just how far philosophy should prescind from anticipating the results of such discourses is a matter for debate. Habermas is after all a success theorist (rather than an error theorist) in the sense that he believes that there are some universally valid moral norms. It is surprising, then, that he is so reticent about what these are. Very occasionally, he uses the examples of human rights and the principle of equality (JA, 91), but in general he does not offer examples.[4] As noted earlier, this is one respect in which Habermas's discourse ethics is very different from standard normative ethics.

The fourth criticism made by Habermas is that the ideals that Rawls puts into practice in the original position are merely theoretical devices constructed by the theorist. By contrast, the idealizing presuppositions of discourse are not merely constructed ideals; they have a foot in actuality "because its idealized, partly counterfactual presuppositions are precisely those that participants in discourse do in fact make" (MCCA, 198). Here, I think Habermas overcooks the contrast. For one thing, he is prone to underplaying the degree of idealization involved in moral discourse, in which participants who may well be few in number (at the limit, two) have to agree on principles that can be accepted by "all affected" (at the limit, every human being now and in the foreseeable future). For another, Rawls insists that the values and ideals that the device of the original position assumes—for example, the equality of free and equal persons—"are ones we do in fact accept" (TJ, 587).

The fifth and final criticism that Habermas levels at Rawls is a repeat of his earliest criticism, namely that Rawls's contractarian theory presupposes the atomistic social ontology of possessive individualism. Habermas objects, "Rawls fails to distance his theory from the voluntaristic implications of a contractual model for the justification of principles of justice" (JA, 28). This, he claims, gives the wrong kind of account of the social bond. The obligations that social agents owe one another, on such a view, are justified merely instrumentally on the basis of the interests of individual agents.

There is an important difference here. Discourse ethics indeed gives a completely different picture of the social bond. Habermas's conception of society as a complex of universal ties of justice-qua-morality and human solidarity is based on the idea that autonomous individual agents are essentially dependent on a preexisting web of intersubjective relations. In *The Division of Labour in Society*, Durkheim famously remarked, "Not everything contractual is in the contract" (Durkheim 1997, 158). Analogously, Habermas argues, not everything moral is in the moral domain; rather, the latter is embedded in a web of pre-moral relations. Thus, Habermas owes to Durkheim the central claim that relations of justice are essentially rooted and embedded in a "web of intersubjective relations of mutual recognition" (MCCA, 200, 202; see also JS, 244).

Still, one is entitled to ask, as Rawls himself does in response to a similar criticism, made by communitarians, of the social ontology of *A Theory of Justice*, "What is this objection? What does it mean?"[5] As Habermas understands it, it means that Rawls accepts the liberal ideology of possessive individualism as a face-value correct description of the social bond. What that description leaves out, as Habermas puts it in his earliest criticism, is any view of "social relations in which mutuality predominates," rather than relations in which individuals cooperate for the sake of individual accumulation alone (CES, 198).

One can understand why Habermas might think this criticism applies to Rawls. If one considers only the first part of *A Theory of Justice* and focuses entirely on the argument from the original position, as Habermas does, rather than on part III of the book, one might be led to conclude from the fact that Rawls stipulates that the parties to the original position are "mutually disinterested" rational maximizers that justice as fairness presupposes the atomistic social ontology of possessive individualism that supposedly also characterized much of classical liberalism (TJ, 13, 187).

That said, Habermas's exclusive focus on the original position is misleading. The original position is a *model*, and the risk-averse rational choosers in the model are the stylized *representatives* of actual citizens. If one wants to know about Rawls's actual social ontology, one has to look at the actual citizens whom the rational choosers in the original position represent and at what Rawls says about these citizens in part III (Freeman 2003; Pettit 2005). On these grounds, defenders of Rawls have countered that even in *A Theory of Justice*, Rawls's social ontology is very different from that of classical liberalism. And Rawls for one is very clear that it is. For example, in his 1958 article "Justice as Fairness," he writes that "people engaged in just or fair practices can face one another openly and support their respective positions, should they appear questionable, by reference to principles which it is reasonable to expect others to accept" and that this mutual acknowledgment amounts to "a true community between persons in their common practices" (CP, 59). The objection, insofar as there is one, cannot be that Rawls remained satisfied with a social ontology of possessive individualism, but that he failed to fulfill his aim of reaching beyond it toward a more humane and inclusive vision of society.

2.3 THE COMMUNITARIAN CRITIQUE OF RAWLS AND HABERMAS

In the second phase of the development of his early critique of Rawls, Habermas becomes embroiled in the liberal–communitarian debate, which comprises arguments levied by a number of "communitarians," such as Alasdair MacIntyre, Michael Sandel, and Charles Taylor, at Rawls and Kant.

2.3.1 SANDEL'S CRITICISM

The first objection by Sandel was not the most original or telling but was one of the most influential (see Baynes 1992, 129–32).[6] Indeed, the very lack of originality of this criticism makes it useful to us, for it represents a widely shared line of argument that inflects the whole early debate. In his article "The Procedural Republic and the Unencumbered Self," Sandel criticizes a certain picture of the person that goes hand in glove with a certain vision of liberal democratic society. The former is "the picture of the unencumbered self, a self understood as prior to and independent of its ends" (Sandel 1984, 86). The latter is what Sandel calls "the procedural republic," a social ontology of independent, antecedently constituted atomic persons who are bearers of rights and liberties and who contract with one another to found the laws that preserve their freedom and allow them to pursue their individual goods (Sandel 1984, 91–94).

One thing to note about Sandel's critique of Rawls's representation of the person is that it is entirely based on what Rawls says about the parties in the original position. Recall that Rawls stipulates that the parties are economically rational, mutually disinterested, and deprived of information about their social roles as citizens. In part III of *A Theory of Justice*, when discussing the question of whether justice as fairness is congruent with the good of rationality, Rawls remarks that the original position imposes certain restrictions that force us "to consider the choice of principles unencumbered by the singularities of the circumstances in which we find ourselves," and it does so to prevent us from "shaping our moral view according to our particular attachments and interests" (TJ, 516). In other words, it is a device for ensuring the equality of the participants and the impartiality of their judgments. Sandel's slogan "the unencumbered self" alludes directly to this passage. However, in so doing, he distorts Rawls's point, for an "encumbrance" in normal English parlance generally means an unwanted burden, one that is good to throw off. As is clear from Rawls's passage, it is indeed bad to be "encumbered," that is, burdened, loaded down, and made to suffer. Thus, most people like to see their nearest and dearest, and their community and culture, as more than just "encumbrances," even if they are not the ones they ideally would have chosen. Yet for Sandel it seems that being *un*encumbered is a bad thing. Such selves (as depicted by Rawls), he claims, mistakenly value their choice of ends above the ends themselves. They lack any "constitutive ends," ends that, as it were, make them who they are; therefore, he contends, they are "wholly without character, without moral depth" (Sandel 1982, 179). Just exactly what the alleged badness of unencumbrance consists in is unclear. Is it a real but pathological feature of a person in a liberal society? Or is it a flaw in the theory that misrepresents what real persons are like?

Once the polemical smoke lifted, it turned out there was at best a difference of emphasis between the position Sandel claimed to endorse and the position he intended to criticize. The target of his criticism is Rawls's claim that "the self is prior to the ends which are affirmed by it" (TJ, 560).[7] This can be interpreted either as the relatively innocuous empirical observation that in a liberal society no attachment or end, however deep, is beyond re-examination and revision, or as the normative claim that each person should be free to interpret and reinterpret his or her own life as he or she sees fit, compatibly with everyone else's similar freedom (TJ, 560).

But in the final analysis, Sandel was reluctant to deny either the empirical or the normative claim. If what Sandel meant by the rejoinder that selves are, *pace* Rawls, "encumbered" was only that "some relative fixity of character appears essential to prevent the lapse into arbitrariness," Rawls could perfectly well agree (Sandel 1982, 180).

One problem with Sandel's criticism of "the procedural republic"—that is, of what he takes to be Rawls's underlying social ontology—is that it is deeply ambiguous. On the one hand, he convicts Rawls of a philosophical failure because of a lacuna in his theory of society, namely the lack of an underlying democratic ethos or thick conception of the good holding society together. Rawls's theory is thus, Sandel alleges, false. On the other hand, Sandel strongly suggests that Rawls's account of liberal democratic society, as a complex of contractual agreements and procedures between self-interested individual agents, is true, *more's the pity*.[8] Thus, Sandel indicts Rawlsian liberalism for legitimizing, and hence contributing to, a pathological society. And the main thing Sandel claims is pathological about Rawlsian liberal democracy is that it corrodes "the kind of community on which it nonetheless depends" and hence is self-stultifying (Sandel 1984, 94).

The ambiguity need not be fatal, however. Sandel's claims can be reinterpreted to make them consistent: Insofar as Rawls's atomistic social ontology of possessive individualism is false, it hides a deeper, shared, thick conception of the good on which society nonetheless depends; insofar as it is true, the liberal idea that society is based on an agreement between autonomous, instrumentally rational individuals has won out and begun to erode that deeper underlying conception of the good.

I should note in passing that I find Sandel's criticism of Rawls wholly unconvincing for the simple reason that the original position is not the place to look for Rawls's account of the self or his social ontology.[9] Rawls has a complex argument that is meant to show that justice is congruent with the good and that one therefore has reason to care about justice, not only for the extrinsic reasons of one's own good, the achievement of which it facilitates, not only for the sake of a "true community" of fellow citizens, but also for its own sake. Whether that argument is successful, or whether it is vulnerable to a different version of Sandel's objection, is another question, but it certainly is not impugned by Sandel's critique of the original position.[10]

Habermas, though, does find Sandel's criticisms convincing. He cites Sandel's critique approvingly as evidence that Rawls's *A Theory of Justice* presupposes an atomistic social ontology of possessive individualism that is supposedly characteristic of classical liberalism (JA, 121n8).[11] And the reason he does is probably because he reads *A Theory of Justice* according to the "standard blueprint." At the same time, he denies that these objections apply to discourse ethics. So together these claims make up the early debate with Rawls. To be sure, the debate is indirect and does not involve Rawls personally. Though, as we saw in the introduction, in the autumn semester of 1986, he held a graduate seminar on discourse ethics, which went into the respective advantages and disadvantages of the original position and principle (U).[12] So they were at least asking the same questions.

Habermas does not even attempt to reject these social-ontological objections to his own theory, since he, rightly in my view, claims that "they do not apply to the basic concepts of discourse ethics" (JA, 91). Recall that in Habermas's view, the social bond consists in relations of justice and solidarity, whereby, provided socialization processes meet the demands of justice-qua-morality halfway, all mature moral agents either implicitly or explicitly (once they enter into discourse) acknowledge the fundamental interests of all other humans equally. This is what it means for a moral consciousness to develop through structures of communication and discourse toward a "decentered understanding of the world" (CES, 106; MCCA, 132).

2.3.2 TAYLOR'S CRITICISM OF THE MORAL DOMAIN

That said, there are other objections leveled by communitarians that Habermas does, and should, find more threatening.

One such is Taylor's criticism, aimed at both utilitarianism and Kantianism, of the view "that there is a single consistent domain of the 'moral,' that there is one set of considerations or mode of calculation, which determines what we 'morally' ought to do" (Taylor 1982, 132). Prima facie, this applies to discourse ethics at least in its first phase, because it has a uniform and singular conception of the moral domain. And presumably, the fact that discourse ethics undergoes such a significant modification in the second phase of its development indicates that

Habermas accepts the criticism. Habermas's accommodation of ethical discourse within the "moral" domain broadly understood deflects Taylor's criticism (insofar as it applies to the broad moral domain), for in the new picture, ethical and pragmatic discourses make their own distinctive kind of "ought" claims (JA, 1–15). However, even on the modified view, "moral discourse," which is now more strictly and more narrowly construed, is still central to the moral domain (even if it is now broadened to include the ethical and the pragmatic), and it is still exclusively concerned with the justification of norms.

The real trouble is that this modification opens up discourse ethics to a third set of criticisms that target Habermas's strict distinction between morality and ethics and the associated priority of the former over the latter. For, as we saw in chapter 1, Habermas thinks principle (U) makes a "razor-sharp" cut between ethics and morality, or, as he says, between "evaluative statements and strictly normative ones, between the good and the just" (MCCA, 104). The point of a moral discourse according to (U) is to eliminate all values as non-universalizable content. Only thus can moral discourse fulfill its function of universal rational consensus formation. Habermas wants to remove any lingering suspicion that (U) is an ethnocentric prejudice, that is, that it depends on a raft of historically contingent cultural (or ethical) values (MCCA, 78, 197). Smudging the distinction between morality and ethics, moral norms and values, the right and the good (he takes these to be equivalent), from either direction—values that, in a pluralistic society, are a source of possibly intractable conflict—would make it impossible to achieve rationally motivated consensus on universally valid norms.

Moreover, Habermas takes it that stage 6 moral consciousness requires not only an "abstract separation between the right and the good" (which he equates with morality and ethics, respectively), but also a prioritization of the right over the good, such that ethical questions only ever arise within the bounds of moral permissibility (JA, 122). Different versions of the third criticism target the very idea that there is a strict separation between ethics and morality as Habermas understands them, and the further thesis that the moral is prior to the ethical, or the right prior to the good.

That said, as Thomas McCarthy and Hilary Putnam, among others, have pointed out, the distinction is not as watertight as Habermas claims (McCarthy 1991, 191–92; Putnam 2002, 132–34). This is not only because Habermas is too quick to relativize values (while absolutizing norms).

By his own lights, Habermas maintains that needs and interests are always already shaped and interpreted in the light of cultural values. Yet he also claims that moral norms embody interests, albeit universalizable ones. This means that moral norms depend essentially on values as the indispensible basis on which agents and participants in discourse interpret their interests and needs. Thereby Habermas inadvertently lets the Trojan horse of value-pluralism and reasonable disagreement in through the back door.

Habermas completely rejects this line of criticism with two arguments. On the one hand, he claims that need interpretations are not fixed but a "public . . . and discursively negotiable affair," which itself can be taken up in discourse (JA, 90). This response is unconvincing, however. Moral discourse is supposed to arise from conflicts of interest in the lifeworld that agents seek to resolve by achieving consensus on norms of action. But if interests are themselves brought into flux as soon as discourse thematizes need interpretations, the participants in discourse will lose their grasp of what their interests are (until the discourse is resolved), in which case the conflict of interest that gave rise to moral discourse in the first place would lose its point, along with the discourse designed to resolve it. On the other hand, he claims that contested ethical issues can be hived off into the realm of ethical discourse, while moral discourse, which remains focused only on questions amenable to rational consensus, "shrinks" to a core domain (JA, 91). However, this response does not answer so much as beg the question, for moral norms are supposed to be valid if, and only if, they are in the equal interests of all, and interests are needs interpreted in the light of values that are not shared. He moves the boundary between morality and ethics—by contracting the domain of the moral—but it is the very existence, and sharpness, of the boundary that is in question, not its position. Hence, although Habermas rejects Taylor's criticism, neither of his two answers convincingly rebuts it.[13]

2.3.3 TAYLOR'S CRITIQUE OF THE SOURCES OF SELFHOOD

Finally, there is another communitarian argument, made most forcefully and subtly by Taylor, targeted at all broadly Kantian conceptions of morality, including those of Rawls and Habermas.[14] Taylor not only denies that morality is a single uniform domain, and that there is no sharp boundary between morality and ethics, the right and the good, but he argues that these assumptions, together with the false prioritization of morality over ethics, have disengaged modern moral selves from the sources of selfhood, resulting in moral disorientation. These sources, he claims, are "constitutive goods," or "hypergoods," whose historical role was always to provide the underlying ground of moral action in the broadest sense. But in the kind of Kantian moral theory that Habermas (and Kohlberg and Rawls) endorses, such goods are occluded by attempts to define morality (and moral justification) in procedural rather than substantive terms and to draw a strict distinction between morality and ethics, the effect of which is to banish substantive goods from the moral domain. It seems that such theories

> are motivated by the strongest moral ideas such as freedom, altruism, and universalism. These are among the central moral aspirations of modern culture, the hypergoods that are distinctive to it. And yet what these ideals drive the theorists towards is the denial of all such goods.... They are constitutionally incapable of coming clean about the deeper sources of their own thinking. (Taylor 1992, 88)

The problem to which this gives rise is that, as Taylor claims, these theories "leave us nothing to say to someone who asks us why he should be moral or strive to the 'maturity' of a 'post-conventional' ethic" (Taylor 1992, 87).

Habermas rejoins that his modified position can handle this objection. It is a mistake, he claims, to attempt to give a substantial reason or justification to a moral agent for why they should care about questions of justice-qua-morality, as he thinks those who argue, like Taylor, for the priority of the good over the right are doing: "A moral theory that no longer claims to know the telos of the good life must leave the question 'Why be moral?' unanswered" (JA, 75–76, 127). It is just a fact that mature moral agents at stage 6 in post-conventional societies tend to act for the sake of morality, and the extent that they do not is down to a failure of socialization and moral education. As for the objection to the priority of the right and the historical shift of the grounds of morality from substance to procedures, Habermas holds that this is not a theoretical *parti pris*, but rather an accurate reflection of the way modernization processes actually take effect and shape individual moral consciousness (JA, 16).

One of the most important interpreters of Habermas's discourse ethics, William Rehg, who has been influential in refining Habermas's theory, has gone further than Habermas. Rehg argues that Habermas can accept and indeed make use of Taylor's argument about the priority of ultimate "constitutive goods" over narrow moral considerations of the right provided he gives these goods a deflated, discourse theoretical interpretation. Rehg proposes that there is indeed a unique meta-good or set of meta-goods that moral discourse and communicative action protect and preserve and that can thus be claimed to be prior to morality. These would include "respect for the personal integrity of all other beings" and the idea of a society of agents who are disposed to coordinate actions and resolve conflicts, where possible through communication and discourse, namely "the good of rational or autonomous cooperation" (Rehg 1994, 136–38). Importantly for Rehg, the acknowledgment of such a meta-good does not amount to a doctrine of the good life, for it is thin and universal in the sense that it is culturally invariant and not a good that any rational agent can reasonably reject (Rehg 1994, 147).

The difficulty is to see what, if anything, is added to discourse ethics by Rehg's conciliatory talk of a constitutive meta-good. If he is just elaborating and reiterating what it is, according to Habermas, to be an agent at stage 6 of moral consciousness, disposed to prioritize the demands of justice-qua-morality, then he is simply reiterating Habermas's position rather than extending it. He is conceding the language of "good" but denying the crucial point of the objection that the good in question is substantive. Alternatively, when Rehg talks about "respect for personal integrity and well-being," he looks like he is acknowledging the existence of a substantial good (Rehg 1994, 136). But if he goes that way, and essentially takes Taylor's side, he violates Habermas's methodological constraints of post-metaphysical theorizing, which specifically rule out a normative moral theory that bases morality on a fundamental substantial norm, principle, or value. Besides, the more substantial the meta-good is supposed to be, the more difficult it is to show that it is indeed universal, and it cannot be reasonably rejected by people who don't share it. (Just asserting that it is universal is not enough.) In the final analysis, then, Rehg's brave attempt to co-opt and defuse Taylor's communitarian challenge adds little to Habermas's straight rejection of it.

2.4 THE FEMINIST CRITIQUE OF RAWLS AND HABERMAS

The communitarian objections to Rawls, which Habermas accepted as valid criticisms, were subsequently taken up by some feminist theorists and turned against Habermas's discourse ethics with mixed results. In addition to these objections, there is another distinctive and significant feminist contribution to the early debate.

The year 1982 saw the publication of Carol Gilligan's *In a Different Voice*; this was ostensibly a critique of Kohlberg's theory of moral development, but it became extremely influential in feminist social criticism, providing the basis for a powerful and sustained feminist attack on moral philosophy and liberal political theory.[15]

2.4.1 *IN A DIFFERENT VOICE*

According to Gilligan, the empirical evidence thrown up by Kohlberg's experiments suggests that women are less likely to reach the higher stages of moral development, stages 5 and 6, the "post-conventional, autonomous, or principled level." They are more likely to remain at the "conventional level," clustering especially around stage 3, at which Kohlberg situates approval-seeking, "good boy/nice girl" behavior and conformity to social roles (Gilligan 1982, 18).[16] Gilligan accepts this finding but offers an explanation that challenges Kohlberg's view. In experiments she conducted on both genders, she began to notice that women had a recognizably different way of approaching moral problems from that of men: one that accentuated care and sensitivity to and responsibility for others rather than rights and duties, and one that emphasized relationships and interconnections rather than separation and individuality (Gilligan 1982, 18–19). She noticed that when faced with moral dilemmas, women tend to seek different solutions from those of men, that they have a different order of priorities, and that they are sensitive to different evidence and to features of situations often ignored by men. She put forward the thesis that in moral matters, women have a "different voice" to men.

This hypothesis allows Gilligan radically to revise Kohlberg's conclusions. Instead of inferring that women have failed to develop into fully mature moral beings, she infers that there is something awry with Kohlberg's scale of moral development (for example, see Gilligan 1982, 6–18, 31). Rather than seeing women as immature, she argues that women have an "alternative conception of maturity" (Gilligan 1982, 22). Women's apparent inadequacy is a function of Kohlberg's definition of adequacy as the satisfaction of the formal criteria of universalizability and reversibility. In other respects, such as the awareness of the complexity and ambiguity of situations and the relevance of personality, their moral outlook is more refined, nuanced, and, in that sense, more adequate. She views Kohlberg's six-stage theory of moral development as skewed in favor of certain ways of formal reasoning to which Kohlberg's male subjects were more inclined than were his female subjects (Gilligan 1982, 18–23, 31). So although Kohlberg's stage 6 might represent the highest stage of *male* development, it does not represent the highest stage of *child* development. Gilligan suggests that women have an alternative conception of the moral standpoint, conceived not as a hierarchy of ever more general principles, but as an interconnected web of substantive reason-giving considerations, the force and relevance of which are context sensitive (Gilligan 1982, 62–63). Gilligan concludes that her study of women's experience and of what she calls the "ethic of care" has helped to expand "the concept of identity" to include "the experience of interconnection" and to expand "the moral domain" (at the post-conventional level) to include the aspects of responsibility and care in relationships (Gilligan 1982, 173–74).

Gilligan's *In a Different Voice* is a profound, original, and suggestive study, but it hovers uneasily between two conclusions: that women and men have different and incompatible styles of moral reasoning, and that the ethic of care and the ethic of justice are complementary post-conventional moral outlooks and that the Kohlbergian model needs to be adjusted to adequately account for women's, as well as men's, moral experiences (Gilligan 1982, 105, 173).[17]

Although they arose within different disciplines, Gilligan's criticism of Kohlberg and the communitarian objections to Rawls have similarities. They take aim at the same targets: the Rawlsian–Kantian conception of the moral standpoint as interpreted by Kohlberg, the privileging of questions of the right over questions of the good, the overemphasis on autonomy and separation, and the occlusion of the self's constitutive relations to others. Moreover, there is an ambivalence in Gilligan's work that recalls a similar ambivalence in Sandel's criticism of Rawls. Is she merely arguing that Kohlberg's model of post-conventional morality is incorrect because it is not sufficiently inclusive (that is, of women's voices and the various phenomena to which they are responsive) and that his moral phenomenology is therefore incomplete? Or is she making the deeper, normative criticism that moral agents who think predominantly in terms of rights and duties (in her view, most men) are somehow deficient? Is the upshot of her critique that there is something wrong with Kohlberg's theory of moral development or that there is something wrong with the actually existing moralities that Kohlberg ranks at stage 6?[18]

Habermas replies to Gilligan at the level of the theory of moral development. He believes that she does not adequately distinguish between the "moral philosophical question of the justifiability of norms" and the separate questions of the application of moral principles and the motivation of agents to comply with moral requirements (MCCA, 179–81). He sticks to the claim, with which he responded to Taylor's communitarian critique, that the separation of ethical questions from moral questions is not a flaw in the theory but a requirement imposed by the aim of moral discourse and the circumstances in which modern moral agents find themselves. Hence, he concludes, "it does not make sense to try to . . . revise the stages of moral judgment" (MCCA, 180). Rather, Gilligan's work calls for Kohlberg's theory to be supplemented by further research into hermeneutic questions of application and questions of moral motivation that does not disrupt the sequence of stages.

2.4.2 FEMINIST CRITICISMS OF MORAL THEORY AND MORALITY

The feminist social theorists Iris Marion Young, Seyla Benhabib, and Nancy Fraser took Gilligan's critique of Kohlberg as indirect confirmation of the communitarian critique of Rawls and attempted to combine them into a full-fledged feminist critique of morality and a critical theory of society.[19] They develop three familiar lines of argument directed toward

Kantian moral theory, Rawls, and what they take to be the liberal conception of society:

1. The moral self is conceived as a formal and abstract person, the holder of certain rights and duties.
2. The moral standpoint is narrow and uniform.
3. The moral standpoint restricts morality to questions of justice and excludes questions of the good from the moral domain.

Morality so conceived, it is argued, cannot account for the kind of moral experiences that, Gilligan maintains, are more characteristic of women. It is blind to the importance of considerations of care and responsibility for others. Gilligan's criticisms are directed in the first instance at Kohlberg's model of stage 6 moral consciousness, and they assume, rather than show, that care, responsibility for others, and their attendant emotions, affections, and attitudes are in fact central moral concerns and that their exclusion from the moral standpoint and omission from Kohlberg's higher stages is a distortion of moral phenomena.

This raises the question of how arguments originally developed within the theory of moral development, Kohlberg's developmental moral psychology, could be so readily pressed into the service of a feminist political criticism of society designed to explain (and where possible to counteract) women's exclusion, subordination, and oppression (see Benhabib 1992, 75, 152, 184; see also Benhabib and Cornell 1987, 7–9). The short answer is that the broadly Kantian shape of Kohlberg's stage 6, and of Rawls's liberalism, appeared to present a common target, such that arguments aimed at the underlying moral assumptions yielded socially and politically relevant conclusions. To take just one example, Benhabib remarks that "the restriction of the moral domain to questions of justice" results in "the privatization of women's experience" and leads to "epistemological blindness towards the concrete other" (Benhabib 1992, 164).[20]

At the heart of Benhabib's argument is her seminal distinction between the generalized and the concrete other. Although the distinction is now part of the lingua franca of feminist theory, and critical theory more broadly, it is not straightforward. At bottom, it is a distinction between two different conceptions of the other person and is compounded of three separate layers. The first layer is a distinction between *general* and *particular* selves or others, namely between other people who have things in common with everyone else and a another person considered as a single and unique individual. The second layer is the distinction between *abstract* and *concrete* selves or others.[21] A concrete other is a determinate and existing individual person. By opposing "generalized" to "concrete," Benhabib aligns the *relata* of the two distinctions general/particular and abstract/concrete, suggesting that generalized others are abstract and concrete others particular. The third layer has to do with process and state: The first term of the distinction, but not the second, has the suffix "-ize," which has the grammatical function of turning a noun or adjective into a verb. The past participle of the verb "to generalize" is used as an adjective meaning "has been made general" or "has become general as a result of a process." A "generalized other" is a conception of another person reached through a process of generalization (and abstraction), a process that makes salient those features someone has in common with all other people and that abstracts from those features peculiar to them. Generalization need not be understood as a mental act; it can also be construed as a real social and historical process. For example, Marx and Weber have argued that the inhabitants of modern mass societies are formed by various processes of rationalization and abstraction.[22] Roughly this means that they cannot but think of themselves and others in general ways and relate to all other people according to general rules and notions.[23]

Benhabib, it should be noted, uses Mead's label the "generalized other" but applies it to moral agents at Kohlberg's stage 6 and to Rawls's chooser in the original position and the veil of ignorance (Benhabib 1992, 158–59, esp. nn22–23).[24] By contrast, "the concrete other"—Benhabib's label—denotes the other person as a unique "individual with a concrete history, identity, and affective-emotional constitution" (Benhabib 1992, 159). She claims that "in contemporary moral theory these two conceptions are viewed as incompatible, even as antagonistic," whereas viewed properly, they "lie along a continuum" (Benhabib 1992, 158).[25]

In 1985, Benhabib argued against Kohlberg that the three lines of argument listed earlier lead to the "privatization" or "personalization" of women's experience (Benhabib 1986, 415–18). She also argued against Rawls that the historical injustices and oppression that women have suffered are concealed by the gender system and that they cannot be recognized as such from the standpoint of justice because they are considered domestic or internal family matters.[26] Initially, discourse ethics, which enjoyed a friendly reception by feminist philosophers, was spared these criticisms, perhaps because it exhibited the supposed virtues of a *dialogical* theory.[27] If the basic defect of stage 6 moralities is that they are deaf to women's distinctive moral voice, discourse ethics, with its emphasis on the inclusion of actual others in real discourse, offered a less abstract, idealized, and exclusionary alternative. However, in 1992, Benhabib turned these same arguments against discourse ethics, too. With the help of her distinction between the generalized and concrete other, she argued that Habermas limits "procedures of universalizability to the standpoint of the generalized other" and thereby makes the concrete other vanish from discourse (Benhabib 1992, 10, 161).[28]

Though the feminist critique of Rawls and Habermas was certainly influential, it is questionable how successful it was.

Criticism 1, that liberal political theory presupposes "disembodied and disembedded" selves is another version of the communitarian critique of the moral person. As we saw, that applied to Rawls only on the mistaken assumption that the original position was the place to look for his conception of the self and his social ontology. As a criticism of discourse ethics, it fares no better. It certainly does not apply to the actual participants in discourse, since Habermas insists that these are concrete individuals.

Does it apply more readily to the hypothetical members of the moral community into whose perspectives participants must project themselves in advocatory discourses?[29] Recall that the objection is that in moral discourse that conforms to (U), participants cannot but disregard the viewpoints of concrete other people. However, proper consideration of the ideal role-taking imposed by moral discourse shows that such discourse in no way opposes or excludes the viewpoints of concrete particular others. Consider also the constituency of "all affected" by a norm, namely the moral community. According to Habermas, in discourse, each participant accedes not only to the viewpoint of every other actual participant, but also to the viewpoint of every member of the moral community, in order to assess whether a norm can be welcomed by all affected. Evidently, that cannot be done if each participant abstracts from all particular and concrete features of the person and the situation and merely generalizes over them. Rather, each person has to fill in the relevant details and particularities of every other affected person as they proceed in order to see whether they can assent to it.

So, while it is true that (U) requires each participant in discourse to switch perspective with every other person qua member of the moral community, these others are not, and should not be, conceived as the generic, abstract, "disembodied and disembedded" individuals of which Benhabib complains, but rather as concrete and situated individuals.[30]

In which case, it does not follow that moral discourse (as Habermas understands it) makes the concrete other vanish from discourse or blinds agents to the viewpoint of the concrete other.

Benhabib's argument is not leveled at universalism per se, but at what she calls "substitutionalist" universalism. In contrast to this, she proposes "interactive universalism," which allegedly does not confine itself to the standpoint of the generalized other but sets out to "recognize the dignity of the generalized other through an acknowledgement of the moral identity of the concrete other" (Benhabib 1992, 164). To my mind, however, Benhabib's attempted counterproposal is not so much a criticism of Habermas's conception of moral discourse as a proper explication of it.[31] She and Habermas are on exactly the same page.

Criticism 2 does not apply so much to Rawls because the original position is an account of the moral point of view not generally but for matters of social justice. It is correct to claim, though, that both Kohlberg and Habermas have a conception of the moral domain that is both narrow and uniform, and this does open them to criticism.[32] For example, Taylor criticizes Kantianism for assuming "that there is a single consistent domain of the 'moral,' that there is one set of considerations or mode of calculation which determines what we 'morally' ought to do" (Taylor 1982, 132). As early as 1954, Kurt Baier criticized theories of moral development for assuming that it is a process by which agents learn to do one thing ever more adequately, rather than a way of learning to perform different tasks well (Baier 1954, 135).

Such a criticism, however, applies much more readily to discourse ethics in phase one, before Habermas had made room for ethical discourse alongside moral discourse. If one takes them as objections to the discourse theory of morality in phase two, though, the picture is more complicated. Some of the differences are merely terminological. Benhabib uses the terms "morality" and "the moral standpoint" in a broad sense. By contrast, in phase two of discourse ethics, Habermas uses the terms in a narrow sense restricted to a central core of impartial moral norms and their justification in discourse. Once one acknowledges that, Benhabib's claim might just be that notions of "care" and "the good" and judgments of the concrete particularities of moral agents and their situations belong to morality in the broad sense and as such enjoy priority and centrality with respect to all nonmoral values. Habermas does not deny that, and he need not deny Benhabib's claim "that relations of justice do not exhaust the moral domain even if they occupy a central position within it" (Benhabib 1992, 10–11). It is just that he puts the point differently, namely by saying that discourse ethics needs to say something about (what he calls) morality and also about (what he calls) ethics.

However, Benhabib's claim might be that the moral domain narrowly construed should not be confined to norms of justice nor moral discourse to their justification. Rather, notions of care and the idea of the good have their place there, too. If this is the intended criticism, then it looks like Benhabib and Habermas differ about what morality is. For Habermas, moral discourse is confined to the task of justifying norms of justice and as such enjoys priority over any ethical considerations of care or the good. Not even the good of friendship or the love of family can be weighed against moral demands. That said, Habermas is keen to point out that even justified moral norms need to be applied through judgment or through discourses of application, practices that might involve other evaluative considerations. And, as we have seen, in phase two of discourse ethics, he also maintains that solidarity with every member of the moral community is the other side of justice (JS, 244).

Criticism 3, as we have already seen, applies to Habermas's discourse ethics insofar as it makes a "razor-sharp" distinction between issues of justice and the good life and his insistence on the priority of the latter over the former (MCCA, 104). His response, however, is to insist it is a distinction that he, the moral theorist, simply reconstructs. Habermas attempts to demonstrate this by providing *both* a genealogical and historical account of the emergence of modern morality *and* a rational reconstruction of the moral standpoint, which dovetail together.

In the final analysis, the feminist critique of the moral standpoint is more or less one with the various communitarian criticisms of Kant and Rawls. It attempts to turn these criticisms against discourse ethics but, in my view, does so with only limited success.

2.5 CONCLUDING REFLECTIONS ON THE EARLY DEBATE

So much, then, for the early debate, in which the exchange between Habermas and Rawls took shape. As noted earlier, Rawls does not participate personally, even though justice as fairness figures centrally. Insofar as it has a focus, the core issue lies between Kohlberg's and Habermas's differing views about whether Rawls's idea of the original position or Habermas's idea of discourse conforming to principle (U) is the most adequate basis for reconstructing the moral point of view of a mature moral agent at stage 6. And this issue is about how best to operationalize (and reconstruct) a procedure for choosing and validating impartial norms of justice as the substantial principles of a general moral theory.

Many of the arguments between the communitarians and feminists on the one side and Rawls, Habermas, and Kohlberg on the other result in stalemate.

Some of the apparent disagreement is merely terminological. Take for example the central notion of justice. When Kohlberg, Habermas, and Gilligan talk about justice, they are referring to what I have been calling justice-qua-morality, which they take to be the central (and indeed single) principle of a general theory of right conduct. But when Rawls, Sandel, and Benhabib talk about justice, they are talking about a political value that can be enshrined in law and, where necessary, enforced by the courts. But political-cum-legal justice is distinct from justice-qua-morality in its scope and in its nature. Moral actions cannot be coerced or enforced by external authority without losing their specific mode of validity. True, the two conceptions are related. But in the early debate, neither the distinctiveness nor the relatedness of the two concepts of justice is brought into focus.

The reasons for this may have to do with an ambivalence at the heart of discourse ethics. By the early 1990s, in the second phase of its development, around the time of the publication of *Between Facts and Norms*, Habermas is clear that discourse ethics is a moral theory—not a normative ethical theory in the standard sense, but rather a social theory of morality. And yet this is not how it is understood by many of Habermas's followers, many of whom construe it as a nascent political theory or theory of democratic legitimacy.[33] To take just one example of many, Simone Chambers writes, "I agree that discourse ethics makes its strongest showing as a theory of political justice and democratic legitimacy," but goes on to argue, against the defenders of the political reading, that discourse ethics offers insight into "the world of morality" (Chambers, 1996, 144). Rehg calls this the "political reading" of discourse ethics (Rehg 1994, 32–34).[34]

The political reading is not a simple mistake. It is motivated by peculiar but central features of discourse ethics that invite the political reading. For example,

1. According to Habermas, the primary function of moral norms is to resolve conflicts of interest and to facilitate social cooperation, which looks like a political, rather than moral, task.
2. Discourse ethics is broadly contractarian in nature, and, with one or two prominent exceptions, contract theories are more common in political, rather than moral, theory.[35]
3. The central normative concept of discourse ethics is justice, which more often figures as a political concept than the central idea of a moral theory equivalent to moral rightness.[36]

To this extent, the political reading reflects a fundamental ambivalence at the heart of discourse ethics itself between moral theory and the theory of democratic legitimacy, an ambivalence that was not fully resolved until Habermas came up with his own political theory, a theory of democratic legitimacy, in the early 1990s. Only at that point, as we will see, does Habermas come to a clear view of what is specific to political justice in the context of the domestic politics of a liberal constitutional democratic state as opposed to justice-qua-morality in the context of a general theory of right human conduct.

Now, this ambivalence at the heart of discourse ethics reflects a similar ambiguity at the heart of Rawls's justice as fairness as set out in *A Theory of Justice*. As I have mentioned, in *Political Liberalism*, which will be the focus of part II of this book, Rawls admits that in *A Theory of Justice*, he was unclear about whether justice as fairness was intended as a theory of institutional design or as a "moral doctrine of justice general in scope" (PL, xvii). And, seizing on this ambivalence, an influential interpretation of Rawls's early book pulled it in just the opposite direction. Though Rawls mainly used the term "justice" in the narrow sense tailored to the basic structure of society, already in the 1970s and increasingly so in the 1980s, justice as fairness came to be treated as a moral theory in the broad sense—as a general moral doctrine and as a theory of right conduct. Many first-generation Rawlsians argued that his principles of justice and the use of the original position for moral deliberation could be applied to domains other than the basic structure of society without much, if any, modification. If anything, they were surprised when Rawls later rejected what they thought were natural extensions of his view. (This is most notably the case in respect of international justice and individual conduct within the basic structure, specifically when it comes to wage demands.)

My contention is that the moral reading of *A Theory of Justice* and the political reading of discourse ethics pushed each theory from opposite ends toward what looked like a shared center ground in which they could be understood as rival theories of the moral point of view for identifying and justifying impartial principles of justice. This is, I believe, how the early debate between Rawls and Habermas is usually understood. But for the various reasons adumbrated here, I believe this view is misconceived. Still, anyone who knows anything about hermeneutics will not be surprised to know that misinterpretations based on misconceptions can be as significant and influential as any other interpretations. And, as we will see, these misconceptions from the early debate do indeed go on to color the understanding and reception of the 1995 exchange and the broader Habermas–Rawls dispute.

II

HABERMAS'S AND RAWLS'S MATURE POLITICAL THEORIES

3

HABERMAS'S *BETWEEN FACTS AND NORMS*

Habermas's 1992 book on law and democracy, *Faktizität und Geltung*, translated into English as *Between Facts and Norms* in 1996, was the book the imminent completion of which was responsible for holding up the meeting of minds that was to have taken place in Bad Homburg in 1992. It is a vital piece of the jigsaw, not just because it is the indispensable backdrop to the dispute, but also because it contains a number of important new criticisms of Rawls, criticisms that, in contrast to those in the early debate, focus primarily on the idea of "political justice": justice in the context of domestic politics in a liberal constitutional state.

3.1 HABERMAS'S CRITICISM OF RAWLS IN *BETWEEN FACTS AND NORMS*

In chapter 2 of *Between Facts and Norms*, Habermas advances a criticism of Rawls that is at the same time a justification of his own discourse theory of law. The section in which it is advanced is entitled "The Return of Modern Natural Law and the 'Impotence of the Ought,'" which tells us two things. Habermas thinks Rawls's political theory is a kind of modern natural law theory and that it is vulnerable to one of Hegel's well-known criticisms of Kant's moral philosophy.

3.1.1 THE NATURAL LAW CRITICISM

The natural law criticism[1] recalls Habermas's earliest criticism of Rawls, in which Habermas situates Rawls in the tradition of the social contract theories of the state of Hobbes and Locke (CES, 184). What makes Rawls a natural law theorist in Habermas's eyes are the following features of his position.

It focuses mainly (indeed too much) on "the legitimacy of law" and not enough on "the legal form as such and . . . the institutional dimension of law backed by sanctions" (BNR, 64). Rawls has a "morally oriented theory of political justice," which is unrealistic (BNR, 64). Furthermore, Habermas claims, Rawls formulates and justifies a conception of justice philosophically. Habermas claims Rawls's theory is "developed in vacuo" (BNR, 57), "first grounded in abstracto" (BNR, 64), and is "justified before philosophical experts" (BNR, 59).

This last criticism is directed by Habermas at the two-stage justification of Rawls's theory, whereby the first stage is a normative and philosophical justification of the political conception of justice, and the second stage asks whether that conception can be stable under conditions of political actuality. Habermas takes this to be the structure of political liberalism, as his reference to Rawls's 1989 essay, "The Domain of the Political and Overlapping Consensus," shows (BFN, 60). That said, many of the criticisms seem better calibrated to *A Theory of Justice* and the arguments set out there.

By contrast with Rawls, Habermas situates himself and his own political theory in the broad tradition of what he calls "rational natural law," namely of Kant and Hegel, both of whom, Habermas claims, distinguish clearly between morality and law. Habermas does also, and this affords him, he contends, the advantages of a "normatively informed reconstruction of the historical development of the constitutional state and its social basis" (BFN, 65). There is another implied criticism of Rawls here: that he does not adequately distinguish between morality and law and fails to interrogate adequately the social and institutional basis of the constitutional state.

Just what are the advantages of a "normatively informed reconstruction of the historical development of the constitutional state and its social basis"? In Habermas's view, there are three important methodological advantages to his approach.

The first advantage is that it allows Habermas to offer a more complete account of the legal system. For Habermas argues that an adequate theory of law must do justice to its *two* dimensions: the normative dimension that it has as a repository of reasons and the factical or positive dimension it has as a system of action. Habermas argues that Rawls fails to grasp the "normative self-understanding" of law because he approaches the legal system from the observer's perspective alone (BFN, 65). By contrast, Habermas's approach offers both a reconstruction of the beliefs and attitudes of citizens toward the law (a participant's perspective) and an empirical, sociological account of the legal system from the observer's perspective as a system of action. The empirical analysis from the observer's perspective "aims at the total complex built of beliefs about legitimacy, interest positions, sanctions and circumstances" and can therefore explain the "de facto acceptance" of laws by those subject to them (BFN, 69).

The second advantage, Habermas claims, is that that these two accounts provide interlocking perspectives from "above and below" or, more accurately, from inside and from outside (BFN, 69). And because of that, they are able to throw light on the various ways in which the system of law mediates the tension between validity and facticity and harnesses it for the purposes of facilitating social integration and reproduction and maintaining social order. By contrast, Habermas argues, Rawls offers a foreshortened account of the normative dimension of law, because he approaches it only from the observer's perspective.

The third advantage of Habermas's approach, he claims, is that it brings to light the tension between facticity and validity in the various places in which it manifests itself. The most important of these for our purposes are what he calls the "internal and external tensions." The internal tension is the "tension between facticity and validity inhabiting law itself," namely the way in which law simultaneously canalizes moral and ethical content, expressing the norms and values of everyday life, while also acting as a coercive system for ensuring compliance through "empirical" motivations, such as the threat of punishment. The external tension is the way in which the normative and evaluative dimension of legitimate law exerts pressure on a recalcitrant reality, namely the complex of institutions, practices, and existing laws and regulations. Habermas claims that by focusing more or less exclusively on questions of justice and legitimacy, Rawls is blind to the internal tension and pays attention to only one aspect of the external tension, namely to the way in which legitimate laws resolve the problem of value pluralism (BFN, 64–65).

3.1.2 THE EXTERNAL CRITICISM

The natural law criticism gives rise to an associated criticism of the two-stage structure of Rawls's theory, namely that it brings the ideal conception of justice to bear externally on political actuality. Habermas claims that Rawls's normative principles "seek contact with social reality in an unmediated way" (BNR, 64). He also notes the "weakness of Rawls's attempt to bridge the chasm between ideal theoretical demands and social facts" (BFN, 64). He makes a broadly similar point in an interview with Michael Haller in 1991: "As opposed to my famous American colleagues . . . I've never had any ambition of sketching out a normative political theory. Although it's perfectly sensible, I don't design the 'basic norms' of a well-ordered society on the drafting table" (PF, 101). This is more than the usual disparaging remark about transcendent criticism, which, because it is based on external standards, is supposed to suffer from various defects (for example, irrelevance) compared with "immanent" criticism, which, by virtue of being based on standards internal to the society that is the object of criticism, is supposed to be appropriate and fruitful.[2] It is also repeating one of the main methodological principles of discourse ethics: that it is not up to the theorist to determine the normative content of moral norms, principles of justice, or legitimate laws.

3.1.3 THE SERENDIPITY OBJECTION

As regards the second stage of justification, Habermas seems to think that insofar as at the second stage, the political conception of justice is justified only on the basis of the ideas that belong to an overlapping consensus—that is, a political culture shared among citizens in spite of a plurality of diverse world views—it is tantamount to a justification on the basis of what he calls "latent potentials that we can awaken from traditions we just happen to inherit" (BFN, 63).[3] In other words, the second-stage justification is a matter of the serendipitous bequest of history and is not apt to provide the normative foundation of a conception of justice.

3.1.4 THE "DESCRIPTIVIST" CRITIQUE

Finally, Habermas maintains that because his theory reconstructs the "development of the constitutional state in concrete societies," it "can play a role in a critical description of actual political processes" (BFN, 65). There are two different critical points in play here. The first is the implication that whereas Habermas's theory is immanent and therefore *appropriately critical*, Rawls's is not. The second is the objection that Rawls's theory is not critical at all. This is what Todd Hedrick calls the "descriptivist critique." Hedrick gives this label to a number of criticisms that have been aimed by various critics, foremost among them Habermas, at justice as fairness advanced as a political conception, as in *Political Liberalism*.[4] Hedrick claims such criticisms boil down to two objections: (1) that Rawls's later theory "is a pragmatic form of advocacy that merely gauges what reasonable people are likely to accept, and suggests we tailor our normative proposals accordingly" and (2) that it is "unable to support the normative claims he would like to make" (Hedrick 2010, 27). It is not very clear whether Hedrick endorses claim (1) or whether he merely thinks Habermas endorses it. He does, however, make clear that both he and Habermas endorse claim (2). I agree that Habermas endorses claim (2). One could put the claim more starkly: Because Rawls's political conception of justice is based on a set of liberal values supposedly common to reasonable citizens, it is unable properly to criticize a liberal society.[5] Whether Habermas endorses claim (1) is harder to determine.

Note that in making such criticism, Habermas is once again drawing unfavorable comparisons between *Political Liberalism* and discourse ethics. For example, take the claim that in limiting itself to the "narrow circle of political-moral questions of principle for which an 'overlapping consensus' may reasonably be expected," Rawls is engaged in a search for "principles or norms that incorporate generalizable interests" (BFN, 61). In other words, the implication is that Rawls needs to rely on moral principles to ground his criticism but for various reasons cannot, whereas Habermas's theory can. This thought, as we will see, runs throughout *Between Facts and Norms* but is most clearly expressed in Habermas's second contribution to the exchange, in which he argues that philosophy has at its disposal an "objective and impartial" standpoint from which society can be criticized, which it "encounters in society itself," namely "the moral point of view" (MW, 89/110).

Since we are not yet in a position to assess these arguments, we must be content with noting them. We will consider Habermas's claims about his own theory again at the end of this chapter, once we have his whole theory in view. Our assessment of Habermas's criticisms of Rawls's *Political Liberalism* will have to wait until the end of chapter 4.

3.2 THE STRUCTURE OF *BETWEEN FACTS AND NORMS*

Most of the criticisms of Rawls that Habermas makes in the second chapter of *Between Facts and Norms* are made from the perspective of his own discourse theory of law and argued on the basis of the assumptions he makes there. To see what those assumptions are, we have to look in more detail at the structure and argument of *Between Facts and Norms*. The key to the structure of this work is in the original German title, *Faktizität und Geltung*, which marks the centrality of the distinction between the facticity and validity of law. It is noteworthy that in the original title, it is not the plural nouns (facts and norms) that are counterposed, but rather the general properties of "facticity" and "validity." And it is clear from the German title that these terms are unsaturated—for it is the facticity *of law* and the validity *of law* that are in question, not just any old facts and norms.

There is no single third term between the facticity and the validity of law, just various different ways of resolving the tension, or rather of holding the two terms in tension and putting the tension to productive use. The emphasis is on the first term—"facticity"—not on the mediating relation "between." Indeed, it is significant that the word "facticity" comes first, rather than its counterpart "validity." In itself, that is a covert criticism of approaches to law such as Rawls's (or Ronald Dworkin's for that matter), which, as we have just seen, Habermas thinks overemphasize and prioritize the normative dimension of law. Not that Habermas comes down on the side of the legal positivists such as John Austin and H. L. A. Hart. On the contrary, the "and validity" part of the title indicates the necessity of validity (the normative component of law, which is itself complex), without which positive law would not be possible.

The distinction (and tension) between facticity and validity reoccurs within each of the individual conjuncts. And this is not just an analytic move, but also an attempt to capture the actual legal phenomena to which the distinction refers, namely the various real tensions between the normative dimension of law and its institutional reality.[6]

In other words, the *facticity* of law itself has both positive and normative dimensions. Law ensures social order by imposing its monopoly on legitimate violence. The monopoly is *legitimate*, and so are its means of coercion, and that means, in this case, that they are consonant with the everyday norms of justice, proportionality, the moral value of human dignity, equal respect for persons, and so on. Law keeps order by dint of sanctions, but not any old sanctions: legitimate ones. This means that *validity* qua the normative dimension of law—its legitimacy—is operative at the heart of its *facticity*, its positive dimension. Conversely, an element of facticity exists within the validity dimension of law. A law or policy that is valid needs not only to be moral (justified by moral norms) and ethical (consonant with ethical values), but also to be enforceable and, beyond that, laid down correctly according to a legally recognized process.[7] So there is also a positive dimension to law inherent to its validity.

The structure of *Between Facts and Norms* reflects this complex of tensions between facticity and validity. The first chapter, "Law as a Category of Social Mediation Between Facts and Norms," lays out the distinction between facticity and validity and rehearses some of the copious background theories of discourse ethics and communicative action. The second chapter, "The Sociology of Law Versus the Philosophy of Justice," is a general synoptic reckoning with existing theories of law. Both the philosophies of justice—normative theories such as those of Dworkin and Rawls—and the sociologies of law, such as those of Weber and Parsons, seize on important aspects of law, but they do so in a one-sided way, Habermas contends. According to Habermas, the dominant theme in these opening chapters is the facticity dimension—the social and institutional reality—of law (BFN, 288).

In chapters 3 and 4, Habermas puts forward his rational reconstruction of the "validity" of law. Hugh Baxter argues that these chapters are further distinguished by the former's being about the validity component (of legal validity), namely the principle of democracy and the system of rights, and the latter's being about the facticity dimension of legal validity, namely the "principles of the constitutional state" and the legal mechanisms by which the basic rights developed in abstraction in chapter 3 are legally implemented (Baxter 2011, 63). Habermas himself claims that chapters 3 through 6 adopt the perspective of legal theory (BFN, 288).

Chapters 7 and 8 return to the dimension of facticity and do so from the perspective of social theory. In chapter 7, Habermas turns his attention to the procedural conception of democracy and in particular looks at this from a sociological perspective, whereas in chapter 8 he looks at the circulation of communicative power and its transformation into administrative power (BFN, 287, 315). Finally, chapter 9 is a concluding reflection on paradigms of law that also deals with several outstanding matters not yet covered.

Another way of thinking of the structure is that while chapters 1, 2, 7, and 8 focus predominantly on the *external* tension between validity and facticity ("the normative self-understanding of the constitutional state" and its relation to "the social facticity of political processes" [BFN, 288]) from a social-theoretical perspective, chapters 3, 4, 5, and 6 primarily examine the *internal* tension between validity and facticity inhabiting law itself from the perspective of legal theory. Of course, these themes and approaches are more closely interwoven than this distinction makes it seem.

3.3 THE ARGUMENT OF *BETWEEN FACTS AND NORMS*

This overview of the structure of *Between Facts and Norms*, if correct, gives a sense of the balance that Habermas attempts to strike between social theory and legal theory and between the facticity and validity dimensions of law. Now we must turn to an exposition and analysis of the argument. This is a huge task, and I cannot hope to do justice to what is already a rich and burgeoning literature on the topic (on which I am very fortunate to be able to draw). However, my limited aim is to throw light on the aspects of Habermas's theory that feature importantly in the exchange and the broader dispute with Rawls. Consequently, I confine my exposition to the following five topics: the co-originality thesis, the principle of democracy, the system of rights, the two-track conception of democracy, and the relation between communicative power and administrative power. This means that the main focus of my exposition is on the validity dimension of law and the internal tension—within law itself—between facticity and validity. The reason for this is that this is the territory in which Habermas conducts his more detailed internal criticism of Rawls's political liberalism in the 1995 exchange. The caveat, though, is that there is much more to *Between Facts and Norms* than merely those aspects of it made salient by Habermas's subsequent debate with Rawls. As McCarthy cautions, we forget that at the price of making Habermas look more like an ideal theorist, and like Rawls, than he really is.

3.3.1 HABERMAS'S RECONSTRUCTION OF MODERN LAW

Habermas's *Between Facts and Norms* is not an analysis of law and democracy as such, but rather a rational reconstruction of law *in modern societies* with liberal constitutional democratic states (Zurn 2011, 157). That is, it reconstructs the basic features of a certain historical configuration of the legal and political system that has emerged in twentieth-century Europe and the United States. To understand what this means for his project, we need to recall our discussion of modernity and the rationalization of the lifeworld. According to Habermas, modernization and rationalization comprise a number of closely related processes.

The first is that individual life histories and collective traditions become *reflexive*. Instead of being naïvely assumed and continued, they are subject to reason and justification. Habermas claims that once "the transmission of culture and processes of socialization become reflexive," individualism and pluralism arise, and both developments give rise to problems of possible conflict and require social coordination. A second part of the rationalization process, closely related to the tendency to become reflexive, is the tendency for substance to give way to procedure. For example, moral substance, the fixed moral code of substantive moral norms, gives way to discursive procedures by which individuals as participants in moral discourses determine the validity of moral norms for themselves. This is because, as Habermas argues, once "the meta-social guarantees of the sacred have broken down" (BFN, 27)—because, say, a single religion no longer sets the moral agenda—modern subjects have no option but freely to thematize, rationally agree, and institute the terms of their continued peaceful coexistence in the medium of communication and discourse. A third significant part of modernization are the tendencies toward value generalization and, in particular, toward the separation of moral consciousness from the ethical self-understanding of the community. Gradually this leads to the ascendancy of universalist value orientations and the priority of the right over thick conceptions of the good life.[8]

The importance of Habermas's focus on law in modern society is not to be underestimated. Habermas offers a reconstruction of *modern* law, law in a highly complex, socially differentiated society in a liberal constitutional democratic state. This colors all of the basic concepts in Habermas's discourse theory, including what he calls "the form of law," which refers to the form law takes *under these specific conditions.*

3.3.2 THE FUNCTION OF LAW IN MODERN SOCIETIES

Recall that one consequence of the demanding condition that any valid moral norm must meet, namely that it should be in the equal interest of "all affected," is the diminution of the number of valid moral norms and the consequent shrinking of the moral domain (narrowly construed). This means that a universal procedural morality is unable on its own to take up the burden of social integration and to meet the challenges of individualism and value pluralism. Consequently, in modern societies, Habermas argues, the social order "becomes more intensely concentrated in the legal system," and law increasingly takes up the burden of social integration from morality (BFN, 98–99). And of course, law is subject to exactly the same social pressures that affect morality. It is equally true of law that under modern conditions, it cannot borrow the sources of normativity from the past but must "create its normativity out of itself" (PDM, 7). What that means is that modern law cannot base its authority on an antecedently given ethical life, or moral order.

For Habermas, modern law is a compensation and counterweight for the loss of moral and ethical substance and thus a mechanism for coping with the individualism and value pluralism that modernization brings about.[9] Not that law supplants moral and ethical substance, but rather it complements and also canalizes moral norms and ethical values for the purposes of social integration and reproduction. For law, as Habermas argues, "borrows its binding force . . . from the alliance that the facticity of law forms with the claim to legitimacy," and its claim to legitimacy, as we will see below, consists in part in its consonance with ethical values and valid moral norms (BFN, 39).

Moral norms are binding on human beings qua human beings in virtue of their universal form and also in virtue of the reason for them. But moral norms cannot be administratively enforced on pain of losing their moral meaning. For moral actions, in Habermas's broadly Kantian view of morality, must be performed out of insight into the reasons for them: They cannot be coerced without vitiating their specific form of validity. In post-conventional societies, mature (that is, stage 6) moral agents are charged with the task of identifying and establishing valid moral norms; in addition, they are disposed to act on them for their own sake, even in the face of countervailing interests and wants. Legitimate laws, however, are different. Habermas likes to say that they are "Janus faced" (BFN, 448). Laws are normatively binding qua legitimate (because they are justified by good moral and ethical reasons), but they are also factually binding insofar as they are backed up by a judicial system that can, where needed, enforce them, and insofar as this fact about them is widely known and understood among citizens.[10]

Because of this dual *binding* force, laws can compensate for the moral frailty of citizens who are not always motivated to do what is morally right, and for the cognitive limitations of citizens who don't always know what is morally right to do. For laws are promulgated and thus tell citizens what they are required to do. Moreover, they demand *only* compliance; they don't demand that the motivations for compliance be the appropriate moral motivations. This is one way in which the internal tension in the law can be shown to be socially useful. The tension between "the coercive force of law, which secures average rule-acceptance" and "the idea of self-legislation (or the supposition of the political autonomy of the united citizens), which first vindicates the claim of the rules themselves," lifts the motivational and cognitive burden of morality (BFN, 39).

3.3.3 THE PRINCIPLE OF DEMOCRACY

The centerpiece of Habermas's political theory is the principle of democracy, which states, "Only those statutes may claim legitimacy [*legitime Geltung*] that can meet with the assent of all citizens in a discursive process of legislation that in turn has been legally constituted" (BFN, 110). It is this principle, Habermas claims, that "confers legitimating force on the legislative process" (BFN, 121). This is an oblique way of saying that the principle reconstructs formal elements of the democratic and legislative process, and it is this process that confers legitimacy.

This is actually rather different from saying that what confers legitimacy on a law, much like what makes a norm justified according to the discourse principle (D), is that it can meet with the reasoned consensus of all affected, where "all affected" refers to the narrower group of all members of the legal community. That would make Habermas's view look like a kind of sophisticated, hypothetical consent theory of legitimacy. However, he knows that in highly complex mass societies, what actually makes laws authoritative for us, or imparts some claim to validity to them, is merely that they received majority support in an essentially bureaucratic decision procedure. (This is the lesson he takes from Luhmann's theory of legitimation by procedure. [Luhmann 2001].) To be sure, Habermas does not want to deny that if a law is legitimate (or valid), it can, and probably will, be accepted by all citizens. What he denies (and Luhmann asserts) is that such acceptance is "motiveless" or "reason free," that it has nothing to do with "freely bestowed acceptance" on the basis of rational insight into the law or the grounds of its justification, but has everything to do with a "social climate that institutes the acceptance of binding decisions as the apparently self-evident . . . consequence of the validity of the administrative decision" (Luhmann 2001, 34).

So instead of claiming that validity (or legitimacy) consists only in the motiveless and routine acceptance of administrative decision, Habermas argues that it is because of the normative richness of the democratic procedures (when properly followed) that they transform facticity into validity by producing legitimate laws. This is the significance of the reference in the principle of democracy to a "legally constituted . . . discursive process of legislation." The discursive process in question is modeled on principle (D) and involves different kinds of reasons specifically excluded from moral discourse, such as ethical and pragmatic reasons. Habermas claims,

> Matters in need of legal regulation certainly do not raise moral questions only, but also involve empirical, pragmatic, and ethical aspects, as well as issues concerned with the fair balancing of interests open to compromise. . . . Unlike the clearly focused normative validity claim of moral commands, the legitimacy claim of legal norms, like the legislative practice of justification itself, is supported by different types of reason. (BFN, 452)[11]

But what this implies is that politics is a mixed discourse that cannot be modeled after the pattern of any of its individual components—whether moral, ethical, or theoretical discourse. This is, I believe, an important point that Habermas sometimes neglects to factor into his discussions.

That political discourse is mixed raises a number of questions about how the various kinds of reasons work together. Habermas makes several different claims about this, but his main claim is that moral reasons have priority (BFN, 103, 108, 113; FG, 64–66; JA, 13; TIO, 42–43). Ethical reasons have validity—and thus can play a role in the determination of the legitimacy of law—only within the bounds of moral permissibility. In this specific sense, there is what Habermas calls an "absolute priority of the right over the good"—and note that by "the right" here, he means moral rightness (TIO, 27). Indeed, when Habermas insists on the priority of the right over the good in his work up to and including *Between Facts and Norms*, he means the priority of questions of justice (which, recall, he takes to be equivalent to moral rightness, hence my label "justice-qua-morality") over questions of the good life, the priority of moral norms over ethical values.

Habermas talks of the "conceptual priority of the right over the good" (BNR, 286). And he makes claims like the following: "The perspective of justice and that of evaluating one's own life are not equally valid in the sense that the morally required priority of impartiality can be leveled out and reversed in favor of the ethical priority of one's particular goals in life" (BNR, 287). What this amounts to is a thesis I call the "moral permissibility constraint," or MPC for short. Habermas often observes that laws, if they are to be legitimate, must "harmonize with the universal principles of justice and solidarity" (BFN, 99, 155). He also says that "a legal order can be legitimate only if it does not contradict basic moral principles." And by "moral principles" (*moralischen Grundsätzen*), he means valid moral norms (BFN, 106; FG, 137)—so not principle (U) but the substantive norms, the validity of which is established by participants in discourse.[12]

Note, though, that Habermas's formulation of the MPC is ambiguous. It is presented both as a positive requirement of coherence—that legitimate law "must harmonize with" morality—and as a prohibition against inconsistency, that is, that no legitimate law may violate any moral norm. The latter condition is much weaker and is easily met by any law that does not bear one way or the other on moral norms and values.

Perhaps this is why some commentators take the requirement to consist in the much stronger claim that there should be some positive relation of fit between a "core morality" and legitimate laws (Baynes 2016, 135).[13] But there are at least two difficulties with this strong interpretation of the MPC. The first is that it undermines a central plank of Habermas's theory of modernity, which is that in modern societies, political discourse and legitimate law take up the burden of social integration from moral discourse. One way they do so is by occupying areas in which behavior regulation is needed but morality is silent or too general to be much use. If there needs to be a positive fit between morality and legitimate law, then democratic agreement will be almost as difficult to achieve, and hence as scarce, as rationally motivated consensus in moral discourse.

The second difficulty is that this interpretation sits ill with Habermas's central theoretical claim that the authority of legitimate law is not borrowed from an antecedent moral order but is "morally freestanding" (BNR, 80). Hence, I maintain, contra Kenneth Baynes, that Habermas can help himself only to the weaker claim: that legitimate law must, on pain of cognitive dissonance, operate within the bounds of moral permissibility.[14]

In addition to legitimate law's being morally permissible, Habermas states that it "must also harmonize with . . . ethical principles" (BFN, 99). Let's call this the "ethical harmonization requirement." This is quite a controversial claim for Habermas to make, for he is an avowed pluralist about conceptions of the good. So the ethical harmonization requirement cannot imply that a legitimate law must cohere with all ethical values, for they are many, and some of them inevitably conflict. Nor can it mean that if someone's—or some group's—ethical self-understanding conflicts with any law, then that law is not legitimate. That would make legitimacy almost impossible to achieve. Besides, Habermas explicitly equates conceptions of the good with religious and metaphysical world views, so, methodologically speaking, such a move would be incompatible with the presuppositions of post-metaphysical thinking. For these reasons I believe that what Habermas must mean, and what we should take him to mean, is just that legitimate laws should aspire to garner as much support from ethical values as possible.

The final thing to note about the principle of democracy is that the "discursive process of legislation" that is to yield laws that can be accepted by all citizens is—unlike moral discourse, which is constrained only by the inherent pragmatic rules of discourse—also constrained by established institutional rules enshrined in law. This is another the way in which law (specifically the facticity dimension of law) figures in the production of legitimacy.

3.3.4 THE DERIVATION OF THE PRINCIPLE OF DEMOCRACY

The central contention of *Between Facts and Norms* is that "the principle of democracy derives from the interpenetration of principle (D) and the legal form" (BFN, 122–23). Principle (D) states that "only those norms are valid that could meet with the assent of all those potentially affected, insofar as they participate in rational discourse" (BFN, 107; TIO, 41). It is a rule of practical argumentation in general. It is supposedly anchored below the threshold of morality (and politics) in the deep structure of social action—that is, the pragmatic presuppositions of communication and discourse—and as such expresses a necessary condition of the validity of action norms in general: political, legal, and moral norms.[15] Habermas claims that it is "neutral" or "initially indifferent vis à vis morality and law" (BFN, 107, 121). (This is what Habermas refers to when he later claims—with a nod toward political liberalism—that the principle of democracy is "morally freestanding" [BNR, 80].)

The legal form, for its part, is a matter of institutional, empirical, and historical fact. It includes, but is not exhausted by, what in Anglophone theory is called the "rule of law." But, as Baynes remarks, contra Joshua Cohen, it is a more substantive concept (Baynes 2016, 166). Recall that Habermas is offering a reconstruction of *modern* law, so "legal form" refers to a complex of features that law has under modern conditions in a liberal constitutional democratic state. In no particular order, these include the following:

- It has been passed by a legally recognized body (for example, parliament) correctly, according to its rules and procedures.
- It applies to every citizen and person who falls under its jurisdiction.
- It is consistent with other laws.
- Its observance is enforceable by various legitimate means.
- There exist generally effective and legitimate mechanisms for applying it.

The main claim Habermas makes is that the principle of democracy derives from the "interpenetration" of principle (D) and the legal form. Importantly, this derivation is separate from, and sits as it were side by side with, the derivation of principle (U) (which, as we saw in chapter 1, is also derived from principle [D]).

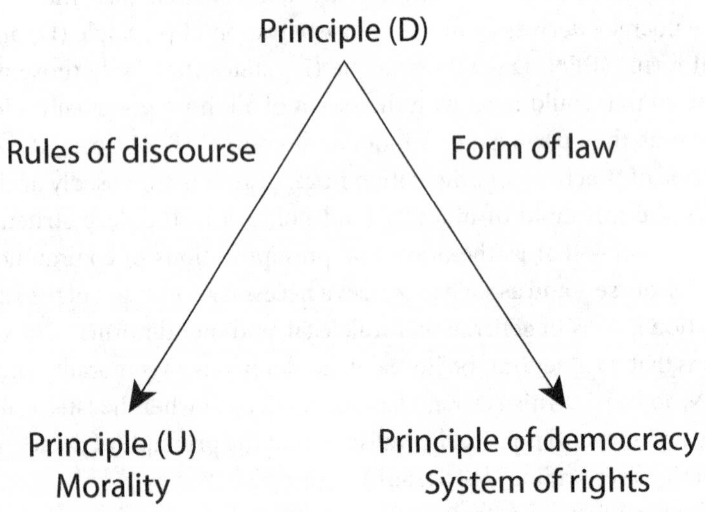

FIGURE 3.1 The underlying structure of Habermas's theory in *Between Facts and Norms*.

The structure of Habermas's theory, specifically the relation among the three principles—(D), (U), and the principle of democracy—reflects Habermas's view that in modern societies, political legitimacy does not derive from an antecedent moral order. The principle of democracy is supposed to rationally reconstruct "the democratic procedure for the production of law," which is the sole source of legitimacy in modern Western societies (BFN, 448). In other words, according to Habermas, the normative force (or the rational authority) of law, as opposed to its positive authority or facticity, is sui generis; it is not borrowed from the normative force and rational authority of morality. To hold the contrary, Habermas maintains, is the mistake that thinkers such as Kant and the natural law theorists make, along with Rawls, Dworkin, Charles Larmore, and Karl-Otto Apel (BFN, 103–105; BNR, 78). Rather, Habermas contends, the normative force of law is ultimately anchored in and derived from "the validity basis of action oriented to reaching understanding" (BFN, 297). This is not just a theoretical point, that is, a feature of Habermas's reconstruction of democratically legitimate law. It is also, he maintains, a feature of the actual (modern, constitutional, liberal, democratic) system of legitimate law that his theory reconstructs.

3.3.5 THE SYSTEM OF RIGHTS

Habermas argues that the "interpenetration" of the legal form and the discourse principle can be understood as "a logical genesis of rights" (BFN, 121). Elaborating on this claim, he states that the "logical genesis of these rights comprises a circular process in which . . . the legal form and the mechanism for producing legitimate law—hence the principle of democracy—are *co-originally* constituted" (BFN, 122). Habermas also claims that the legal form "presupposes rights that define the status of legal persons as bearers of rights" and that the "general right to liberties" is "constitutive of the legal form" (BFN, 119, 121). His point is that the law presupposes a legal subject as rights bearer no matter what the content of those specific rights is.

Habermas is pretty clear about the conclusion of this argument, which is that a system of basic rights is given along with the principle of democracy as its necessary correlate. This system comprises five kinds of basic rights:

1. Basic rights that result from the politically autonomous development of the *right to the greatest possible measure of equal individual liberties.*
2. Basic rights that result from the politically autonomous development of the *status of a member* in a voluntary association of consociates under law.
3. Basic rights that result immediately from the *actionability* of rights and from the politically autonomous development of *legal protection.*
4. Basic rights to equal opportunities to participate in the processes of opinion and will formation in which citizens exercise their *political autonomy* and through which they generate legitimate law.
5. Basic rights to the provision of living conditions that are socially, technologically, and ecologically safeguarded, insofar as the current circumstances make this necessary if citizens are to have equal opportunities to use the civil rights listed in (1) through (4).

These are not actual concrete rights. They are general categories of rights, or schemas, that are "unsaturated" stand-ins for actual concrete rights (BFN, 125). They represent the kinds of rights that citizens must grant one another if they want to "legitimately regulate their living together by means of positive law" (BFN, 125). And Habermas is talking about *democratically* legitimate laws here (for the system of rights advanced here is a necessary correlate of the principle of democracy). When citizens actually do this, he allows, they grant one another "specific rights," rights that are "developed in a politically autonomous manner," that is, interpreted and concretized in the light of their own political culture and tradition (BFN, 129).

We cannot go into a full discussion of Habermas's theory here. We should note, though, that these schemas of basic rights (*Grundrechte*) are fully legal entities justified as functional prerequisites of the legal order in a democratic constitutional state. Just as Habermas claims of the principle of democracy, the system of rights stands free from (and thus is not justified by) any antecedently existing substantive moral norms or ethical conception of the good (BFN, 104). And this is what we should expect from a rational reconstruction of modern law, for just as modernity in general generates its own normative resources, so the legal order in a modern democracy must generate its own legitimacy (PDM, 7).

Habermas's theory claims to reconstruct the inherent rationality in law itself, which in a democratic society presupposes nothing as "given prior to the citizens' practice of self-determination" save the discourse principle and the legal form (BFN, 127).[16]

It is much less clear how Habermas's conclusion follows from his argument. Baxter is right to say that Habermas's argument is "difficult to follow" and also that Habermas's claim is not that the legal form itself implies any particular rights or system thereof (Baxter 2011, 70). For the system of rights Habermas "derives" is a scheme of five kinds of basic rights that are "unsaturated" and supposedly co-originally constituted with the principle of democracy from the "interpenetration" of the legal form (of modern societies with a liberal democratic constitution) and the discourse principle.

That is important to remember because Habermas has come in for criticism from various quarters for offering a merely legal-functionalist justification of basic rights that supposedly does not draw on moral premises. It is widely argued that his justification is normatively too thin and that he should have rested his justification more explicitly on some normative basis, whether democratic political values (Joshua Cohen), moral rights we owe to each other (Rainer Forst), a core morality consisting in a principle of equal respect (Charles Larmore), or the preconditions of the practice of moral discourse (Stefan Rummens).[17]

Let's take a closer look at a couple of these objections. Cohen claims that "legality as such—the very existence of a legal code . . . implies only that some individuals have some rights of private autonomy" (Cohen 1999, 392). So nothing so normatively demanding as the principle of equal liberties flows from the form of law. But, as Baynes points out, Cohen's objection trades on a very minimal understanding of the rule of law (Baynes 2016, 164). Habermas's notion of "legal form" is normatively much richer than the rule of law minimally understood (Baynes 2016, 166). Baynes is right. Recall that there is a legitimacy component internal to legality itself.[18] On Cohen's reconstruction of Habermas's argument, the requirement of equal liberties is supposed to flow from the other premise, the discourse principle. Cohen then argues that the latter, as a principle of impartiality, is too weak to generate a principle of equal liberties. But Habermas clearly also denies that the system of rights follows from the discourse principle *alone*. So it is misleading and uncharitable to claim that for Habermas, either the normative basis of law (its legitimacy) is based *solely* on the legal form or that it must rest entirely on the discourse principle instead. Habermas's view is that *both* are necessary, and they are *jointly* sufficient (BFN, 128). Cohen's point might be correct, but it does not count as an objection to the theory under discussion, Habermas's theory in *Between Facts and Norms*.

Jeffrey Flynn also has a counterargument to the objection that Habermas's derivation of basic rights is too functionalist and not normatively rich enough to justify its conclusions, namely the five kinds of basic rights. The logical genesis of the system of rights, he points out, is a first step that "does not exclude . . . the moral justification for specific rights—indeed it requires it"; that is, it calls for a second stage in which citizens themselves fill out the unsaturated schema in the context of their own historical and political traditions (see Flynn 2003). And at that stage, moral arguments will be appropriate. Indeed they will be necessary, for, as we saw in our discussion of the principle of democracy, Habermas claims that the "legislative practice of justification" is subject to the MPC in that it draws on the whole gamut of normative reasons: moral, ethical, and pragmatic.

A more trenchant criticism might be that here, as in discourse ethics, Habermas claims to be doing rational reconstruction, an approach that is supposed to prescind entirely from substantive normative argument. Accordingly, the moral philosopher reconstructs principle (U) but does not derive specific moral norms. Not so the political philosopher it seems, because although Habermas does not derive any specific rights, he does manage to derive a fairly detailed schema of what those rights should be. Either Habermas is in violation of his own methodological tenets or he has dramatically changed his view of rational reconstruction.

3.3.6 THE CO-ORIGINALITY THESIS

Alongside the central argument of *Between Facts and Norms*, concerning the principle of democracy and the system of rights, is a central thesis—the co-originality thesis—that is as important as the thesis enunciated in the title concerning the relation between facticity and validity. The idea of co-originality (*Gleichursprünglichkeit*) refers to a relation of equiprimordiality between two *relata*: namely that neither has priority over the other and that both are equally important. "Co-originality" also means that neither one can be reduced to the other. Finally, in a co-original relation, each mutually presupposes the other as its necessary complement, and they are thus interdependent (BFN, 314). In sum, the relation of co-originality has four axes: equal priority, equal weight, mutual irreducibility, and complementarity or interdependence.

"Co-originality" pops up everywhere in *Between Facts and Norms*. There are several different *relata* that exhibit this relation. We have already seen Habermas claim that such a relation exists between the system of rights and the principle of democracy (BFN, 122). In the same sense, Habermas claims that moral and civic autonomy are co-original.[19] What he means by this is that the subjective freedom of the individual citizen and moral autonomy are on the same level. He makes the same claim about private and public or political autonomy.

The thesis that private autonomy and public (or political) autonomy are co-original carries most of the load in his theory. Private autonomy is the freedom of the individual citizen to do what he or she likes, consistent with the private autonomy of all others. Public (or political or civic) autonomy refers to the democratic self-legislation of the people, who are simultaneously addressees of the law, insofar as they have to obey it, and—in some sense to be specified—authors of the law. Thus, for example, Habermas writes, "The co-originality of private and public autonomy first reveals itself when we decipher, in discourse theoretic terms, the motif of self-legislation according to which the addressees of law are simultaneously authors of their rights" (BFN, 104; see also 314, 409). The sense in which citizens of modern societies can meaningfully be said to be "authors of their rights" or authors of the laws needs specifying, for in a modern mass society, and representative democracy, it is not actually necessary for every citizen to be directly involved in parliamentary business.[20]

So what is being claimed? Is it enough that citizens actually participate in the flows of discourse and communication that, on Habermas's account, make up civil society, provided there is representative democratic government? Or is being an inhabitant of such a society enough?

There are three distinct but related dimensions to the co-originality thesis in *Between Facts and Norms*, which we can call the historical dimension, the theoretical/architectonic dimension, and the sociopolitical dimension.

a) The Historical Dimension of the Co-originality Thesis

The historical thesis follows the broad outlines of the genealogical account Habermas gives of the emergence of universal justice and solidarity as the basis of secular morality in the course of the rationalization of the lifeworld. Once "the normative substance of an ethos embedded in religious and metaphysical traditions has been forced through the filter of post-traditional justification," that is, once communication and discourse have taken up the burden of social integration and reproduction from a shared thick conception of the good, then only ideals of self-realization (ethical-existential and ethical political discourse) and of self-determination remain as possible sources of legitimation for modern law (BFN, 99). And, at least in the West, Habermas maintains, these ideals are mobilized by two rival traditions of political justification for the coercive impositions of law: On the one hand, the liberal tradition rests political justification on the basis of human rights as the expression of moral autonomy; on the other, republican traditions invoke the idea of popular sovereignty bound to a shared ethos and a conception of civic autonomy.

Habermas cites Kant and Rousseau as the major exponents and representatives of these two rival traditions. Kant belongs to the liberal tradition (along with the natural law theorists) insofar as he takes morality in the form of human rights to be the basis of political justification. In Kant's view, a legal order is legitimated "prior to its differentiation in the shape of positive law on the basis of moral principles, and hence independently of that political autonomy of citizens first constituted only with the social contract" (BFN, 101).[21]

By contrast, the tradition of civic republicanism in which Rousseau stands rests political justification entirely on the sovereign will of the people as expressed in the general will. To do this, Habermas contends, Rousseau conceives popular sovereignty as expressed through the social contract as a kind of "existential act of sociation through which isolated . . . individuals transform themselves into citizens oriented towards the common good of an ethical community" (BFN, 102). He can do this only because he presupposes that citizens have the political virtues of the inhabitants of small, ethically homogenous communities, and he makes this move at the expense of the individual interests of private persons.

Broadly speaking, according to Habermas, these two rival traditions exhaust the historical options, and each rival tradition suffers from an equal and opposite problem. Essentially, the liberal tradition fails to do justice to the public autonomy of the political community, and it subordinates the democratic process to the liberal requirement to guarantee the freedom of individuals, whereas the republican tradition sacrifices the private autonomy of individuals (or individual freedom) to the democratic will of the citizen body. Thus, each tradition fails to do justice to an essential dimension of autonomy and fails to account for the co-originality of private and public autonomy.

According to Habermas, both traditions are essential to the political heritage of Western liberal democracy, and what is needed is a theory that does not draw on just one of these at the expense of the other. The advantage of Habermas's discourse theory of law is that it reconfigures political justification so that it draws on both of these sources of normativity at the same time, in a form that makes them compatible with a modern, post-traditional mass society characterized by social differentiation, complexity, and value pluralism. Thus, discourse theory does justice to the co-originality of private and public autonomy insofar as it manages to combine and to give a place to the notions of popular sovereignty and human rights while simultaneously deflating their substantive presuppositions.

b) The Architectonic Dimension

So how does it do this? The argument that we have just outlined concerning the interdependence of the principle of democracy and the system of rights is one example. This argument shows how, by means of the democratic process (political autonomy), private autonomy can be given legal shape. In a passage cited earlier, Habermas refers to the "circular process in which the . . . legal form, and . . . the democratic principle—are *co-originally constituted*" (BFN, 122). Ingeborg Maus gives a detailed account of the circularity the process involves (Maus 2002, 90–98). He rightly insists that the fact that Habermas begins with three categories of subjective rights, which emerge from the application of the discourse principle to "the general right [in a non-legal sense] to have liberties," does not of itself show that Habermas subordinates the democratic process to a higher (and prior) law. And that is because the fourth right shows how the previous three categories of right in turn depend on the democratic process, of which the participatory rights outlined in category 4 are constitutive. Habermas's co-originality thesis does not assert that neither private autonomy—and the rights that enable it—nor public autonomy enjoys priority; it asserts that both do. Habermas's argument demonstrates the co-originality of private and public autonomy by showing how the basic rights are called into being by the democratic process and vice versa. The important feature of this argument, Maus shows, is that it subordinates neither the subjective basic rights of citizens (and the liberties those rights enable) nor the democratic process to external constraints exerted by an antecedent moral order of rights.

c) The Sociopolitical Dimension

Finally, there is the sociopolitical dimension of the co-originality thesis, which is an argument about the actual social and political conditions of the production of legitimate laws rather than about the form of the theory of legitimacy and its adequacy to existing conditions: "A legal order is legitimate to the extent that it equally secures the co-original private and political autonomy of its citizens; at the same time, however, it owes its legitimacy to the forms of communication in which alone this autonomy can express and prove itself" (BFN, 409).[22] The latter half of this sentence refers to the way in which democratic decision-making institutions are both receptive to, and hence dependent on, communication and discourse flowing into them from the public sphere, and shows how they thereby involve and in part consist in democratic deliberation and discourse. To understand how subjective rights and the private autonomy they enable, as well as the democratic process and the public autonomy it involves, combine in the real world to produce legitimate law, we have to consider the co-originality thesis within the context of Habermas's sociological theory of democracy and law.

3.3.7 HABERMAS'S TWO-TRACK CONCEPTION OF DEMOCRACY

According to Habermas, democracy functions well to the extent that a body of citizens enjoys political autonomy, or popular sovereignty (which, as we have seen, in turn calls for and depends on its private autonomy), and political autonomy in its turn is obtained only when citizens can understand themselves not only as the subjects, or addressees, of the law, but also—in a relevant sense—as its authors. I say "in a relevant sense" for the reason I gave earlier. Presumably, Habermas cannot be claiming that citizens understand themselves as authors of laws just in case they really are authors of the law, that is, just in case they directly participate in the drafting, hearing, and passing of legislation. For in modern democratic societies, those roles are left up to a small number of representatives. In small-scale democratic republics of the kind envisaged by Rousseau, it might have been possible for all or most citizens to participate in the legislative and administrative affairs of the republic. But in modern mass societies, the parliament or assembly does not provide a model for society as a whole. This raises two questions:

1. What does it mean for the citizens to be able to understand themselves in an appropriate sense as authors of the law?
2. What form does political autonomy take in a modern representative democratic state?

Habermas's short answer to the first question is that citizens can be politically autonomous and understand themselves as authors of the law provided that only legitimate law "programs" the political system and "determines the direction in which political power circulates" (BFN, 187). However, the short answer needs unpacking. In particular, how can legitimate law "program" the political system? And how does this programming make it the case that citizens can rightly understand themselves as authors of the law even when they don't participate directly in the legislative and administrative affairs of the state? We can understand all this better in the light of the answer to the second question.

The form that political autonomy takes in a modern representative democracy is best illustrated by Habermas's remark that the democratic system is characterized by two distinct tracks. Habermas sometimes refers to these as the formal and the informal public spheres (BFN, 307–308). In a different metaphor, borrowed from Bernhard Peters, he refers to a "center–periphery axis" (BFN, 314). In both cases, what distinguishes one track from the other, the formal from the informal public sphere, or the center from the periphery, is the degree of formal organization determined by legitimate law.

At the center lies the political system, or what Habermas refers to as "the parliamentary complex," itself an ensemble of administrative, judicial, parliamentary, and other bodies (BFN, 299). And parliament itself, which is formally programmed and authorized to "act" and to "take decisions," lies as it were at the heart of the center. By contrast, the periphery, or the informal public sphere, comprises an "open and inclusive network of overlapping subcultural publics having fluid temporal and social . . . boundaries" (BFN, 307). In this informal sphere, public opinion and will formation come about spontaneously to form a " 'wild' complex that resists organization as a whole." At the same time, although they are unruly and unregulated, the flows of public communication and discourse can be channeled by mass media and are vulnerable to the "oppressive and exclusionary effects of unequally distributed social power" (BFN, 307).

Before we move on to show how the political system thus construed produces legitimate law, it is worth noting in passing that it is in the role of civil society in the democratic process that Habermas sees a sublimated form of the idea of popular sovereignty.[23] According to the republican model, civil society (which is coeval with political society) is conceived as a macro-subject that gives laws to itself. By contrast, in discourse theory, civil society has an indirect influence on the political system, and "in no way does it occupy the position of a macro-subject supposed to bring the society as a whole under its control and simultaneously act for it" (BFN, 374). In fact, discourse theory paints an "image of a decentered society" in which the political system vies for influence with the economic and administrative subsystems, which are steered by the media of money and power, respectively, and attempts to counter-steer these through the medium of legitimate law (BFN, 327).

The fact that modern societies are decentered does not sit well with the claim that the political system stands at the center of the democratic process. However, these are merely spatial metaphors, albeit discrepant metaphors used for different purposes. The political system stands at the center of the democratic process, and parliament stands at the center of the center to the extent that it is the only body that *acts* and is geared to *take decisions*. Society as a whole, however, is decentered to the extent that the body politic is not a macro-subject that acts as a self-legislating, sovereign will, but rather consists in an ensemble of subsystems that vie with one another for control. Popular sovereignty lives on in a modern, complex, and differentiated society to the extent that the will of the people is not concentrated "concretely in the people" but dispersed in civil society: "The 'self' of the self-organizing legal community disappears in the subjectless forms of communication and discourse that regulate the formative process of public opinion in civil society" (BFN, 301). In this way, the public sphere "is not conceived simply as the back room of the parliamentary complex, but as the impulse-generating periphery that surrounds the political center: In cultivating normative reasons it affects all parts of the political system without intending to conquer it" (BFN, 442). Indeed, Habermas claims that the flows of communication and discourse in civil society "besiege the political system, without however intending to conquer it" (BFN, 487). When the democratic system "works," and the siege is successful, the flows of communication and discourse are able to enter the parliamentary complex through the "sluices" and "portals" of representative government (BFN, 354). Since these have been rinsed through the filters of moral, ethical, and pragmatic discourse, the "input" into the political system comprises public reasons consistent with morality and congruent with the ethical self-understanding of individuals and groups with common sense, so far as this is possible. Thereafter they are subject to further discursive treatment in the formal public of the parliamentary system. For parliament does not simply react to public opinion: It is set up to solve problems raised in civil society and given to it by the "impulse-generating periphery." In drafting, hearing, and passing legislation, and through its "output" of laws and policies, the political system aims to solve those problems but aims to solve them legitimately, that is, in a manner that is legally correct and consistent with moral, ethical, and pragmatic reasons that flow into the center from the periphery. This is effectively what liberal constitutional democracy does through the production of legitimate law. Legitimate laws, insofar as they provide good solutions to actual social problems in need of regulation, and because they fit with the moral and ethical self-understandings of the citizens, will tend to find acceptance among citizens.

This exposition answers the first question: What does it mean for the citizens of a modern society to be able to understand themselves in an appropriate sense as "authors" of the law, even though they do not participate directly in the legislative and administrative affairs of government? It means that the citizens participate indirectly simply by virtue of being members of civil society in a modern liberal constitutional democratic state in which democratic will and opinion formation crystallize. By Habermas's lights, this suffices for citizens to be able to consider themselves "authors" of the law. Outvoted minorities, who make their voices heard but lose the argument for one reason or another, still count as "authors" of the law in Habermas's view. So the notion of "authorship" in play here is fairly weak and very broad.[24]

That said, there are many forces at work in civil society besides discourse and the "unforced force of the better argument," including mass media outlets directed by powerful private interests. Habermas knows this and makes a further point: "Politically autonomous citizens can understand themselves as authors of the law to which they submit as private subjects only if legitimately generated law also determines the *direction* in which political power circulates" (BFN, 187).

Political power originates in civil society in the "wild" and "anarchic" currents of communication and discourse, in which, as Habermas puts it, political and public opinion and will formation spontaneously arise. Habermas calls this "communicative power" because it arises among citizens in common causes and general interests and takes the form of shared reasons. Communicative power, thus construed, arises in the periphery and flows toward the center, where, when combined with administrative power in the political system, it becomes political power in the form of legitimate laws.

Why is the direction of the circulation of power important? The answer, according to Habermas, is that there are three sources of integration in modern societies: money, in the economic system; power, in the administrative system; and what Habermas in *Between Facts and Norms* calls "solidarity." Now, money and power are "steering media," which work instrumentally and internally govern spheres that are largely autonomous. They result in what Habermas in *The Theory of Communicative Action* calls "system integration" as opposed to communication and discourse, which work non-instrumentally to facilitate "social integration" (TCA II, 117–18).[25] Now, as Habermas uses the term in *Between Facts and Norms*, "solidarity" represents "the other side" of political justice, and it is not a steering medium that brings about system integration. Solidarity is a basis of social integration produced by the "rationally motivated agreements" that result from discourse. So the legal system, insofar as it generates legitimate laws, can institute social solidarity provided that communicative power (in the form of the shared reasons that result from discourses) percolates into the political system from civil society.

The question now is, how can the media of money and power, which steer the economic and administrative systems, respectively, be on the one hand left to their own devices and on the other made congruent with the demands of moral solidarity?

Habermas's answer is that the political system "programs" the economic and administrative system through legitimate law. It can do this because law is, as we have seen, "Janus faced." Earlier we described this as the conjunction of the normative dimension of legitimacy with the positive dimension of enforceability, but these can equally be redescribed in terms of communicative and administrative power. Political power in the form of legitimate law (in Habermas's sense) is both at once. Legitimate law acts as a "hinge between the system and lifeworld" (BFN, 56). More pertinently, since one of the main functions of legitimate law is to bring the economy and the administration in line with the common good of citizens, it can function as a "transformer."[26]

Earlier we observed that moral norms have only a weak motivating force and that this limits their social integrating effect. However, legitimate law, which as we have seen must obey the MPC, not only has a moral content, but, beyond this, is also enforceable. Thus, law canalizes, strengthens, and broadens the socially integrating effect of morality (BFN, 118). Furthermore, because of the dual structure of legitimate law, the political system is able to counter-steer (or instrumentally affect) the economy and administration through the administrative power of legitimate law. But this means that it can, when all goes well, program the economy and administration in the direction of the common good or the general interest. Indeed, the implication of the passage from *Between Facts and Norms* cited earlier—the claim that legitimately generated law must also determine the *direction* in which political power circulates—is that only if the political system effectively programs (or counter-steers) the economic and administrative systems to realize the common good can citizens realize their political autonomy. Left to their own devices, the capitalist economy and the administrative system would steer their own courses, set by money and power, respectively, in blithe indifference to the common and individual good of citizens. The upshot is that political autonomy can be achieved only when, as Zurn puts it, "the power of solidarity, through legitimate mechanisms of constitutional democracy, controls the political state, which in turn regulates the major sources of functional social power" (Zurn 2011, 161).

However, the threat is that the economic and administrative systems either remain unaffected by the political system's attempt to program them "because they are stronger," or, worse still, that the unequal social powers (whether individuals or multinational corporations) use "the legitimating force of legal forms to cloak their merely factual strength" (BFN, 40). Thus, law is "profoundly ambiguous" as a medium of social integration because while it can, when legitimate, be a force for the common good, it can also be used to further the illegitimate interests of unequal social power and to lend these the illusion of legitimacy.

3.4 *BETWEEN FACTS AND NORMS* AND DISCOURSE ETHICS

To conclude this chapter, I want to return to Habermas's opening criticisms of Rawls in *Between Facts and Norms* in order to assess not the criticisms themselves but the implied contrast with his own theory, which underlies them. There are two in particular that we need to reexamine.

The first, as we saw in chapters 1 and 2, is that Habermas is apt to contrast Rawls's conception of justice with his own discourse ethics, in particular with principle (U). Indeed, Habermas often claims that the moral point of view is one that underlies the social criticisms of a society by its own social critics and social movements. That may be true, but to what extent can discourse theory avail itself of that moral point of view as the basis on which it holds society to account? Habermas argues that it can and that it does (see, for example, MW, 98/110). On what grounds does he do so?

Is it on the grounds of the MPC? The trouble is, as we have seen, that the status of the MPC is ambiguous and its role in Habermas's theory problematic. There is also Habermas's claim that because the legal system is anchored by the system of basic rights, which although they are legal entities have a fully moral content, to a principled morality of rights and duties, it can "spread morality to all spheres of action" (BFN, 118). But neither view properly explains the normative basis of Habermas's theory. And neither would justify Habermas's tendentious habit of inviting invidious comparisons between discourse ethics and Rawls's justice as fairness, or of mistakenly presenting agreement in democratic discourse as a "rationally motivated consensus" that is, as a consensus in moral discourse that satisfies the validity requirement.

The second contrast Habermas draws is that whereas Rawls focuses too much on the normative dimension of law (its legitimacy) and pays too little attention to its social reality or facticity—the form of law, its institutional embodiment, questions of enforceability, and so on—Habermas gets the balance right. He avoids the mistake of "natural law" accounts by putting forward a theory of democratic legitimacy that remains entirely within the domain of the political, as he understand it, that is, as the domain of enforceable law. This is the rationale of Habermas's "logical derivation" of the system of basic rights from the form of law and principle (D).

That said, critics such as Benhabib and Larmore have questioned the "pre-moral" status that Habermas assigns principle (D), as the principle of discourse as such, and claimed rather that (D) is itself a moral principle. Others, such as Rainer Forst, have criticized Habermas's attempt to give a purely immanent justification of basic rights that does not rest on moral grounds. If either of these objections holds, then one obvious response to Habermas's criticism is that his theory, too, ultimately trades on substantive normative premises. Whether he pays adequate attention to the institutional dimension of law is one question. Whether he succeeds in evincing all his conclusions (in particular, but not only, the system of rights) without smuggling in substantive moral considerations is another. I shall say no more on the latter question, for it reemerges in the exchange. Further analysis of Habermas's specific criticisms of Rawls's political liberalism in *Between Facts and Norms* will have to wait until the next chapter.

4

RAWLS'S *POLITICAL LIBERALISM*

Our task of providing a chronicle of the development of Habermas's debate with Rawls and of staging the intellectual context of the exchange is not yet complete. We have yet to examine Rawls's political liberalism as set out in the book of the same name. Needless to say, *Political Liberalism* is another long and difficult book, and I cannot hope to lay it out in full or to do justice to the entire work here. Once again, I will stick chiefly to the exposition and interpretation of the key ideas and arguments relevant to the exchange and the subsequent dispute with Habermas, and I will engage with Rawls's critics and commentators when their criticisms and comments clarify his position. In passing, I will draw attention to any ambiguities or niceties that later gave rise to notable misunderstandings or significant differences in interpretation, so that, in the course of our later discussion, we can refer back to them.

4.1 *POLITICAL LIBERALISM* AND THE RETROSPECTIVE DIAGNOSIS OF *A THEORY OF JUSTICE*

Rawls's *Political Liberalism* came into existence as a result of his dissatisfaction with certain features of his presentation of justice as fairness in *A Theory of Justice*. To put it crudely, he came to believe that his presentation of justice as fairness—its justification—in his first book and in some later works was incompatible with what he came to call the "fact of reasonable pluralism." The use of the term "fact" is not accidental. Rawls is not just making a claim about a contingent feature of our social and political situation that is liable to change. His claim is not that there cannot be a society that is not pluralist. Rather, the claim is relative to present social and historical circumstances—conditions of modernity—that are unlikely to change in the medium to long term. The fact of reasonable pluralism, he assumes, is a deep-lying characteristic of modern democratic society and an (enduring) social fact with which all political philosophy must reckon.[1]

Rawls distinguishes "reasonable pluralism" from the mere "fact of pluralism": "A modern democratic society is characterized not simply by a pluralism of comprehensive religious, philosophical, and moral doctrines, but by a pluralism of incompatible yet *reasonable* comprehensive doctrines" (PL, xvi). The fact of pluralism is just the fact that the sources of value are many and often conflicting and incommensurable. The fact of *reasonable* pluralism is the fact that this is also true of the subset of reasonable doctrines espoused by reasonable citizens.

Charles Larmore has argued that the idea of reasonable pluralism conflates two distinct theses: a metaphysical thesis about the source of values (pluralism rather than monism) and an epistemological thesis about reasonable disagreement, namely that reasonable people will inevitably tend to disagree about matters concerning the meaning of life and other deep moral questions.[2] Larmore thinks the distinction is vital because pluralism about values is itself a controversial metaphysical theory about which reasonable people can disagree. In my view, Rawls understands the claim about pluralism as a relatively uncontroversial descriptive empirical and historical claim about Western liberal democratic societies. To that extent, it is part of common knowledge and not a controversial claim that is reasonable to dispute. But I agree with Larmore to the extent that the more important claim, and the one fundamental to Rawls's political liberalism, is the epistemological claim about the inevitability of reasonable disagreement arising from the diversity of citizens' reasonable comprehensive doctrines.

4.1.1 WHAT IS A COMPREHENSIVE DOCTRINE?

One of the key ideas in Rawls's *Political Liberalism* is that of a "reasonable comprehensive doctrine." To get that idea in full view, we need to know what he means by "reasonable" and "comprehensive doctrine."

A doctrine is a body of belief, and it is comprehensive when it informs and gives shape to every aspect of an individual citizen's life. A Christian can live an entire life (every part of it) as Christian doctrine holds one should, and so can a Stoic, or for that matter a Kantian or a utilitarian. Comprehensive doctrines are pervasive. The idea is close in meaning to a conception of the good or the right life, though it has a much broader sense: "It covers the major religious, philosophical, and moral aspects of human life" (PL, 59; see also xxxvii). This is an important point, more important than it initially appears, even to Rawls himself. A comprehensive doctrine can be (a) a religion or world view, (b) an actually existing morality (or moral theory), or (c) a philosophical doctrine or theory (not necessarily a moral philosophy).

On the one hand, these are similar and interrelated. Consider that Kantianism and utilitarianism would count as comprehensive in at least two senses since each can be construed as a first-order moral doctrine, a repertoire of duties and obligations; a moral theory, a theory about how such duties are derived; a theory of the good; and a philosophical theory. And each of these senses of 'comprehensive doctrine' is marked by a similar relational feature, namely that they can be rejected by reasonable persons. That said, they are distinct, and they pose different problems for politics and for political theory. For example, whereas the commitments proper to religious world views and, to an extent, also to moral doctrines, are constitutive of moral personality, theoretical commitments are not. Under conditions of reasonable pluralism, justifying a policy or law to citizens generally on the basis of comprehensive reasons in senses (1) and (2) poses a moral problem in that it impugns the moral integrity of the citizens who reasonably reject the doctrines on which those reasons rest. That is not the case with theoretical commitments. Justifying a policy or law on the basis of a disputed economic theory of general equilibrium poses no such moral problem, even if it may needlessly embroil the law or policy in theoretical controversy (Lister 2007, 12–13).

As Rawls notes, the idea of a comprehensive doctrine is meant loosely; it is not limited to named religions, such as Islam or Buddhism, or to philosophical theories, such as Kantianism or utilitarianism (PL, 59). Rather it is meant to include any pervasive body of belief that gives shape to a life. That includes, for example, the kind of scientific world view that the unabashed secularist Richard Dawkins espouses, along with all kinds of other people far more tolerant than he. It is thus a fact (and an enduring one with which politics and political theory will have to reckon) that "no one comprehensive doctrine is affirmed by citizens generally" and that a reasonable person can reasonably reject any such doctrine (PL, xvi).

A comprehensive doctrine is one that is presented as, and held by its practitioners as, true or correct.[3] Moreover, to put it in other words, words that Rawls himself uses, a comprehensive doctrine, generally speaking, claims to be "the whole truth" or is claimed to be the whole truth by those who hold it and live by it (PL, 216). It thus contrasts naturally with a political conception, such as political liberalism, that claims only to be reasonable (PL, xx).

4.1.2 REASONABLENESS

In *A Theory of Justice*, Rawls uses the term "rational" widely, sometimes as a semi-technical term, but he uses the word "reasonable" in its everyday sense. In *Political Liberalism*, the term "reasonable" becomes a term of art that bears much of the weight of his argument.[4] In the later work, "reasonableness" is both a virtue that pertains to persons and a quality that a principle, or a body of principles, such as a comprehensive doctrine, may have or may lack.

Reasonable persons, Rawls claims, view society as a system of fair cooperation over time between free and equal persons. They are thus disposed to be cooperative and naturally will be inclined to adopt principles that others can share. Since reasonableness is linked to a "sense of justice," it forms part, though not the whole, of a person's "moral sensibility" (PL, 42). "Reasonableness" is thus a normative moral concept, albeit of a specifically political kind. For example, the reasonable person is not required to be altruistic or impartial. Rawls claims that reasonable persons are disposed to reciprocity. They not only propose fair principles and terms of cooperation, but also are inclined to abide by them, provided others do likewise. Hence, some kinds of partiality are reasonable because they are reciprocal.

Closely connected to cooperativeness and reciprocity, "reasonableness" is a social virtue. Unlike rationality, it rules out egoism, selfishness, and action that is merely self-interested. For example, in Rawls's account of rationality, the assumption that a person is rational means that his or her default setting is a disposition to act out of self-interest, as do the individual choosers in the original position. And rationality can be fully realized by an individual acting in isolation, whereas reasonableness is a social virtue that cannot be properly exercised by an individual acting alone. (To put it in Habermas's terms, the ideal of rationality is monological, but the ideal of reasonableness is not.) As Rawls puts it, "the reasonable is public in a way that the rational is not" (PL, 53).[5] The idea of the reasonable and the virtues of fairness, cooperativeness, and reciprocity associated with it are linked to the idea of public life and its demands. It thus forms a central part of "a political ideal of democratic citizenship" (PL, 62).[6]

More controversially, Rawls includes a willingness to accept what he calls the "burdens of judgment" among the defining features of reasonable persons.[7] The burdens of judgment are a cluster of considerations that incline to the view that, in many cases of judgment, even conscientious and well-informed people, even after full discussion, will not expect agreement from similarly well-informed and conscientious reasoners (PL, 58).

So much for the reasonableness of persons, but what about the reasonableness of principles or doctrines? Some of the earlier discussion also applies here. If principles or bodies of belief are fair and reciprocal, then they are reasonable. But the reasonableness of doctrines and principles goes beyond this. The reasonableness of a doctrine is what Rawls calls "an exercise of theoretical reason" (PL, 59), albeit one, Rawls adds, that is more properly political than merely epistemological (PL, 62). A reasonable doctrine will be a "consistently and coherently organized body of belief" that expresses "an intelligible view of the world" (PL, 59). (This sense of reasonable is weaker than saying that a doctrine is justified in the sense that it is supported by good reasons and likely true, but it does carry the sense of "justified by coherence with a wider frame of beliefs.") On that account, it will tend to be stable rather than unstable, although not fixed. In virtue of these features, a reasonable comprehensive doctrine will be apt to support a viable political morality and a just democratic regime that citizens as free and equal persons can accept as the basis of their shared life.

However—and this significance dawns on Rawls only gradually—not all comprehensive doctrines that are "reasonable" are liberal (PL, xxxvii). Just as religious doctrines can be reasonable in Rawls's sense, so illiberal doctrines can be reasonable. Of course, not all are. But the point is that they can be, and some are. Political liberalism outlines a conception of the political that can be affirmed by illiberal—but nonetheless reasonable—citizens, from the perspective of their illiberal—but nonetheless reasonable—comprehensive doctrines. This is in fact a consequence of the term "reasonable" having the weaker meaning of "coherent within a set of beliefs."

4.1.3 RAWLS'S RETROSPECTIVE VIEW OF *A THEORY OF JUSTICE*

Returning now to Rawls's diagnosis of *A Theory of Justice*, he claims that, mainly owing to the way in which it was presented in the earlier book, justice as fairness is vulnerable to certain objections. To be more specific, in his early book, he did not manage to show that justice as fairness is the best political conception for a political community given the fact of reasonable pluralism. Why was that? The short answer is that in *A Theory of Justice*, justice as fairness rests on a comprehensive liberalism, or liberalism as a comprehensive doctrine. Reasonable persons can *reasonably* reject that doctrine and thus refuse to accept justice as fairness as the most appropriate (or even as *an* appropriate) basis for the institutions of a democratic society (PL, xv).

Moreover, the argument in *A Theory of Justice* fails in another way. For it rests on a premise that *Political Liberalism* assumes to be false, namely that "in the well-ordered society of justice as fairness citizens hold the same comprehensive doctrine" (PL, xl). There is no single comprehensive doctrine that all citizens affirm; rather, there are several, among which some, though not all, are reasonable.

Political Liberalism thus sets out not to alter the content of justice as fairness but to indemnify it against these two kinds of justificatory failure, both of which are linked to the fact of reasonable pluralism. To this end, Rawls identifies several other faults in his earlier defense of justice as fairness, which lead to the failure just outlined:

1. It makes no distinction between moral and political philosophy.
2. It does not distinguish adequately between "a doctrine of justice general in scope" and a "strictly political conception of justice."
3. It does not distinguish between comprehensive moral doctrines and "moral doctrines . . . limited to the domain of the political"; therefore, it fails to adequately characterize the moral basis of political democratic legitimacy.

By rectifying these faults in the presentation of justice as fairness, *Political Liberalism* aims to make good the two justificatory failures outlined here and to propose and defend justice as fairness as the best—or at least as a good—basis of the legitimacy of constitutional liberal democracy.

4.2 THE QUESTIONS OF *POLITICAL LIBERALISM*

This change in the presentation of the doctrine of justice as fairness reflects a shift in the question that animates political liberalism. The animating question is the question of stability, which, Rawls claims, "has played very little role in the history of moral philosophy" (PL, xvii).[8] As a matter of fact, Rawls addressed that question at length in *A Theory of Justice*, where he argued that affirming and acting on the principles of justice in a well-ordered society would be congruent with a rational person's good (TJ, 450–64).[9] But his argument there was premised, he later realizes, on various controversial claims about human flourishing and, to that extent, rested on a comprehensive moral doctrine, and also crucially on the assumption that every citizen in a just society would and could affirm that same doctrine. And this, he notes in the first introduction to *Political Liberalism*, renders his earlier treatment of the question of stability "unrealistic" (PL, xvii).[10]

Taking into account the fact of reasonable pluralism, the guiding question is, "How is it possible that there may exist over time a stable and just society of free and equal citizens profoundly divided by reasonable though incompatible religious, philosophical, and moral doctrines?" (PL, xviii). In the second introduction, written after the 1995 exchange, he claims that this question is not formulated sharply enough. There is no problem with how exponents of otherwise conflicting versions of comprehensive liberalism, in Kantian, Millian, or Rawlsian variants, should be able to endorse a just democratic constitutional state. The real puzzle is, "How is it possible for those affirming a religious doctrine that is based on religious authority, for example the Church or the Bible, also to hold a reasonable political conception that supports a just democratic regime?" (PL, xxxvii). Furthermore, how can "citizens of faith," as he calls them, do so "wholeheartedly," without "simply going along with it in view of the balance of social and political forces" (PL, xxxviii)?[11]

There is a passage from Weber's *Economy and Society* that Habermas cites in chapter 2 of *Between Facts and Norms*, where Weber observes that social orders based on custom and tradition are much more stable than those merely based on force but that the most stable social order of all is that which "bears the prestige of 'legitimacy' " (BFN, 68). In a way, that is what Rawls is asking here. How can a just liberal democratic regime acquire the prestige of legitimacy and be affirmed and accepted as legitimate by all citizens, even those who, though reasonable, are illiberal and who reasonably reject comprehensive liberalism? Rawls's answer is that a liberal and just democratic polity can be justified to all reasonable citizens, including citizens of faith and illiberal citizens, as a "political" (but not "metaphysical") conception. To justify a liberal democratic constitution on the basis of a "political" conception of justice means to justify it in a way that all citizens can accept in the light of their reasonable comprehensive doctrines. To understand this claim, we have to look at *Political Liberalism* in more detail.[12]

4.3 THE ARGUMENT OF *POLITICAL LIBERALISM*

4.3.1 OVERLAPPING CONSENSUS

The central idea of *Political Liberalism* is that a political conception of justice can be "the focus of an overlapping consensus of reasonable comprehensive doctrines" (CP, 423; PL, 141). The idea of an *overlapping consensus* of reasonable doctrines is, in my view, rather unclear and ambiguous. But it is not ambiguous only in the sense Rawls takes it to be—because of the meaning of *consensus* in everyday politics as referring to a coalition of interests skillfully put together for strategic purposes (PL, 39). The other ambiguity stems from a tension between the notion of an overlap and the notion of a consensus.

One easy way to think of an overlap is by picturing reasonable comprehensive doctrines as the circles of a Venn diagram and the overlap as the intersection. (This is indeed how Habermas thinks of it [BFN, 61; JA, 93]). For example, Rawls likes to adduce the examples of a religious doctrine of faith (such as Catholicism), a Kantian comprehensive liberalism, and a Millian comprehensive liberalism, represented as circles (a), (b), and (c) in figure 4.1, which model their respective sets of beliefs and values. The overlap of these doctrines is represented as the intersection of the circles, which contains every belief and value (and idea), religious, moral, and philosophical, that these comprehensive doctrines have in common.[13]

This diagram reveals an ambiguity in the notion of a comprehensive doctrine. Does the comprehensive doctrine include everything that falls within circles (a), (b), and (c), regardless of whether they overlap with other, or all other, doctrines? Or does the term "comprehensive doctrine" refer only to the ideas and values outside the intersection set? Generally speaking, Rawls assumes the latter.[14]

Now it is fair to assume that the contents of the overlap—the intersection set—will comprise all kinds of beliefs that won't form part of a political conception of justice since those beliefs and values are not germane to a just democratic regime. These might include certain attitudes toward hygiene, or of disgust, that may be hardwired in us or culturally invariant for other reasons. In other words, their being part of the overlapping consensus is only a necessary and not a sufficient

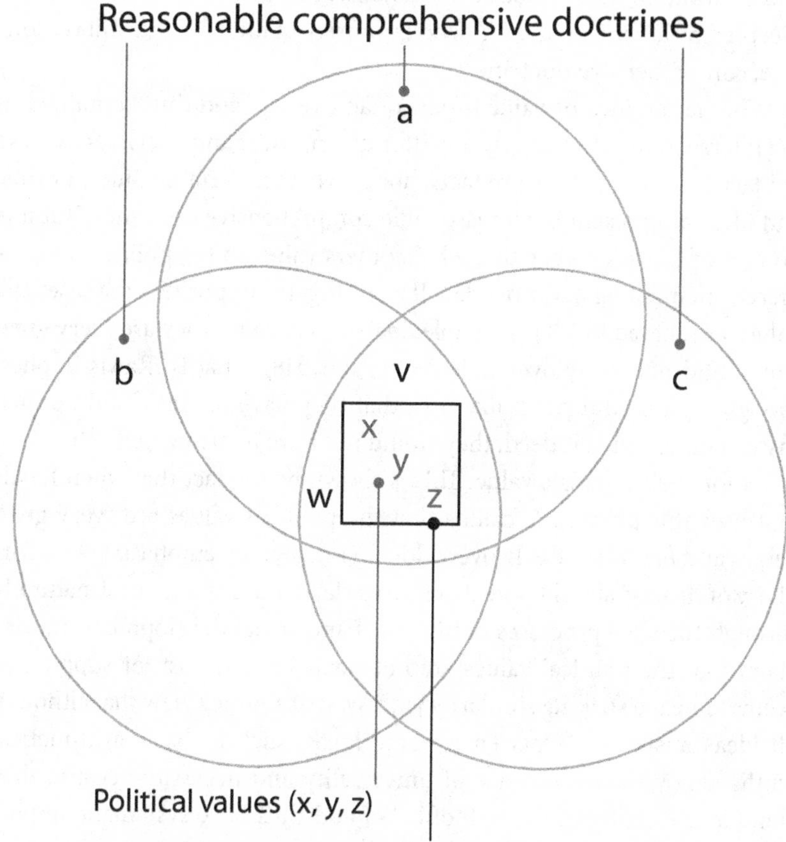

FIGURE 4.1 This figure shows that (1) the module is not coextensive with the intersection set; (2) the module comprises a subset of the values falling in the overlap: (x), (y), and (z) are political values, but (v) and (w) are not; and (3) comprehensive doctrines are best conceived as including and hence congruent with the module but can be conceived as excluding it.

condition of their being political values, and thus apt to be part of a political conception. That said, all the political values, the ones that, as Rawls puts it, are to "govern the basic framework of social life" and to "specify the fundamental terms of political and social cooperation" must fall within the overlap (PL, 139). So to continue our example, the right to religious freedom is an individual liberty supported by Catholic doctrine and by Kantian and Millian comprehensive liberalism. It would also be accepted by a "citizen of faith" who espoused an illiberal, but still reasonable, comprehensive doctrine.

Whether an idea or value is part of an overlap, and thus contained in the intersection set, is largely a matter of empirical and social fact. These are facts, insofar as they are facts, about whether certain values, norms, and ideas are present in all reasonable comprehensive doctrines. But it is no part of Rawls's theory that what confers value on the political ideas is merely their falling in the overlap. If anything, the opposite is the case. The values are shared by all reasonable doctrines because they are "very great values and not easily overridden" (PL, 169, 218). That is, Rawls implies, though he does not put it like this, that they have intrinsic and not just instrumental value; indeed, they would not have instrumental value were it not for their intrinsic value. This is shown by the fact that when Rawls first uses this phrase, he claims that the political values are "very great values and *hence* not easily overridden" (PL, 139, my emphasis). As a corollary of this, we should note that the overlap comes about quasi-naturally through the slow processes of historical and social development. Rawls's claim that the political values are not easily eroded, lost, or supplanted seems to bear a striking similarity with W. v. O. Quine's view that although all ideas answer to experience, some ideas, such as basic arithmetical truths, enjoy the appearance of universality and necessity because they stand at the center of the web of belief and thus have systematic import for all the rest.[15]

So much for the notion of the overlap of reasonable doctrines. Consensus, though, is rather different:

1. Consensus as distinct from the overlap is an agreement not of doctrines but of people, and it is an agreement on a political conception. In other words, the consensus of reasonable citizens on the political conception involves the recognition and endorsement of the political conception as a conception, as a complex of ideas, that is more than the doxastic and axiological commitments to the individual ideas and values out of which it is constructed. To that extent, the consensus of reasonable citizens on the political conception is epistemically and theoretically richer than the overlap.

2. The consensus of reasonable citizens involves a practical commitment to the conception that consists in what Rawls often refers to as a "willingness to propose and abide by fair terms of cooperation provided that other citizens do likewise" (PL, 49, 54, 81, 94). This commitment is more robust than the doxastic and axiological commitment to the several political ideas and values that form the overlap. It is more robust partly because the beliefs and commitments that fall in the overlap may be first order only, and tacit rather than explicit. This cannot be the case with the consensus. Since it involves the willingness to live by it, it must involve the second-order belief that the conception is correct and worth affirming. This is related to a further point.
3. The overlap obtains just where all reasonable people either tacitly or explicitly believe the same political ideas and values, whatever their comprehensive doctrine. An overlap can obtain even where people are not yet conscious of it. By contrast, the consensus of reasonable citizens on the political conception involves the consciousness that other reasonable people can affirm it; otherwise, there could be no willingness to abide by it provided other people do likewise. And this reflexive dimension of consensus also deepens and strengthens the commitment to it, because the fact that other people recognize and affirm the political conception gives each citizen assurance that their commitment is valid and a further reason to endorse it.

So, to my mind, there are some notable differences between the notions of an overlap of reasonable doctrines and of a consensus of reasonable persons.[16] On a political conception of justice, they differ both in their object and in the kind and degree of the commitment.

4.3.2 OVERLAPPING CONSENSUS VERSUS *MODUS VIVENDI*

For Rawls, the idea of an overlapping consensus of reasonable doctrines is contrastive. It contrasts with the idea of a *modus vivendi.* We can get a better idea of what Rawls has in mind by an overlapping consensus of reasonable doctrines if we know why Rawls thinks it a superior basis for political agreement to a *modus vivendi.*

The latter is essentially a compromise: an equilibrium reached on the basis of an ongoing estimation of the balance of forces. Each party will tolerate the other provided neither party has the power to impose its view on the other. Gerald Gaus puts it somewhat more precisely:

> Agreement X is a modus vivendi between agents A and B if and only if:
>
> 1. X promotes the interests, values, goals, etc. of both A and B;
> 2. X gives neither A nor B everything they would like;
> 3. The distribution of the gains of the compromise (how close X is to A's or B's maximum reasonable expectation) crucially depends on the relative power of A and B; and
> 4. For both A and B, the continued conformity by each to X depends on its continued evaluation that X is the best deal it can get, or at least that the effort to get a better deal is not worth the costs.
>
> (Gaus 2003, 59)

According to Rawls, such an agreement (really a kind of truce) does not issue in stability for the right reasons, even though it might produce stability of a kind, namely one that rests on a contingent and provisory alignment of interests. By contrast, the overlapping consensus of reasonable doctrines does yield "moral grounds" (more precisely, a subset of moral reasons that inhere in all reasonable comprehensive doctrines and that are germane to a just constitutional regime) on which rest the political conception of justice, which is itself a "moral conception" (insofar as it is worked up from the "very great values" in the overlap [PL, xxxix]). Rawls argues that these two aspects of an overlapping consensus, "moral object and moral grounds," issue in a stability not only more worthwhile than that of a *modus vivendi*, but also more robust and enduring, since "those who affirm the various views supporting the political conception will not withdraw their support of it should the relative strength of their view in society increase and eventually become dominant" (PL, 148).[17] Essentially this is what Rawls means by "stability for the right reasons" rather than mere stability, and it is central to his conception of democratic legitimacy (PL, xxxix–xli, 385–90).[18] Though both Habermas and Rawls have public reason accounts of legitimacy, albeit different ones, they both agree with Weber that a social order that is legitimate (based on legitimate law) is more stable than one based on custom or force and is more stable than a social order based on a *modus vivendi.*

4.3.3 JUSTICE AS A POLITICAL CONCEPTION

Rawls begins *A Theory of Justice* by noting the distinction between the *concept* of justice and the several different *conceptions* of it. The role of the various conceptions of justice is to "specify the rights and duties and to determine the appropriate distributive shares" (TJ, 6). The underlying concept of justice, as distinct from the conceptions, is "specified by the role which these different . . . conceptions have in common" (TJ, 5). Fortunately, there is a measure of agreement between the conceptions. The different conceptions converge on a single view—the concept—that there should be no arbitrary distinction between persons in assigning basic rights and duties and determining a proper balance between the competing claims to social advantages. In sum, at least as set out in chapter 1 of *A Theory of Justice*, Rawls's approach appears to consist in conceptual analysis, the description of a single abstract object, "justice." There is one concept of justice. But there are various *conceptions* of justice, which are interpretations of the role of the principles of justice (TJ, 10), and such conceptions can be, and can be shown to be, better or worse according to how well they capture the concept.

This view is not the approach Rawls takes in *Political Liberalism*. In the later book, he holds on to two thoughts, expressed at the beginning and at the end of the earlier work. The first is that "some measure of agreement in conceptions of justice is . . . a prerequisite for a viable human community" (TJ, 6). The second is that "the argument for the principles of justice should proceed from some consensus. This is the nature of justification" (TJ, 581). These thoughts, which are incidental in the earlier work, shift to the center of the later work, in which his approach—specifically his approach to justification—broadly speaking, is social and pragmatic. The rationale for the new approach is his acknowledgment that the fact of reasonable pluralism is not only endemic in culture and society but also in philosophy. There just is no settled consensus on many fundamental philosophical questions. They are a matter of ongoing controversy and are likely to remain so, and the theory of justice has to take cognizance of that fact. This means Rawls can no more present justice as fairness as the best approximation of the concept of justice than he can justify it on the basis of any single comprehensive moral doctrine—such as the comprehensive liberalism of Kant or Mill. To do so would be to advance a conception of justice that is, to adopt his terms, "metaphysical, not political." By contrast, Rawls offers a social and pragmatic justification of justice as fairness that is political, not metaphysical (CP, 388–415; PL, 10, 97).

Political, Not Metaphysical

Rawls uses the word "political" as a term of art, in contrast to "metaphysical." Now, a lot of twentieth-century philosophy has a strong theoretical animus against metaphysics, including the kind of analytic pragmatist philosophy prominent in midcentury Harvard (that of Goodman and Quine). However, Rawls's reason for abandoning his earlier analytical philosophical approach to justice is practically, rather than philosophically, driven. A conception of justice is not metaphysical when it does not presuppose a philosophical doctrine that citizens can reasonably reject; if it did, that would mean that it could not meet with the consensus of reasonable citizens (as free and equal).

A Political Conception Is a Moral Conception

Consensus could be blocked if the justification depended on any one comprehensive doctrine, whether religious, moral, or philosophical. Does this mean that a political conception of justice cannot be a moral conception? No. It means only that a political conception of justice cannot rest on any one *comprehensive* moral doctrine, or any set of such doctrines. As Rawls insists many times throughout *Political Liberalism*, "a political conception is a normative and a moral conception" (PL, xxxix, 147). Moreover, it is affirmed on *moral* grounds (PL, 147–48). The ideas and values that fall within the overlapping consensus of reasonable doctrines, and that are germane to what he calls "the special domain of the political," are a subset of moral values in general. It is because the overlapping consensus has two moral aspects, a moral object (the political conception) and moral grounds (the values and ideas in the overlap), that it can provide stability for the right reasons.

A Political Conception as Freestanding

Although it is a moral conception, since it is not a comprehensive doctrine but a political conception (and thus shared by all reasonable citizens), the political conception cannot be reasonably rejected. Moreover, since it rests on moral grounds (the "very great values" at the center of the overlap [PL, 139]), it follows that these, too, cannot be reasonably rejected. This brings us to the third and probably the most important feature of a "political conception" of justice as Rawls understands it. It is "freestanding" in the sense that it contains no "metaphysical or epistemological doctrine beyond what is implied by the political itself." In other words, it prescinds from any controversial philosophical or other theoretical assumptions (PL, 100). Or, as he puts it later (after the 1995 exchange), "it is not presented as derived from, or as part of, any comprehensive doctrine"; hence, insofar as it is a moral conception, it "must contain its own intrinsic normative and moral ideal" (PL, xlii). The crucial point is that, as a freestanding view, the political conception is indemnified against certain kinds of argumentative defeat. Qua freestanding, the political conception is guaranteed to be at least consistent with every reasonable comprehensive doctrine.

A Political Conception as a Module

The fourth feature of a political conception is that it is constructed as "a module, an essential constituent part that fits into and can be supported by various reasonable comprehensive doctrines" (PL, 12, 145). Rawls is speaking loosely here. The political conception as a module must be able to fit into all and any reasonable comprehensive doctrines, which means that it cannot put in play any idea or value that does not fall within the overlapping consensus. Where its being freestanding guarantees that it is at least *consistent* with all reasonable comprehensive doctrines, its being a "module" ensures that it *coheres* with all reasonable comprehensive doctrines, because the political values of which it is composed lie at the center of the overlapping consensus and have weightiness and preeminence. But this raises the ambiguity we noted earlier, namely whether the notion of the comprehensive doctrine should be understood *exclusively*, as designating the doctrine *excluding* the module, or inclusively, as designating the whole doctrine, *including* the module. When Rawls uses the term "comprehensive doctrine" to contrast with the idea of the political conception, he uses it in the exclusive sense.[19] So there are inclusive and exclusive senses of the notion "reasonable comprehensive doctrine," and Rawls uses now one, now the other sense.[20] But the proper sense of "reasonable comprehensive doctrine" should be one that includes the module, because otherwise the doctrine is neither "reasonable" nor "comprehensive" in Rawls's sense.

Finally, Rawls acknowledges that although he uses justice as fairness as "the standard example" of a political conception of justice, he realizes that it is more realistic to allow that there can be more than one political conception. Indeed, he allows that the focus or object of the overlapping consensus can be "a class of liberal conceptions that vary within a certain more or less narrow range" (PL, 164). And, indeed, in the second introduction to *Political Liberalism*, he allows that this family includes "different and incompatible political conceptions of justice" that are nonetheless reasonable and that the question of which is the most reasonable is a matter of reasonable disagreement (PL, xlvii).

4.3.4 THE TWO-STAGE JUSTIFICATION

Let us return to the ambiguity in the idea of an overlapping consensus I noted earlier. Rawls claims that the justification of justice as fairness now takes place in two stages. At the first stage, justice as fairness—or any other political conception—is given a freestanding justification (PL, 64). One way to do this is via the argument from the original position, now reinterpreted so as not to presuppose any comprehensive doctrine, religious, moral, or philosophical. As I interpret it, this ensures that the conception will be consistent with any reasonable doctrine, such that no citizen has reason to reject it in the light of their (reasonable) comprehensive doctrine.

At the second stage, one asks whether justice as fairness is "sufficiently stable" (PL, 141, 144). Rawls tends to speak as if the overlapping consensus comes into play only, or primarily, at the second stage. But in fact, he presents the role of the overlapping consensus in two slightly different ways:

1. Rawls claims that to assess the stability of the political conception, citizens must check whether it can be "the focus of an overlapping consensus" (PL, 141, 143). Insofar as this differs from presenting the political conception as freestanding, it involves checking that the political conception coheres with every reasonable comprehensive doctrine, that it is thus a "module" (PL, 145, 12).
2. Rawls also claims that we must see whether justice as fairness is "acceptable to citizens" as reasonable and rational and free and equal, and whether it can "gain the reasoned support of citizens who affirm reasonable though conflicting comprehensive doctrines" (PL, 143).

Claims 1 and 2 spell out the test of consensus differently. According to claim 1, stability is ensured if the political conception coheres with all reasonable comprehensive doctrines. It is a question of fit. According to claim 2, stability is ensured if every reasonable citizen accepts and affirms the political conception—in the rich sense set out in section 4.3.1. I presume here that to affirm a conception is to avow or to demonstrate one's willingness to abide by it, rather than just to hold a belief about it.[21]

Rawls has come under heavy criticism for this way of construing the two-stage justification and the role of the overlapping consensus. Jonathan Quong, among others, has leveled a powerful criticism of what he sees as a "common view" of the role of the idea of the overlapping consensus in political liberalism. The common view, as Quong understands it, assumes that the subject of the overlapping consensus (which Rawls calls the "focus" or "object") is the political conception (in Rawls's account, justice as fairness). He therefore argues that "public justification of justice is not complete until we show that the principles within the political conception can be the subject of an overlapping consensus amongst all the reasonable comprehensive doctrines" (Quong 2011, 162). So, on the common view, achieving an overlapping consensus on the "module" is seen as the final stage of public justification, which completes the process, and not as the initial point of departure. It is the conclusion, not the premise, of Rawls's argument. (This is significant because among those who subscribe to "the common view" are Habermas and some of his most influential supporters, including Kenneth Baynes, Rainer Forst, and Todd Hedrick.[22])

Quong has a whole raft of arguments against the common view (as a view, rather than as an incorrect interpretation of Rawls) (Quong 2011, 162). In his view, consensus is focused on the political ideas and values, rather than on the political conception. This is not the place to examine Quong's critique in detail, but one of his worries is that, since there is a family of political conceptions of justice rather than only one, it will be harder to achieve a consensus of reasonable persons on it.

To my mind, Rawls's acknowledgment that there may be several different and incompatible political conceptions does not render the goal of achieving consensus on a political conception impossible. For each is a module that fits with all reasonable comprehensive doctrines, and so each can be affirmed by all reasonable citizens as reasonable, even if in practice citizens might reasonably disagree over which is best. What is crucial is that they can be endorsed by all reasonable citizens as the basis of a viable liberal constitutional regime.

I agree that Rawls is a little unclear about whether the political ideas and values should be amenable to a consensus of reasonable citizens, as well as about the political conception that is an arrangement of them. But it seems that Rawls can argue that *both* the very great values that are the constituent ideas of the political conception *and* the political conception itself can be supported by a consensus of reasonable citizens. This is implied by his statement that that the overlapping consensus issues in stability because it has two aspects: "moral object and moral grounds" (PL, 148, xli). It is true that achieving a consensus on a political conception is more difficult, since it requires a deeper kind of theoretical appraisal and practical commitment, but it is nevertheless desirable and feasible, providing one bear in mind, as Rawls does, that consensus is not an all-or-nothing affair: "Reasonable citizens . . . know that in political life unanimity can rarely if ever be expected on a basic question, and so a democratic constitution must include procedures of majority or other plurality voting to reach decisions" (PL, 393).

4.3.5 THE PRIORITY OF THE RIGHT

One of the central ideas of political liberalism is that of the priority of the right over the good. This doctrine was also a central idea of *A Theory of Justice*, in which it is explicitly identified with the Kantian interpretation: It is a "central feature" not only of justice as fairness, Rawls writes, but also of "Kant's ethics" (TJ, 31). Just how Kantian the doctrine of the priority of the right is in *A Theory of Justice* is a matter of debate, but it is probably not so much as Rawls claims—or, let us say, some Kantians dispute how "Kantian" Rawls's theory really is (Höffe 1984; O'Neill 2015).

Samuel Freeman argues, contra Kymlicka and Sandel, that, even as set out in *A Theory of Justice*, Rawls's thesis of the priority of the right cannot fairly be thought of as the priority of deontological moral principles over conceptions of happiness. For the priority thesis does not describe how moral principles primordially "relate the concepts of the right and the good"; rather, it refers to the "lexical ordering of the principles of right and justice in individual and social deliberation" (Freeman 2009, 62). I want to make two remarks on this point. First, if Freeman is right, which I believe he is, then Rawls's reference to Kant's ethics in the passage cited earlier (TJ, 31) gives at the very least a highly misleading impression of what he is up to. Second, if Freeman is right, then even in *A Theory of Justice*, Rawls construes the thesis of the priority of the right in a completely different way from Habermas, who, as we have seen in previous chapters, does indeed think of it primarily as the priority of deontological moral principles over ethical values (in his sense of those terms). In short, Habermas construes the thesis in the same way that both Kymlicka and Sandel do; but whereas they attribute the view to Rawls and repudiate it themselves, Habermas endorses the thesis, with the proviso that his way of construing, and defending, it is different from and superior to Rawls's.

In any case, by the time of *Political Liberalism*, the thesis of the priority of the right was so much altered as to render the very phrase "priority of the right over the good" rather misleading. In *Political Liberalism*, the priority is a priority of the "very great" political values and ideas over the nonpolitical values and ideas, or the priority of the political conception over comprehensive doctrines. What is most misleading is that in *Political Liberalism*, the right, which is prior, in part comprises ideas of the good, albeit a subset of ideas of the good that are also "political ideas" insofar as they "belong to a reasonable political conception of justice for a constitutional regime" (PL, 194, 176). These include the good as rationality, the idea of primary social goods, the idea of permissible conceptions of the good, the good of political virtues, and the good of political society, all of which meet the criteria of falling within the overlap of reasonable comprehensive doctrines and being germane to a just constitutional regime (PL, 173).

This alteration in the way in which the priority of the right is conceived in the two works means that Rawls's other memorable slogan—"Justice draws the limit, and the good shows the point"—is also an oversimplification, since we are talking about justice as a political conception, and that conception includes "political" ideas of the good (CP, 449; PL, 174). What he means by that slogan, when expressed more fully, is that the political conception of justice and legitimate law draw the limits to individual actions in pursuit of a thick conception of the good, whereas reasonable comprehensive doctrines indicate much of what makes life worth living. Furthermore, Rawls admits that the political conception, though neutral in aim, insofar as it does not aim to promote any particular comprehensive doctrine, is not neutral in effect or influence and so will inevitably over time shape reasonable comprehensive doctrines in its own image (PL, 193). So even if we allow that "the good shows the point" in the sense that reasonable citizens are free to shape their lives according to their comprehensive doctrines, over time the right—in the form of a just constitutional democratic regime—will inevitably end up gradually influencing and reconfiguring the good. But that means that the right, eventually, also shows the point.

4.3.6 POLITICAL LEGITIMACY

I have argued that the central question of *Political Liberalism* is that of political legitimacy. It is true that Rawls seldom uses the term "legitimacy" in that book, but this does not mean that it is not the central question. Rather it shows that he tends to put the question in different terms. For Rawls states explicitly that the guiding question of *Political Liberalism* is how the institutions and the constitution of a society of free and equal citizens under conditions of reasonable pluralism can achieve "stability for the right reasons" and that is equivalent to asking how they can be legitimate. And if we recall Weber's statement, cited by Habermas, that legitimate social orders are the most stable, we can see that the two questions are closely linked (BFN, 68). Occasionally, though, Rawls does use the language of "legitimacy" to express the central idea of his theory. For example, the "liberal principle of legitimacy" claims that "political power is fully proper only when it is exercised in accordance with a constitution the essentials of which all citizens as free and equal may reasonably be expected to endorse in the light of principles and ideals acceptable to their common human reason" (PL, 137).

Thus, on Rawls's account, the legitimacy of laws and policies—that is, their stability for the right reasons—is achieved when they can be adequately justified by a political conception of justice that itself comprises only ideas and values inherent in the overlap of all reasonable comprehensive doctrines and to which as a consequence all reasonable people as free and equal can agree.

Standard accounts include three conditions generally taken to be jointly sufficient for political legitimacy: (1) conformity to law, (2) congruence with the values and ideas of the governed, and (3) agreement of the governed.[23] All three are in evidence in Rawls's liberal principle of legitimacy. A legitimate law must be enacted according to a constitution, so it meets condition 1. The essentials of that constitution must be justifiable to all citizens on the basis of principles of public reason, which means on the basis of the political values of reasonable citizens. Recall also that nonpolitical, nonpublic values (comprehensive values in the exclusive sense) are *ex hypothesi* at least consistent with (and at best cohere with) the political conception. Thus, Rawls's principle of legitimacy also meets condition 2. And it meets condition 3 insofar as there is a consensus of reasonable citizens on both the political values and the political conception.

Having said that, in *Political Liberalism*, Rawls is a little vague on the relation between political justice and legitimacy.[24] Later, in his "Reply to Habermas," he adds that the two are distinct, though related, and that legitimacy is a weaker constraint, since laws enacted in accordance with the constitution might still not be perfectly just (RH, 175–7/87–8). They have to be just to some extent, however, since, at some point, the unjustness of the laws will corrupt their legitimacy too.

Rawls considers this conception of legitimacy to be distinct from three other conceptions to which it is superior in that it can produce stability for the right reasons under conditions of reasonable pluralism.

The first are theories that see political legitimacy as falling entirely within the domain of politics and law. The paradigm example of a theory from this camp is legal positivism, which understands legitimacy merely as a technical matter of conformity with legal procedures and not at all as dependent on the authority of ethical or moral norms.[25]

The second are conceptions that are "realist" enough to allow condition 3 to be satisfied by the agreement of citizens on the basis of a *modus vivendi*, that is, an assessment of the current balance of forces in political society. According to Rawls, that might produce stability (that is, effective political domination) but not legitimacy.[26]

The third is any conception of legitimacy based on a comprehensive doctrine (in the exclusive sense) such that conditions 2 and 3 depend essentially on religious, philosophical, or moral values that can be reasonably rejected. And, given the broad and vague nature of the notion of the term "comprehensive doctrine," such a conception might take a range of forms. It might take the form of a shared ethos or conception of the good, such as the one espoused by Sandel and other communitarians. It might take the form of a comprehensive liberalism, such as that of Kant, Mill, or the early Rawls. It might take the form of the theory of "rational intuitionism," such as the one that Rawls attributes to Clarke, Price, Ross, and Sidgwick, which holds that moral beliefs answer to a fixed moral order that obtains antecedently to and independently of our political ideas and that they are true or false according to whether they correspond to that moral order (PL, 94). Or it might take the form of natural law theories of legitimacy, according to which obedience to political authority rests on the perception of moral duties and obligations antecedent and external to the political culture of a society.

All these comprehensive conceptions are ruled out by Rawls's liberal principle of legitimacy. On his account, the first and second types of conception are illegitimate because they don't meet condition 2. The various examples of the third conception also fail to meet condition 2 and hence also condition 3. That is because in a society characterized by the fact of reasonable pluralism, any conception of legitimacy based on a conception of the good or of moral truth or that is derived from an external moral order will not be acceptable to all citizens from the perspective of their several and discrepant comprehensive doctrines.

Notwithstanding his insistence that the political conception of justice is "freestanding" from any comprehensive doctrine, Rawls's conception of legitimacy has come under fire from some realists for being an "applied ethics" or "morality first" conception (Williams 2005; Geuss 2008). It is true, as we saw earlier, that Rawls's conception of legitimacy is based on a conception of justice, which, although "political, not metaphysical," is definitely a moral conception. And it is true also that the liberal principle of legitimacy is based on a substantive conception of justice. Nonetheless, it is not a morality-first conception, in the sense that it bases legitimacy directly on an external moral order and thus fails to account for the autonomy of the political domain. That is exactly the kind of account Rawls's political liberalism is designed to avoid. In other words, Rawls wants his political conception of justice to be a moral conception, and to enjoy moral authority, without its being externally constrained by nonpolitical determining factors and hence having to sacrifice the autonomy of the political. His notion of a political conception of justice worked up from ideas implicit in the public political culture, and comprising only political ideas and values in an overlapping consensus of reasonable doctrines, is supposed to allow him the best of both worlds: a morally authoritative conception of political justice that nevertheless honors the autonomy of the political order.[27]

4.3.7 THE IDEA OF PUBLIC REASON AND THE DUTY OF CIVILITY

One helpful way of looking at Rawls's work in the round is to say that *A Theory of Justice* is, as its title says, a theory of justice, one that tells us what social justice for a liberal constitutional democratic state is and should be, whereas *Political Liberalism* shows that the conception of justice defended in the earlier work, when reworked as a political conception, can serve as an appropriate criterion of political legitimacy in a liberal democratic constitutional state under enduring conditions of reasonable pluralism. One of the fundamental ideas that connects the two projects is the idea of public reason. The idea of public reason is the idea that informs the liberal principle of legitimacy, and its purpose is to shape social institutions according to principles that it is reasonable (even under conditions of reasonable pluralism) for each citizen to accept. As we can see, this was one of the original animating ideas of justice as fairness:

> Persons engaged in a just, or fair, practice, can face one another openly and support their respective positions, should they appear questionable, by reference to principles which it is reasonable to expect each to accept. . . . Only if such acknowledgment is possible can there be a true community between persons in their common practices; otherwise, their relations will appear to them as founded to some extent on force. (CP, 59)

Rawls has a public reason account of legitimacy. What makes a law legitimate is that it is properly justified to citizens from the perspective of every citizen and for that reason honors the equality and freedom of each citizen. It means that citizens can and should understand the operation of coercive law as more than merely an external imposition by a state with a monopoly on violence.

The Scope of Public Reason

Two questions about the scope of public reason much discussed in the literature, and that also arise in the debate with Habermas, are the following: Who owes public reasons to whom? And about what? The first question is about the constituency of public reason: Who should comply with the requirements of public reason? The second is about the content of public reason.[28]

In respect of the first question, it is obvious enough to whom public reasons are owed: citizens of democratic societies. But who should give them? Three answers suggest themselves: citizens, public officials, or both citizens and public officials. Rawls means both (RH, 140/53).[29] Not only does he say this, but it follows from his view. Of course citizens must meet the requirements of public reason: The liberal principle of legitimacy imposes a constraint on the political conduct of citizens. Public reason is the reason of free and equal citizens (PL, 214). And in a democratic society, Rawls claims, a special moral obligation falls on citizens, namely "the duty of civility," the duty "to explain to one another on those fundamental questions how the principles and policies they advocate and vote for can be supported by the political values of public reason" (PL, 217). All this flows from one of the central ideas of justice as fairness, that citizens form part of a "true community" whose members can "face one another openly."[30]

The second question concerns the content of public reason. What matters should be regulated by laws that meet the requirements of public reason? The answer one gives to this question depends on whether one takes a broad or narrow view of the scope of public reason. The consensus in the literature seems to be that Rawls takes a narrow view. And Rawls does indicate this:

> When citizens share a reasonable political conception of justice they have a basis on which public discussion of fundamental political questions can proceed and be reasonably decided, *not of course in all cases*, but we hope in most cases of constitutional essentials and matters of basic justice. (PL, xxi, my emphasis)

By "constitutional essentials," Rawls means the "fundamental principles that specify the general structure of government and the political process" and the "basic rights and liberties" of citizens (PL, 227). By "matters of basic justice," he means the chief structural features of the basic structure of society, namely economic justice, equality of opportunity, income, wealth, and minimum levels of welfare not already covered by the constitutional essentials (PL, 228–29). And if that is not unambiguous enough, in his last statement of justice as fairness, Rawls writes,

> We strive for publicly based justifications for questions regarding the constitutional essentials and basic questions of distributive justice but not in general for all the questions to be settled by the legislature within a constitutional framework. We should distinguish, then, between these two cases, the first attainable (we hope) and desirable, the second *neither attainable nor desirable*." (JFAR, 91, my emphasis)

This interpretation is backed up by the fact that some of Rawls's staunchest defenders, and some of his most sympathetic critics, attribute the narrow view to him (Freeman 2000, 405). In explicit contrast to Rawls, both Larmore and Quong espouse the broad view. Larmore argues that public reason applies to all matters in need of regulation by coercive law, whereas Quong claims that it applies to matters of "ordinary legislation," such as funding of the arts or environmental regulation (Larmore 1996, 137; Larmore 1999, 607–608; Quong 2013, 266).

The main reason Rawls gives for advancing the narrow view is that a political conception of justice needs to be *complete* in the sense that its values, when suitably arranged, can give reasonable answers to all or nearly all questions asked of it, without recourse to any comprehensive doctrines (IPRR, 454). In his eyes, this desideratum can be met only if those questions are confined to those concerning constitutional essentials and basic justice.[31] In *Political Liberalism*, though, Rawls's view is not yet a settled one; there are indications of his canvassing a broader view of public reason. For example, he writes that the strongest case of the application of public reason is to constitutional essentials and matters of basic justice: "If we should not honor the limits of public reason here, it would seem that we need not honor them anywhere. Should they hold here, we can then proceed to other cases." Indeed, he goes on to claim that it is "usually highly desirable" to settle all political questions, including, one assumes, matters of ordinary legislation, by public reason (PL, 215). So it looks as though, as Rawls continued to refine his conception of political liberalism, he gravitated away from the broader view of the scope of public reason's application toward the narrower one.[32]

4.4 A REVIEW OF HABERMAS'S CRITICISMS OF RAWLS IN *BETWEEN FACTS AND NORMS*

With this exposition of *Political Liberalism*, part II is almost concluded. We are ready to begin our critical exposition and analysis of the 1995 exchange and of the Habermas–Rawls dispute proper. However, it behooves us, now that I have set out the main arguments of *Political Liberalism*, to return briefly to the four criticisms that Habermas makes of Rawls in *Between Facts and Norms*.

4.4.1 THE NATURAL LAW CRITICISM

There were three strands to this criticism. One claim of the natural law objection was that Rawls had a morally oriented theory of justice that was unrealistic in the sense that it focused too little on the institutions that produce legitimate law and too much on the normative components of legitimate law.

One aspect of this criticism is that, on Rawls's account, what makes laws authoritative for us is entirely a matter of the moral values that justify them, whereas, for Habermas, it is a matter also of the function of legal and administrative procedures within the political system. This is part of what Habermas means when he calls Rawls's theory "unrealistic."

Indeed, in *Political Liberalism*, Rawls makes a similar criticism of his own *A Theory of Justice*. But what he says is that because some of his arguments, particularly in part III, presupposed a comprehensive liberalism, and thus made moral assumptions that reasonable people can reject, justice as fairness cannot be realized under conditions of reasonable pluralism (PL, xvii). In other words, the moral conception of justice it advances is not a fully "political" conception in his sense. This criticism does not apply to *Political Liberalism*.

What is at issue here, then, among other things, are two discrepant senses of "political" and two conceptions of the relation between the moral and the political. For Habermas, the domain of the political is coextensive with all domains of social life regulated by government legislation, whereas, as we have seen, Rawls's conception of the political domain is far more restricted. For Rawls, political values are a relatively fixed and readily identifiable subset of general moral values, whereas, for Habermas, morality (that is, the norms of right conduct) flows into and around the political system.

Another way in which Habermas considers Rawls's "morally oriented theory" to be "unrealistic" is that it rests the authoritativeness of legitimate laws on the authority of morality. A case in point is that one's duty of civility is a moral, not a legal, duty and thus cannot be enforced by law.

Finally, Habermas objects to Rawls's theory because according to the two-stage justification as Habermas understands it, Rawls first attempts to justify a political conception of justice philosophically and then assesses it for stability. He understands this as first justifying the principle of justice with the argument of the original position and then assessing the conception for its ability to bring about stability, where the first is a matter for normative moral philosophy and the second mainly an empirical and sociological matter. That criticism seems to apply much more readily to *A Theory of Justice* read according to the standard blueprint than to the presentation of the argument in *Political Liberalism*. For one thing, political values are supposed to be ideas inherent in our common political culture, the bequest of history and tradition. Therefore, these ideas are supposed to be amenable to the consensus of reasonable citizens right from the beginning.

4.4.2 THE EXTERNAL CRITICISM

There are two issues here that overlap with those motivating the natural law criticism:

1. Assuming that the standard of political criticism is the principles of justice, reconceived as a political conception, can social criticism on that basis be fairly dubbed external or transcendent criticism? Presumably not, because the standard is composed of ideas that form part of our common political culture and so will not suffer from the supposed deficiencies of "transcendent" standards, such as irrelevance.
2. The second issue has to do with the question of the extent to which justice as fairness in *Political Liberalism* is a merely philosophical construct. True, it took a philosopher—Rawls—to arrange the idea and values of the political culture into a political conception of justice. But since they are held in common, in principle any citizen could have done that. To the same extent, any citizen could deploy the device of the original position or the method of reflective equilibrium. For in the final analysis, according to one insightful commentator on *Political Liberalism*, the canons of justification in political philosophy are simply the everyday canons of political justification.

> If so, then it cannot be fairly claimed, as Habermas does, that the political conception of justice is drawn upon the philosophical drafting table (PF, 101).[33]

Again, the issue of the relation of morality to politics crops up. If political values are internal to, and part of, the domain of moral values, as Rawls maintains, then this undermines the objection that the principles of justice are norms brought to bear externally on political actuality. If they are not, the objection applies.

4.4.3 THE SERENDIPITY OBJECTION

This objection is that if a political justification is made merely on the basis of values we happen to hold in common as a contingent bequest of history, it won't provide a firm normative basis of political legitimacy and won't capture the "epistemic" or "cognitive" content of democratically legitimate decisions. Consequently, an overlapping consensus will never satisfy what Habermas calls "the validity requirement," which states that if a law is valid, all citizens must be able to accept it for the same reasons.

First, if my exposition is correct, the serendipity objection rests on a mistake. While not a priori, the political values and ideas that comprise the overlap of reasonable comprehensive doctrines are not shared merely by accident; they are shared by all reasonable citizens because they are "very great values that are not easily overridden" and because they satisfy other relevant criteria. So not every component idea and value of the overlap is actually a political value, in Rawls's sense, and their value is not conferred merely because they happen to fall within the overlap. Moreover, the second part of the serendipity objection does not follow. If there is indeed an overlapping consensus of reasonable doctrines, as Rawls claims, with a common stock of political values, and if these can form a political conception of justice that can be and is accepted by all reasonable citizens, then the validity requirement can be satisfied. Citizens will be able to agree on the coercive laws that are justified, on the political conception that justifies them, and on the component values and ideas that the conception comprises.

4.4.4 THE DESCRIPTIVIST CRITICISM

The descriptivist criticism, as Hedrick construes it, contains the objections that (1) *Political Liberalism* is uncritical insofar as it merely aims to show that liberal citizens are likely to be able to endorse justice as fairness and (2) Rawls's normative conclusions are unsupported (Hedrick 2010, 26–33).

To my mind, if the descriptivist critique is just the objection that Rawls's principles of justice, in particular the difference principle, lack normative force because they are merely descriptions of what Western liberal democratic societies are like, then Habermas certainly does not endorse it.[34] Habermas well knows that *Political Liberalism* makes normative claims about what a just society should be like. He holds, rightly, that both the global political order, and virtually all liberal democratic states, fall miserably short of Rawls's principles of justice.

That said, Habermas makes the fair point that at the second stage of the two-stage justification, Rawls is too preoccupied with showing that, under conditions of reasonable pluralism, his two principles can nonetheless be accepted by all reasonable citizens. Habermas considers that it is more than just a pluralist political culture that stands in the way of the realization of the principles of justice, which is why he claims Rawls needs to show how his conception of justice can be embodied in legal form, given institutional reality, and thus shape action systems (BFN, 64).

One thing to note about these criticisms is that although the natural law criticism and the external criticism are mutually compatible, each is incompatible with the descriptivist criticism, at least as Hedrick construes it, as implied in his first objection. One cannot claim both that *Political Liberalism* amounts to a description of the conception of justice reasonable citizens of liberal democratic societies can most likely accept and that such a conception, qua transcendent, is inappropriate or irrelevant to liberal democracy. And the incompatibility between the natural law criticism and the descriptivist criticism is even more glaring. If Rawls is right to claim that political values are also shared *moral* values, then a judgment in the light of the principles of justice will definitely be a normative *moral* judgment, not just a judgment about what in fact all citizens can accept.

That said, Habermas is not being inconsistent here. The natural law criticism and the external criticism target the first stage of justification, as

Habermas understands it, namely the argument from the original position, or possibly the argument of *A Theory of Justice* as a whole.

The serendipity objection and the descriptivist criticism target the second stage of justification, as Habermas understands it, namely the attempt to show that a conception of justice as fairness can be accommodated by a pluralist political culture (BFN, 64–65). Habermas also argues that these stages don't mesh well, since the second stage effectively bypasses the "normative self-understanding" of the legal order, while the first stage fails to justify it adequately.

A second important point is that the natural law criticism, the external criticism, and the serendipity objection are all based on a denial of a crucial assumption that Rawls makes, namely that a political morality consists in moral ideas and values that form an identifiable subset of morality in general. If one grants Rawls that assumption, then few of these criticisms go through. And here we hit upon a very important issue in the Habermas–Rawls debate that will play a pivotal role in the exchange: Is there a reliably identifiable political morality shared by all reasonable citizens, and, if so, what is it, and what follows from it?

III

THE EXCHANGE

5

HABERMAS'S "RECONCILIATION THROUGH THE PUBLIC USE OF REASON"

Now we are ready to examine Habermas's criticisms of Rawls in the article that began the 1995 exchange: "Reconciliation Through the Public Use of Reason: Remarks on John Rawls's *Political Liberalism*."[1] The aim will be to initially appraise those criticisms by asking whether they hit their marks—whether, that is, they rest on misinterpretations or miscontruals of Rawls's *Political Liberalism* that can be relatively easily clarified. To the extent that that is the case, we will set the criticisms aside. To the extent that the criticisms are valid, we will subject them to a full appraisal at the end of part III.

Habermas opens his critical review, "Reconciliation Through the Public Use of Reason," with an intriguing remark that has been much discussed: "Because I admire this project, share its intentions, and regard its essential results as correct, the dissent I express here will remain within the bounds of a familial dispute" (RPUR, 110/26). Although in correspondence with Rawls, Habermas had made the same remark about their 1995 exchange, which essentially consisted in his review of *Political Liberalism* and Rawls's response, this remark seems to pertain to what I'm calling the "dispute."[2] If so, a rather important, and perhaps even surprising, question arises: To which family does Habermas think their respective theories belong? Various true answers could be (and have been) given to this question: the family of neo-Kantian political theories, the family of Hegelian Kantian political theories, the family of Kantian pragmatist political theories, the family of theories of Western liberal constitutional democracy, or the family of public justification accounts of liberal democracy. I'll return to this question later.

After making this observation, Habermas offers three sets of criticisms:

1. On the design of the original position
2. On the idea of the overlapping consensus
3. On the relation between private and public autonomy and Rawls's general approach

I shall discuss each set of criticisms in turn. My aim is to identify the good criticisms that, once the misunderstandings are removed, can be seen to hit the mark and then to evaluate them. That most of the aforementioned misunderstandings (though certainly not all) lie on the side of Habermas is only to be expected. After all, the exchange comprised Habermas's critical review of *Political Liberalism*, an unpublished version of which Habermas had obtained at the time of writing and had recently read for the first time. By contrast, Rawls's grasp of his own project was more nuanced and complete, though even he apparently did not have a thorough grasp of all the implications of his own ideas.[3] The other thing to note about the exchange is that Habermas compresses his criticisms into 7,500 words, the standard length of an article in the *Journal of Philosophy*, whereas Rawls replies at far greater length. This put Habermas in a situation in which, owing to word limitations, he had to reel off an array of criticisms without being able to develop them fully.

5.1 "RECONCILIATION THROUGH THE PUBLIC USE OF REASON" I: ON THE DESIGN OF THE ORIGINAL POSITION

Habermas's first set of criticisms focuses on the design of the original position and the veil of ignorance and on the contrast between these devices and Habermas's alternative, principle (U). This was the contrast that formed the focus of most of the early debate. The 1995 exchange, however, purports to be a critical review of *Political Liberalism* by Habermas, followed by a reply and defense by Rawls. And where the argument from the original position to the principles of justice formed the key argument of *A Theory of Justice*, especially when interpreted according to the standard blueprint, it plays a much less prominent role in *Political Liberalism*, where it is not discussed until section 4 of lecture VIII. So why does Habermas begin a review of *Political Liberalism* with arguments aimed at the original position?

In my view, there are two reasons. First, these criticisms are carried over from Habermas's close critical discussion of the original position, which, as we saw in chapter 1 (section 1.2.8), took place in the context of his dispute with Kohlberg over the proper construal of the moral point of view at stage 6 of moral consciousness.[4] Until the exchange, Habermas had had no occasion to put objections directly to Rawls himself, and so he recapitulates them as a preliminary introduction to the exchange, without paying heed to the change of context. (Recall that the early debate was between Habermas and Kohlberg about the correct model of moral consciousness for a general moral theory.) Second, Habermas does not notice many of the significant differences between the two projects, since he initially tends to interpret *Political Liberalism* as an extension of *A Theory of Justice*, albeit one that focuses on the conditions of the institutionalization of justice as fairness under conditions of pluralism.

That said, it is not as if there is no merit in comparing the original position with principle (U). If one sets aside the fact that the original position is the central argument of a political theory tailored in the first instance to the basic structure, whereas principle (U) is the central idea of a general theory of moral consciousness, and instead considers them merely as competing ways of operationalizing the moral point of view (as Habermas puts it)—that is, as devices that help us to identify and validate impartial principles of justice (even in different senses)—then certain interesting philosophical issues arise. So, let us examine Habermas's criticisms in that light.

5.1.1 HABERMAS ON THE ORIGINAL POSITION AND PRINCIPLE (U)

Habermas argues that Rawls gets into trouble by constructing the original position as he does, building morally substantive considerations (of equality and impartiality) into the choice situation through the device of the veil of ignorance, which obliges the choosers to make impartial choices while freeing them up from any moral pressure and allowing them free rein as merely rational self-interested parties, that is, people "disinterested" in others and wanting the best outcome for themselves. Habermas maintains this has three deleterious consequences:

1. Contrary to Rawls's explicit assumption, the highly stylized parties in the original position are unable to grasp the "highest-order interests" of the actual citizens whom they model and on whose behalf they choose (RPUR, 111/27). Consequently, it is not the case that the principles chosen in the original position would be the ones that the actual citizens they stand in for would choose.

The issue here seems to be that while the parties in the original position in *A Theory of Justice* are stylized as merely rational choosers who take no interest in the interests of other parties, the citizens they model, and on behalf of whom they are to choose principles of justice, are not merely rational choosers but fully rounded human agents and citizens. Hence, Habermas suggests, the choices of the former do not also hold for the latter.

This is not an original criticism.[5] And it is brought to bear on *A Theory of Justice* interpreted according to the "standard blueprint," namely as a traditional philosophical theory that proceeds from slender premises of an account of human rationality to justify the rationality of justice through the argument from the original position for the two principles of justice. Still, the important point of contrast here is with the participants in moral discourse, who, Habermas argues, are *real* people participating in an *actual* practice.

While that is so, there is still a related problem here. For the constituency of participants in any actual discourse will be relatively small, whereas the constituency of "all affected" by the norm in question will be virtually unlimited. To that extent, the *actual* participants in the *real* discourse will have to conduct advocatory discourses on behalf of very many hypothetical others. So Rawls might counter that there is a similar "gap" in Habermas's discourse ethics: between the number of moral agents to whom the norm ideally agreed upon is to apply and the number of participants who actually canvass it and endorse it in a real discourse.

Further, as Rawls later makes clear, the choosers are moral persons who have not only a conception of the good but also a sense of justice and who are not only rational but also "reasonable." And as reasonable moral persons, they are willing to propose and abide by fair terms of cooperation, provided others do likewise (PL, 59). This normatively richer starting point in *Political Liberalism* closes the alleged gap between the stylized choosers in the original position and the citizens of the liberal democratic polity they represent. In sum, the problem in *Political Liberalism* is perhaps not as big as Habermas makes it out to be; and, anyway, discourse ethics in spite of its insistence on an actual discourse among real participants suffers from a similar problem.

2. Rawls's argument from the original position misleadingly treats basic rights as primary goods by imposing the prudential perspective of the economically rational chooser. It is thus unable to account for what Habermas calls the "deontological meaning" of basic rights or principles of justice (RPUR, 114–16/29–31).

There are a variety of contrasting concepts of the good and the right in *A Theory of Justice*, and there are a variety of distinctions between them, some sharper than others (TJ, 466–52; PL, 177–79). A distributive conception of justice as fairness is self-evidently one dependent on a notion of the good, since the well-being of representative persons is specified with reference to the goods—the thin goods or primary social goods—whose fair distribution is at issue. So to begin with, it seems wrong to suggest that principles of justice lack "deontological meaning" entirely just because they distribute primary social goods. Such principles specify rights and counterpart *duties* concerning just distributions and impose *obligations* on other citizens, and are *deontological* in that sense. Perhaps Habermas makes this claim because, on his standard interpretation of the argument, the parties in the original position are stipulated to be merely rational choosers who prefer a greater, rather than smaller, share of goods, but this interpretation is one-sided, as we have just seen, since the persons behind the veil of ignorance are also reasonable and have an effective sense of justice. But further, Rawls's argument is supposed to show that the two principles are ones that a reasonable and rational person would choose; its purpose is not to provide an explanation of the "deontological meaning" of those principles, that is, of their normative force or status.

By contrast, that *is* one of the central aims of Habermas's discourse ethics. Habermas's theory does, among other things, set out to account for the normative force of moral norms, but, as we've seen, it is a different kind of theory. Habermas's theory of discourse ethics also presupposes a single, allegedly "razor-sharp" distinction between justice-qua-morality and the good as an ethical value (MCCA, 104).

Habermas is contrasting justice as fairness—a conception of distributive justice for a liberal constitutional democracy—with a general conception of moral rightness that figures in Kohlberg at stage 6, but not in *A Theory of Justice*. This is plain when he describes norms as absolutely binding, universal, and encoding a binary validity claim (RPUR, 114–15/30). And if that were not evidence enough, he goes on to compare Rawls's original position with the categorical imperative and the golden rule (RPUR, 117/32). This means that the deontological meaning of moral norms in Habermas's sense is quite different from the deontological meaning of political norms (as he understands them)—consider just the differences in scope and application—and from Rawls's principles of justice. True, an action can be judged as either permissible or impermissible—which is what Habermas means by the "binary validity claim" of moral rightness.[6] By contrast, social institutions can be more or less just, and in this sense social justice as conceived by Rawls does not exhibit the binary logic that Habermas sees as characteristic of moral rightness. Still, this does not bear out Habermas's conclusion that Rawls has failed to account for the "deontological meaning" of moral norms. It shows, rather, that norms of social justice are not in every respect like norms of general moral rightness and that it is no part of *A Theory of Justice* to provide a phenomenology of the moral.

3. The veil of ignorance does not guarantee impartiality of choice in the original position, insofar as all the basic normative constructs deployed in the construction of the original position would need to be accepted without revision on an ongoing basis by the citizens thus represented (RPUR, 116–19/31–33).

The issue in this third criticism seems to a combination of those in (1) and (2). Impartiality is achieved, Habermas suggests, only at the final stage of the four-stage sequence, when the "veil of ignorance is gradually raised." At that point, Habermas maintains, the principles can be accepted by real citizens in the light of all the relevant information. He suggests that this can happen only because the theorist has already constructed the principles for selection in the light of the very information that the theorist deprives the choosers of in the original position. The underlying objection is that whether each participant in discourse can welcome a norm in the light of their interests and values is a more reliable test of a norm's impartiality than whether a principle of justice can be chosen by moral persons from behind a veil of ignorance.

This is a difficult issue to untangle. Beside the fact that Habermas is comparing unlike conceptions of justice, comparisons are difficult, as Martha Nussbaum notes, since "the original position is a hypothetical situation, and a device of representation, whereas Habermas focuses on an idealized conception of real social dialogue" (Nussbaum 2003, 495). These difficulties notwithstanding, the objection founders because these are not the appropriate points of comparison.

5.1.2 McMAHON'S CRITICISM

This aspect of the debate—the respective roles and merits of the original position and of principle (U) in identifying and validating impartial principles of justice—has been the focus of much of the secondary literature, not only in the early debate but also in discussions specifically concerning the exchange. To that extent, it deserves special attention. Christopher McMahon has been the most incisive critic of Habermas and Rawls in this regard, having produced three important articles on the topic. The results of his analysis are illuminating, and important for both the explication and evaluation of the debate.

McMahon's first important contribution, in his article "Ethics and Dialogue," is to distinguish between two distinct conceptions of dialogicality (McMahon 2000, 520). He calls the first of these "weak dialogicality," which amounts to "simply a de facto concurrence of independent monological judgments regarding which principle would be in the interests of all" (McMahon 2000, 521). He argues that the condition set out in (U), namely that "the foreseeable consequences and side effects of [a norm's] general observance for the interests and value-orientations of each individual could be freely accepted jointly by all concerned," is satisfied by a weak dialogical agreement.

McMahon's second important contribution is to show that Habermas construes the dialogical structure of moral discourse (and principle U) in a much stronger sense, as necessarily involving a collective judgment of all participants in discourse about whether a norm is in the interests of all affected.[7] He calls this "strong dialogicality" (McMahon 2000, 519–21).

According to McMahon, Habermas's conception of strong dialogicality is incoherent. For on Habermas's view of strong dialogical agreement, no individual participant has adequate grounds to judge whether a norm is indeed in the equal interests of all until everyone has been consulted and has finally agreed that it is. This robs each individual participant of any good reason to judge whether a norm is valid from their individual perspective. Furthermore, it makes deviation from a valid norm an impossibility: "As soon as there is deviation the norm is no longer valid. Deviation from a norm or judgment cannot be criticized as mistaken" (McMahon 2002, 529). The upshot is that strong dialogicality, as understood by Habermas as a cognitive requirement on agreement in moral discourse, is untenable:

> If there is such a thing as the rational acceptance of moral principles there can be no cognitive requirement to suspend judgment as long as anyone disagrees. We can still understand (U) as characterizing the endpoint of idealized inquiry for the purposes of a constructivist account of moral truth. But the consensus envisaged must be . . . a piecemeal consensus consisting of the de facto agreement of independently generated (monological) moral judgments. (McMahon 2000, 533)

If McMahon is right, and I believe he is, then his arguments undermine Habermas's claim that principle (U), as a *dialogical* approach to universalization in ethics, is distinct from and superior to *monological* approaches.

In a second, related, article, "Why There Is No Issue Between Habermas and Rawls," McMahon forensically examines Habermas's reasons for rejecting Rawls's device of the original position as a monological, rather than dialogical, model of moral consciousness (McMahon 2002). This article is of especial significance, since it appeared in the same journal as the original exchange, the *Journal of Philosophy*. In this article, McMahon shows that Habermas appears to construe "ideal role taking" as an epistemic process of exchanging perspectives with all affected in order to eliminate bias in the assessment of which norms are in the equal interests of all. This can take either a monological or a dialogical form, but either way, it is "of purely epistemic significance. It is simply a sign that the group has attained a correct understanding of what would be in everyone's interests." Furthermore, he points out that "moral impartiality is constituted by the relevant reasons, those relating to what would be in everyone's interests" (McMahon 2002, 120). Finally, McMahon shows that, where Habermas says nothing about what it is for a norm to be equally in everyone's interests, Rawls does, in that he shows that principles of justice are those supported by reasons of fairness: "Rawls has taken up the challenge of explicating, with the help of his device of choice in the original position, the notion of a fair resolution of the competing interests" (McMahon 2002, 128). But Rawls's contribution on this point is therefore fully compatible with Habermas's broader, more open-ended conception of moral discourse and its epistemic aim of arriving at norms that are in the equal interests of all.

In a third article, McMahon goes on to show that Rawls's devices of the original position and the veil of ignorance provide an interpretation of a moral notion that is indeed central to Habermas's principle (U), namely "the notion of being in everyone's interests" (McMahon 2011, 211–15). Moreover, McMahon contends, Habermas needs such a notion, since his attempt to operationalize the moral point of view such that it "generates moral impartiality from the presuppositions of argument alone" is a failure (McMahon 2011, 215). So Habermas has to draw on a notion of impartiality external to the argumentative procedure.

If McMahon's arguments are right, what do they show?

1. They show that the distinction between monological and dialogical approaches to moral universalization is not as clear as Habermas thinks; indeed, monological universalization is more or less interchangeable with weak dialogical universalization.
2. They show that Habermas must give up on construing discourse ethics—in particular, the ideal of rationally motivated agreement as the result of an ideally prosecuted discourse—as strongly dialogical, that is, as essentially involving a collective judgment whereby every individual participant in discourse has a veto over the adoption of moral norms.

3. They show that, with regard to the choice of impartial principles, the sense in which weak dialogical procedures are superior to monological procedures in ethics is very different from how Habermas construes it. Weak dialogical agreement is a useful supplement to, and corrective for, monological universalization.
4. They show that Habermas's criticism that Rawls's original position fails to guarantee the impartiality of norms because it is monological, but that principle (U) is successful in so doing because it is dialogical, fails to do justice to the complexities of either device.
5. They show that discourse ethics can make use of a device like Rawls's argument from the original position, and indeed needs something like this, because it itself relies on a source of impartiality external to the presuppositions of argument (McMahon 2002, 111; 2011, 221–23).

What McMahon's arguments do not evince, however, is the trenchant conclusion announced in the title of the article in the *Journal of Philosophy*, namely that "there is no issue between Habermas and Rawls" (McMahon 2002). At best, they establish that the issue that Habermas raises in his opening salvo of the exchange, on which McMahon and numerous others focus their entire attention, is a nonissue. Indeed, McMahon himself notes that the contrast between principle (U) and the original position is "one important issue" dividing the two theorists (McMahon 2002, 111). Nowhere does Habermas claim that it is the only issue, and clearly he does not think this, for in parts II and III of "Reconciliation Through the Public Use of Reason," he goes on to discuss two further sets of issues.

Now, McMahon might think not that this is the only issue but rather that it is the key issue dividing the two thinkers, on which all other significant issues depend. In that case, dissolving the issue, as McMahon quite brilliantly does, would indeed show that there are no others. However, for reasons I've already given, namely that the original position and principle (U) are not the salient points of comparison between Rawls's and Habermas's respective *political* theories, it is clear that this cannot be the key issue dividing the two thinkers, on which all other issues depend. Rawls, to be fair to him, acknowledges as much. He notes early on in "Reply to Habermas" that the difference between their respective devices of representation, principle (U) and the original position, is the "second main difference" between them (in his view, there are only two), which presupposes "a more fundamental difference," namely that Habermas's position is comprehensive and that his is not (RH, 132/47). Plainly, Rawls thinks that the issue on which McMahon focuses is ancillary and that the main issues lie elsewhere.[8]

Rawls is right about this. For reasons I have already given, namely that the argument from the original position plays a comparatively minor role in *Political Liberalism*, and that principle (U) is not the central principle of Habermas's *Between Facts and Norms*, I'd go so far as to say that, though they form part of the 1995 exchange, Habermas's first set of criticisms is not central to the broader dispute between *Political Liberalism* and *Between Facts and Norms*. Moreover, I believe that this wrong assumption (encouraged by the political reading of discourse ethics and the moral reading of *A Theory of Justice*) has derailed many commentators, including McMahon, and diverted their attention from the very weighty real issues between Rawls's and Habermas's respective mature political theories.[9] This, in addition to the general failure to pay due attention to the eventual format of the debate, and the concomitant failure to distinguish between the 1995 exchange and the dispute, is responsible for the widespread, and in my view precipitate and largely erroneous, judgment that the debate was much ado about nothing.[10]

5.2 "RECONCILIATION THROUGH THE PUBLIC USE OF REASON" II: ON THE IDEA OF THE OVERLAPPING CONSENSUS

Habermas's second set of criticisms divides roughly into two different but related lines of argument: first, directed at the role of the idea of the overlapping consensus in the justification of the theory and, second, directed at the meaning of the term "reasonable" and at Rawls's method of avoidance.

5.2.1 THE ROLE OF CONSENSUS AND THE JUSTIFICATION OF THE POLITICAL CONCEPTION OF JUSTICE

As for the first line of argument, Habermas objects that in *Political Liberalism*, it is "unclear what needs to be justified" and that it is "unclear how the validity-claim of the theory is to be understood" (RPUR, 119/34).

Habermas takes his point of departure from what Rawls called the "two-stage justification of the political conception of justice." It is first given a "freestanding" justification, for example with the argument from the original position. Subsequently, at the second stage, it is asked whether the political conception is sufficiently stable, which is established by checking that it can be the focus of overlapping consensus.

Habermas asks the following questions: Does the overlapping consensus contribute to the justification of the theory? Or does it only "explicate a necessary condition of functional stability" (RPUR, 119/34)?

As regards the first question, evidently Habermas thinks it should but suspects it does not. On his reading, consensus comes into play only at the second level, where the question of stability arises and at which, as he puts it, consensus "merely expresses the functional contribution that the theory of justice can make to the peaceful institutionalization of social cooperation" (RPUR, 121). This means, he reasons, that the test of whether the political conception can be the focus of an overlapping consensus loses its essential "epistemic meaning" and is "no longer a confirmation of the correctness of the theory" (RPUR, 121–22/36).

One can see why Habermas might think this having read only the first version of *Political Liberalism*. But as our discussion of Quong's challenge to the "common view" made clear, the idea of a consensus of reasonable persons plays a role at the first stage, too. After all, the political ideas and values are ones that all reasonable citizens hold in common. And a freestanding justification of the political conception, such as the argument from the original position, is supposed to show that the principles of justice can be welcomed by all reasonable citizens.

Habermas's implicit point of contrast is the much beefier role that consensus plays in discourse ethics, in which the amenability to consensus in discourse is a necessary (and sufficient) condition of validity for moral norms and, to that extent, constitutes the "cognitive meaning" of valid moral norms, given that validity claims to rightness are in this respect analogous to validity claims to truth.[11] Habermas is right to see that consensus plays a weaker role in *Political Liberalism*, since the fact that the political conception of justice can be supported by an overlapping consensus is not of itself an indicator of the truth of the conception.

As for the second question, note that Habermas tends to frame it as a disjunction. Does the overlapping consensus play a "cognitive" role in the justification of the theory (sometimes he says "epistemic"), *or* does it play a "merely instrumental role" (RPUR, 119)? So he thinks that these are mutually exclusive, that the second stage of justification consists in the ascertaining of a social fact, namely whether reasonable citizens do in fact accept the political conception of justice. If so, the "overlapping consensus would then be merely an index of the utility . . . of the theory" (RPUR, 122/36), that is, its usefulness in yielding social stability.

There are a lot of questionable assumptions behind these criticisms. To begin with, Habermas assumes wrongly that what makes a value "political" is that it happens to fall in the overlap of reasonable comprehensive doctrines and that, as a consequence of that contingent fact, it is politically useful for bringing about consensus and social stability. But as we saw in chapter 4, not every value in the overlap is a political one. There may be values or ideas shared by all citizens but not germane to the justification of a liberal constitutional democratic order (PL, 139). The political values are common to all reasonable doctrines and affirmed by all reasonable citizens *because* they are "very great values and not easily overridden" (PL, 169, 218; RH, 147/61). That is, they have intrinsic and not just instrumental value: Indeed, they have instrumental value only because of their intrinsic value. (Of course, Rawls does not put it like this, for this sounds like a meta-ethical thesis of the kind he wishes to avoid.) Furthermore, in Rawls's view, the political values that fall within the overlap are moral values (PL, 148–49, xxxix). And the reasons that flow from these shared values are moral reasons shared by all reasonable citizens, which is why Rawls writes that "a political conception of justice is a normative and a moral conception" (PL, xxxix; see also xli, 148).[12]

Habermas is not alone in interpreting Rawls's overlapping consensus in the way he does. Rainer Forst also claims that in advancing his political conception of justice only as "reasonable" and in refraining from advancing it as "true," Rawls "relegates the validity of the theory to the contingent fact of its being consonant with various comprehensive doctrines" (Forst 2011, 157).[13] Like Habermas, Forst claims that although the political conception of justice "can be justified in a 'freestanding' way . . . it is not accepted on the basis of shared moral reasons, but rather for the different ethical reasons of citizens" (Forst 2011, 163).

This means that although citizens can agree on a political conception (from the perspective of their several comprehensive doctrines), they do not agree for the same reasons, and hence "the validity requirement," which, in Habermas's view, constitutes their cognitive meaning, is not met. What Rawls's theory lacks, according to Forst and Habermas, and what it needs if it is to account adequately for the "cognitive" or "epistemic" meaning of democratic discourse, is "a common perspective on justice among citizens and a genuine moral consensus" (HRDP, 157). But as we have seen, the freestanding justification, insofar as it appeals only to the political ideas and values in the overlap, is a justification on the basis of shared moral reasons and does give citizens a "common perspective on justice."[14] (Of course, that is not the only perspective citizens have, for the political conception of justice is also justified in the eyes of each reasonable citizen on the nonpublic basis of their reasonable comprehensive doctrines.)

5.2.2 THE REASONABLE

Habermas's second line of argument targets Rawls's conception of the "reasonable" and his so-called method of avoidance. Habermas thinks that what Rawls means when he claims that the political conception is justified as "reasonable" is something like "the reflective attitude of enlightened tolerance" (RPUR, 119/34). He realizes that reasonable agreement must be more than a *modus vivendi*, namely self-interested toleration of a view based on an assessment of the balance of forces, but remains puzzled about what that would amount to. He suggests that it amounts to either reasonable toleration, such as that advocated by G. E. Lessing toward the world religions, or " 'thoughtfulness' in dealing with debatable views whose truth is for the present undecided" (RPUR 123/37; 125/39). One understands Habermas's difficulty, for Rawls is not exactly crystal clear on the status of the reasonable, but neither of these strikes me quite right. (A reasonable conception of justice in Rawls's view is one worth affirming not merely because of our ignorance but because of our need for cooperation with our fellows and our nature as free and equal citizens.)

Where Habermas clearly goes awry is in his construal of the claim that a political conception justified as reasonable prescinds from truth. Habermas takes this to mean that Rawls is claiming that his theory does not so much as aspire to truth. Habermas agrees with this, since, according to discourse ethics, a validity claim to rightness is not a claim to truth but only analogous to a claim to truth. (Rawls's political theory "neither asserts nor denies" the claim to the moral truth of the political conception [PL, 127].) This is not because of a meta-ethical background view according to which normative theories are either not true or, alternatively, not even apt to be true or false. Habermas's odd remark that he concurs with Rawls's "rejection of moral realism" and his "consequent rejection of a semantic truth-predicate for normative statements" (RPUR, 124/39) indicates that he thinks it is. He assumes that Rawls's method of avoidance consists in the theoretical assumptions of noncognitivism plus anti-realism.

The peculiarity of Rawls's approach to political constructivism, which escapes Habermas, is that it avoids, so far as possible, presupposing such meta-ethical background theories and neither asserts nor denies those either. Rawls's strategy, which he calls "the strategy of avoidance," is not any variety of noncognitivism or error theory. It is not a constructivist anti-realism either but a thoroughgoing quietism about all such meta-ethical theories (PL, 29): "As I have said, here it does not speak. It says only that for a reasonable and workable political conception, no more is needed than a public basis in the principles of practical reason in union with conceptions of society and person" (PL, 127). *A fortiori*, he does not deny that either justice as fairness as a political conception or political liberalism is true. He very probably believes that they both are. It is just that such claims would be comprehensive in his view, not "political" (RH, 150/63).

Habermas's overall judgment is that Rawls needs and wants to make a far stronger claim. He quotes a passage from *Political Liberalism* in which Rawls says that if any one of the views in an overlapping consensus is true, then the political conception of justice will be true (PL, 153n19, 128). Habermas reads this passage as showing that (1) the political conception needs to be made true and (2) it can be made true, according to Rawls's own assumptions, only by being derived from a comprehensive doctrine.

Habermas counters that while he agrees that normative statements do not make truth claims, he rejects Rawls's view that world views do make truth claims and can be appropriately appraised as being true or false. The background assumption here is that what Rawls calls a "comprehensive doctrine" is the same as what Habermas calls an "ethical world view" and that these "are measured more by the authenticity of the lifestyles they shape than by the truth of the statements they admit" (RPUR, 126/40).

But Rawls's claim is a weaker one, that "*if* any one reasonable comprehensive doctrine in the consensus is true, then the political conception itself is true."[15]

It may be that no part of the reasonable comprehensive doctrine is true and that, as a consequence, the political conception is not true, but that it would still be one free and equal citizens can affirm as reasonable. Habermas thinks that with this thought, Rawls "makes the legitimacy and stability of the institutions of a well-ordered society dependent on the possible transfer of truth from at least one of these doctrines to the generally accepted conception of justice" (HRDP, 291). But that is not how Rawls intends the claim. He is not offering this thought to the designers of institutions or to professional philosophers as a reply to a worry about the possibility that the political conception might not be true or valid. Rather, it is offered to reasonable citizens as a further justification for supporting the political conception of justice, a justification that is desirable but not necessary.

5.3 "RECONCILIATION THROUGH THE PUBLIC USE OF REASON" III: PRIVATE AND PUBLIC AUTONOMY

In the final section of his article, Habermas levels several wide-ranging criticisms under the heading of "Private and Political Autonomy" (the third set of criticisms described earlier). In this section, he reels off several different lines of criticism, each of which ramifies into more specific criticisms:

1. The first, which is the criticism that squarely belongs under that heading, is that in spite of Rawls's claim of having balanced the liberties of the ancients and those of the moderns, in fact his theory "generates a priority of liberal rights" and "demotes the democratic process to an inferior status" (RPUR, 128/42).

2. The second line of criticism concerns the fact that, in Habermas's eyes, Rawls conceives of "political" as a technical term with three different meanings: It describes a conception that is (1) neutral with respect to world views, (2) scope restricted in its application, and (3) based on a small fund of values held in common. Furthermore, this technical meaning of the political is very narrow and separated from the private sphere by a "rigid boundary" (RPUR, 128–29).
3. The third line of criticism is more methodological in orientation. Although their theories are both modest, Habermas claims, they are modest in different ways, and (implicitly) Habermas's theory is modest in a better way than that of Rawls, since it leaves "more questions open because it entrusts more to the process of rational opinion and will formation" (RPUR, 130/43). Furthermore, he claims, where Rawls's theory is freighted with "substantive connotations," his own is developed in a "strictly procedural" manner (RPUR, 116/32).

5.3.1 HABERMAS'S METHODOLOGICAL CRITIQUE

Let's begin with the last line of criticism, which concerns questions of method and approach. Habermas claims that his approach is both more and less modest than Rawls's (RPUR, 131/44).[16] Both claims are meant as criticisms.

Habermas's theory is supposedly less modest in that it gives a greater role to philosophy in its explication and justification of both morality and political legitimacy. For example, he subtitles the major essay in *Moral Consciousness and Communicative Action* "Notes on a Programme of *Philosophical* Justification" (MCCA, 43, my emphasis). In a criticism that throws one of Rawls's claims in *Political Liberalism* back at him, Habermas rejects Rawls's view that political theory " 'move[s] entirely within the domain of the political' and 'leave[s] philosophy as it is' " (MW, 92; see also RH, 47/93). We shall discuss this argument in more detail in the following chapters when we look at Rawls's criticisms of Habermas. The questions here are what kind of ideas are germane to the justification of political theories, and whether, for example, political theories must also answer to philosophical and social theoretical criteria of justification.

The other point on which Habermas claims his own theory is less modest is that it claims to be true, not just reasonable. He thinks that making a claim to truth is unavoidable, even for a deflated, post-metaphysical theory that is ontologically parsimonious and restricted in scope to the tasks of a stand-in for and interpreter of the sciences (see chapter 1, section 1.2.9). Indeed, qua post-metaphysical, his theory is also defeasible and must, on pain of revision, stand up against the unforced force of the better argument in theoretical discourse. It can do this, Habermas thinks, only if it makes a validity claim to truth. On Habermas's view, if it means avoiding making a truth claim for the theory, Rawls's strategy of avoidance is not even an option.

Habermas argues that his theory is *more* modest in that it leaves *more* up to participants and citizens and imposes stricter limitations on the role of the philosopher: "I propose that philosophy limit itself to the clarification of the moral point of view and the procedure of democratic legitimation" (RPUR, 131/44). Habermas appears to have discourse ethics in mind when he makes this claim. As we have seen, in his political theory, he does a lot more than merely "clarify" the democratic point of view—he derives an entire system of rights. Still, each theory involves different procedures and different relations between its substantive and procedural elements, so we will have to examine this criticism in the light of both theories in turn.

Before we do so, however, the notion of procedure or proceduralism in play requires clarification. Rawls helpfully distinguishes three main forms of procedural justice: perfect procedural justice, imperfect procedural justice, and pure procedural justice (Peters 1996, 116; Gledhill 2011, 189). Perfect procedural justice involves an independent criterion of justice separate from and prior to the procedure. For example, in the case of the procedure by which the person who divides the cake is the last to take a slice, the idea of a cake cut into equal slices is an external criterion against which the outcome can be checked. In this case, provided the procedure is correctly carried out, it is guaranteed to lead to a just outcome. Imperfect procedural justice—for example, a criminal trial—also involves an independent criterion of justice, namely that the guilty are found guilty and the innocent are not, but even when the procedure is properly carried out, there is no guarantee of a just outcome. Pure procedural justice, such as the laying of fair bets, has no independent criterion for the right result. A just outcome is simply whichever outcome results from the properly followed procedure.

As we saw in chapter 1, justice as fairness involves pure procedural justice in the choice of principles in the original position. Pure procedural justice is ensured by the rational autonomy of the deliberating parties modeled by the veil of ignorance, since there is no external criterion independent of the procedure to constrain the choice of principles of justice (Gledhill 2011, 190; TJ, 120).[17] Pure procedural justice also plays a role in Rawls's first principle of justice, the liberty principle, which secures the fair value of the political liberties. The idea of this principle is to "incorporate into the basic structure of society an effective political procedure which mirrors in that structure the fair representation of persons achieved by the original position" (Gledhill 2011, 190; PL, 330).

Discourse Ethics as Procedure

In Habermas's discourse ethics, proceduralism plays a somewhat different role in respect of the choice of valid moral norms (which, for Habermas, are norms of justice). On the face of it, the procedure of moral discourse resembles more closely what Rawls calls "*perfect* procedural justice," since there is a criterion of justice external to the procedure, namely the fact that a valid moral norm is one that is in the equal interests of all, a criterion not contained in either (U) or (D). Also, when the procedure is properly carried out (and runs to completion, namely a rationally motivated consensus), a just outcome is certain. The chief difference is that the theorist does not run the procedure to validate any norms. The role of experts is restricted to explicating the moral point of view.

Habermas contrasts discourse ethics with Rawls's theory, which "claims to elaborate the idea of a just society, while the citizens then use this idea as a platform from which to judge existing arrangements and policies" (RPUR, 131/44).[18] What is at issue here is the role of the theorist. Habermas, as we have seen, interprets the original position in the light of the "the standard blueprint" of *A Theory of Justice*, according to which it is the philosopher, as expert, who establishes the two principles of justice through argument, whereas Rawls allows that this can and should also be done by citizens.

Whether Habermas can rightly claim that his theory, unlike Rawls's, leaves "substantial questions which must be answered in the here and now to the more or less enlightened engagement of participants" is, however, not so obvious (RPUR, 131/44–45). And, as we have seen, Habermas hesitates even to give examples of valid moral norms, although he does sometimes adduce the rather tricky example of human rights.[19] In this respect, Habermas is a success theorist and not an error theorist. He holds that there are some valid moral norms, which is why he assumes his philosophical justification of the moral point of view can defeat the moral skeptic (MCCA, 77–79; see also 44–45, 55–58, 81–85, 97–99).

Recall also that, as we saw in chapter 1, some of what Habermas presents as merely rules of discourse in general—specifically that everyone has an equal right to participation and that everyone has an equal right to express their interest—look suspiciously like moral norms that illicitly import moral substance into the supposedly formal procedure of discourse.[20]

Finally, as Gledhill points out, Habermas acknowledges that there is plenty of "substance in procedure" in the discourse theory of morality. As Habermas writes about the contrast between Kant's moral theory and discourse ethics, the latter "deprives practical reason of all specific normative contents and sublimates it in the form of a procedure for justifying possible normative contents" (TCC, 149). And that is by no means the only sublimation in question. Habermas argues that post-traditional societies emerged from the great world religions, which provided a substantial shared ethos, a tradition that functioned as a fund of shared values, and a fellowship in a common outlook and a common way of life. The post-traditional remnant of this, and its functional equivalent as the basis of social integration, is the procedure of moral discourse, or what he calls elsewhere "the fund of formal features of the performatively shared situation of deliberation" (TIO, 41). In other words, this shared substantial ethos is also sublimated into moral discourse: "The missing transcendent good can be replaced . . . only by appeal to the intrinsic constitution of the practice of deliberation" (TIO, 41). Even in a post-traditional society characterized by a thin and highly general morality of justice, morality's origins in a thick conception of the good live on in a different form as a "remnant of the good at the core of the right" in the shape of a thin, affective relation of universal solidarity among human beings (TIO, 28–29). This web of solidary relations protects "the web of intersubjective relations of mutual recognition," without which, Habermas maintains, moral norms cannot function (MCCA, 200).

We already know that the relation between moral discourse as procedure and the substantive results of the discourse process is very different from the relation between the original position and the principles of justice. But to say that the former is strictly procedural and the latter not is simplistic and misleading. In both theories, morally substantial elements are contained in the procedures themselves.

Democracy as Procedure

A comparison with Habermas's political and democratic theory yields a similar conclusion. Habermas's political theory does not fit into Rawls's typology. Kenneth Baynes thinks the best way of describing it is as what Charles Beitz calls "complex proceduralism," according to which "the terms of democratic participation are fair when they are reasonably acceptable from each citizen's point of view, or more precisely, when no citizen has good reason to refuse to accept them" (Beitz 1989, 23; also in Baynes 2016, 163). However, this description raises as many questions as it answers. What counts as reasonable acceptance, or as a good reason to reject a law or political norm? The MPC says that a political norm violating a moral one is a good reason to reject it. The ethical harmonization requirement allows legitimate laws to be rejected if they do not resonate with citizens' ethical self-conceptions. Looked at in the round, Habermas's political theory resembles a political specification of the moral requirement in principle (U) that a norm be in the equal interest of everyone: For a law to be legitimate, it must be in the equal interest of every citizen and accepted by them in the light of their moral and ethical outlooks. This view would, however, mean that the procedure depended on the external input of substantive ethical values and substantial moral norms.

The picture is complicated because, as Baynes points out, Habermas applies the terms "procedural" and "proceduralism" somewhat indiscriminately to law (BFN, 409), the constitution (BFN, 246), politics (BFN, 273), and popular sovereignty (BFN, 463–91). Indeed, Habermas's political theory contains a whole cluster of different contrasts between procedure and substance.[21] In the context of his political sociology, Habermas contrasts what he calls the "procedural" legal paradigm with the liberal and welfarist paradigms (BFN, 409–10). This throws little light on what he means by "procedural" and instead positions his whole conception of the modern democratic state as being distinct from the welfare state and the liberal state.

In the context of Habermas's reflections on method, he contrasts his own discourse theory with two "substantive" approaches, natural law theories and civic republican theories, which, he claims, make the move of grounding the authority of law on an antecedent moral order or ethical order, respectively. Neither of these normative orders, he claims, is available in post-traditional societies, in which legitimacy is generated as it were on the fly by discursive procedures of deliberative democratic politics (BFN, 285).

None of this really bears out Habermas's criticism that *Between Facts and Norms* is "strictly procedural" by comparison with Rawls's more substantive theory and that it leaves more questions unanswered, up to the citizens to decide. In making such claims, Habermas probably has foremost in his mind the basic architectonic of the theory, whereby he derives only a schema of "unsaturated" rights from the conjunction of the discourse principle and the legal form and thus leaves up to citizens themselves the historical and ethical task of filling these out on the basis of their own values and traditions (see chapter 3, section 3.3.5). In this one respect, Habermas's theory design pays due deference to his insistence that democratic legitimacy flows from the sui generis nature of the normative authority of law rather than from the normative substance of an antecedent moral or ethical order. But that does not mitigate the fact that he does derive an entire schema of rights, which rather suspiciously resembles the classical sequence of civil, political, and social rights examined by the historical sociologist T. H. Marshall.

However, as we noted in chapter 3, Habermas's claim to have advanced a functional justification of basic rights fully immanent to law has come under attack from various critics, including sympathetic commentators such as Forst, Larmore, and Rummens, who argue that the system of rights lacks an adequate normative justification. He has been defended from these criticisms by others, such as Baynes and Flynn, who counter that Habermas's theory can or does contain substantive moral support for basic rights.[22] So, depending on who wins this argument, either discourse theory is more procedural and less substantive in this regard than Rawls's, but that is to its detriment, or it isn't, in which case it is not so dissimilar to Rawls's after all. Neither result is welcome.

Furthermore, Habermas's claim that his principle of democracy, the centerpiece of his political and legal theory, is "morally freestanding" and his rejection of natural law theory are, as I have argued, somewhat undermined by the role of the MPC in legitimate law, and it is not yet clear how Habermas should respond (see chapter 3, section 3.3.3).

Overall, then, in Habermas's account, there is a great deal of substantive moral and ethical content circulating in the legal system. Not only that, but the very idea of the self-legislation of the citizen body, the idea that equal citizens are autonomous just in case they can understand themselves simultaneously as both subject to the law and authors of it, an idea which Habermas explicates in terms of constitutional principles, a system of rights, and the besieging of the formal political system by the informal domain of civil society, remains, Habermas concedes, a "dogmatic core" at the heart of the legal system and of Habermas's reconstruction of it (BFN, 445).[23] This "dogmatic" or "doctrinal" core lies at the heart of the "normative self-understanding of law," and it is only in virtue of the latter that Habermas's "reconstruction of the development of the constitutional state . . . can then play a role in a critical description of actual political processes" (BFN, 65).

In fine, there are various notions of procedure in play in Habermas's discourse theory of law and politics. In some cases, the distinction between procedure and substance is not sharp, since those procedures either contain a degree of sublimated moral and ethical substance or depend on external substantive moral and ethical resources.[24] But the claim that Habermas's theory is more strictly procedural that Rawls's is not borne out.

Something similar is of course true of Rawls's *Political Liberalism* and the role of the original position and public reason (particularly when not evaluated in the light of the standard blueprint of *A Theory of Justice*). The difference is rather that Rawls offers a substantive theory of justice (as a political conception) within which various procedural arguments play different roles. The original position and the idea of public reason, for example, presuppose a substantive conception of democracy "as a political relationship between citizens within the basic structure of society" (PL, 217), relations in which they "can face one another openly and support their respective positions" such that there is "a true community between persons in their common practices" (CP, 59).[25]

All of this suggests that we should take Habermas's criticism that Rawls would be better to keep "the procedural conception of practical reason free of substantive connotations by developing it in a strictly procedural manner" with a large pinch of salt, since both positions are complex and involve procedural and substantive elements that are very closely interwoven. The comparison Habermas draws for polemical purposes is too stark and simple to do these justice. The difference between Habermas's and Rawls's theories is not, as Habermas claims in *Between Facts and Norms*, that Rawls's normative theory makes "contact with social reality in an *unmediated* way" whereas Habermas's reconstruction of the legal system does not (BFN, 65). Rather, the difference is that they offer alternative accounts of where the normative substance of constitutional democratic states lies and of how it relates to legal and democratic "procedures." Gledhill nicely sums this up as a contrast between a Rawlsian theory that embeds procedures in substance and a Habermasian one that locates substance in procedure (Gledhill 2011).[26]

5.3.2 HABERMAS ON RAWLS ON THE "POLITICAL"

Habermas criticizes Rawls for artificially restricting the domain of the "political," and deploying it as a semi-technical term to describe a conception of justice that is (1) neutral with respect to world views, (2) scope restricted in its application to the basic structure of society, and (3) based on a small fund of values held in common.

I've already commented on the neutrality claim (see chapter 4, section 4.3.5). We need bear in mind only that, although Rawls claims that political liberalism must be neutral in aim, insofar as it must not aim to favor any one conception of the good or comprehensive doctrine, he denies that it can be neutral in effect and influence (PL, 192–93).

As for the other two claims, it is true that Rawls's theory of justice has a narrow range of application: The political conception applies only in certain contexts and only to "constitutional essentials and matters of basic justice" (PL, xxl, xliii). Habermas objects that the boundary of the public political domain is too narrowly drawn and that it is too rigid. He talks of a "rigid" boundary, indeed an "a priori boundary," between the "political and the nonpublic identities of the citizens" or their "private and public autonomy" (RPUR, 128–30/42–43).

In part, this first criticism is based on a misunderstanding. Habermas supposes that the political justification is justified only by people's private comprehensive doctrines, given a sufficient but merely serendipitous overlap thereof. He omits to consider that the political conception as a module both fits into each reasonable comprehensive doctrine and is detachable from it. He also neglects to consider that the political values in the overlap are moral values (albeit values that form a subdomain of general morality). So while his own discourse theory conceives morality as "an authority that crosses the boundaries between private and public spheres," Rawls, he contends, allots morality a role only in the shape of citizens' private "ethical" outlooks (for Habermas also takes comprehensive doctrines to be equivalent to ethical outlooks) (BFN, 109).[27]

That said, the criticism is only in part based on a misunderstanding. And once this is cleared up, the objection remains that the boundary between the public political domain, namely "constitutional essentials and matters of basic justice," and matters of ordinary legislation is very hard, perhaps impossible, to draw. Others agree (see, in particular, Greenawalt 1994, 685–86). So why draw it at all, and, in particular, why draw it so narrowly? Why not widen the scope of public reason and the domain of application of public justification to all matters in need of coercive legal regulation, as Larmore and others propose (Larmore 1996, 137; 1999, 607–608)? The objection is that by drawing the boundary of the political domain so narrowly, effectively making the adjective "political" into a technical term, Rawls detaches his conception of "the political" from political sociology and historical actuality. Thus, the operative idea in Rawls's notion of a "political" conception bears hardly any relation to politics or the political domain as normally understood.[28] There is a lot more to be said about this criticism, and we will return to it in the next chapter when we look at Rawls's reply and his criticisms of Habermas.

5.3.3 LIBERAL RIGHTS VERSUS POPULAR SOVEREIGNTY

Habermas's first line of criticism of Rawls for granting the "priority of liberal rights" is arguably Habermas's most promising and certainly the most influential. The criticism is that, in spite of Rawls's attempts to account for both the priority of liberal rights and the democratic process and to strike the right balance between what Constant calls "the liberties of the ancients and the liberties of the moderns," as Habermas sees it, Rawls ultimately gives greater weight to the private rights of individuals than to the democratic process. That is, he prioritizes liberal rights over popular sovereignty.

The contrasting idea here is Habermas's thesis in *Between Facts and Norms* about the co-originality, namely the equal weight and priority, of private autonomy and public autonomy, a claim that, as we saw in chapter 3 (section 3.3.6), works simultaneously on three levels: the historical, the sociopolitical, and the theoretical.

However, there is more at stake than the elegance of Habermas's and Rawls's respective theories in accounting for the equal weight and priority of negative and positive liberties, and of individual rights and the democratic process, a theoretical desideratum at which both theorists aim. Habermas is suggesting that Rawls offers a theory of liberalism that fails to give due weight to democracy: It is a justification of liberalism at the expense of democracy.

In Habermas's presentation, this criticism becomes entangled with the earlier criticism that it is a mistake to entrust the philosopher with settling issues of moral and political substance (RPUR, 118–19/33–34). However, the question of whose job it is to attempt to settle matters of substance is separable from the objection that Rawls's theory wrongly prioritizes liberal rights over popular sovereignty and thus excludes much of the discussion about what a just society is and how it can be achieved from democratic debate and deliberation.

Once we disentangle these two lines of criticism, we are left with a complex objection that is expressed in the following statements:

1. The two-stage character of Rawls's theory leads to the "priority of liberal rights" and the relegation of the democratic process to "an inferior status" (RPUR, 128–29/41–43).
2. Although political autonomy is granted "virtual existence" in the original position, it does not "unfold in the heart of the justly constituted society."
3. The real citizens whom the parties in the original position represent "find themselves subject to principles and norms that have been anticipated in theory and have already been institutionalized beyond their control."

4. "The essential discourses of legitimation have already taken place within the theory."
5. The boundary between the political and the nonpublic domains is "set by liberal rights that constrain democratic legislation . . . from the beginning, that is, prior to all political will formation."
6. These rights delimit a domain of liberties "which is withdrawn from the reach of democratic legislation."

Note that some of these claims are about the principles of justice, and some are about liberal rights and individual liberties. Some are about the way in which the principles are won (by way of theory) and the way these relate to constitutional rights and their institutional existence (namely externally). Others are about the legitimation of these rights (which are theoretically legitimated insofar as they conform to the principles) and the way in which these rights constrain democratic legislation from the outside. The whole argument seems to be as follows. Through the device of the original position, and the four-stage sequence, which is a model for political autonomy, the political theorist constructs and refines principles of justice. These principles are then brought to bear externally on a liberal constitution on which they confer legitimacy insofar as it conforms to these principles. This establishes liberal rights as basic rights, which then, in turn, constrain the democratic process *externally*.[29]

The first part of the objection seems to apply more readily to justice as fairness as set out in *A Theory of Justice* and interpreted according to "the standard blueprint," according to which the argument proceeds from slender rational principles to substantial principles of justice.[30] The way that Habermas states the objection in statement 1, and the way he develops it with reference to the original position and the four-stage sequence, confirm this. As Frank Michelman points out to Rawls, and as the text shows (RPUR, 128–30/41–43), the objection refers explicitly to Rawls's argument that moves from the original position via the four-stage sequence to the application of the principles of justice in actual life. There is just such an argument in *Political Liberalism*, namely in section 4 of lecture VIII. However, that is not Habermas's target. Habermas's phrase "two-stage character" (the feature he claims has such baleful consequences) is naturally interpreted as a reference to the two-stage presentation of justice as fairness (PL, 141–44).[31] So it looks as though Habermas takes this to be a criticism of the argument of *Political Liberalism* as a whole, not just the argument of lecture VIII.[32] Now it is true that Habermas's objection does not really capture how the argument of *Political Liberalism* as a whole is structured or reflect its main lines of justification. To put it crudely, whereas in *A Theory of Justice*, the lines of justification run from premises concerning rationality to conclusions about justice, in *Political Liberalism*, the lines of justification proceed from the idea of the reasonable, including the argument from the original position and the four-stage sequence: "At each stage the reasonable frames and subordinates the rational" (PL, 339).[33] Habermas does not see this, perhaps because the status of the "reasonable" in *Political Liberalism* is somewhat fuzzy, perhaps because he has not yet brought the distinctiveness of the presentation of justice as fairness as a political conception into sharp focus, perhaps because he is apt to interpret Rawls's terms in the light of his own discourse theory.

That said, overall, Habermas's suspicion that Rawls's defense of liberalism does not say enough about democracy is correct. The fact is that Rawls does not have a theory of democracy properly speaking. For all he says about "public justification" and the "public use of reason," he provides very little by way of explanation about how these are supposed to be *institutionalized* and what relation those institutions will have to existing democratic procedures. Institutions, legal and political, remain very much over the horizon in Rawls's *Political Liberalism*, which focuses mainly on the obligations of individual citizens to one another.

5.4 A REVIEW OF HABERMAS'S SURVIVING CRITICISMS

Since we are now encroaching on the topic of chapter 6, we should stop and review our findings. Our aim was to review the three sets of criticisms Habermas directs at Rawls in the light of any misunderstandings clouding the underlying issues in order to identify the "valid" criticisms. Let's call these the "surviving criticisms." Most of Habermas's criticisms concerning the design of the original position (see section 5.1) can be discounted since, as I have shown, they are not central either to the exchange—the critical exchange over *Political Liberalism*—or to the broader dispute between Habermas's and Rawls's respective political theories. Neither the original position nor principle (U) is the central guiding idea of their respective mature political theories.[34]

Some of Habermas's criticisms of the idea of the overlapping consensus (see section 5.2) can also be discounted, because they rest either on his misunderstanding of the role of the overlapping consensus in *Political Liberalism* or on his tendentious reading of the notion of the reasonable. However, genuine worries remain about Rawls's artificial and narrow conception of the political and about his restriction of the constituency of public reason, that is, the claim that public justifications about political issues are owed only to all reasonable citizens. This is an objection that we will review and appraise in the next chapter. Finally, a genuine worry remains about whether Rawls is consistently able to pursue his "method of avoidance."

As regards Habermas's criticisms concerning private and public autonomy (see section 5.3), the surviving criticisms are that Rawls wrongly prioritizes liberal rights and freedoms over democratic discussion, that he isolates the former from the latter and that he thereby relies too heavily on contributions from philosophical theory rather than democratic practice. This is a serious criticism, but it needs to be developed in a way that makes it relevant to *Political Liberalism* rather than only to justice as fairness in its earlier iterations.[35] However, Habermas's suspicion that *Political Liberalism* is more about liberalism than democracy, and that it says far too little about the actual institutions of democracy, is certainly on the mark.

6

RAWLS'S "REPLY TO HABERMAS"

As noted earlier, Rawls replies to Habermas in 1995 at great length, and much of his long reply restates and summarizes the theory of *Political Liberalism* as he understands it in response to what he sees as Habermas's misinterpretations. I have already discussed some of these misinterpretations. To avoid repetition, I shall pass over Rawls's replies where they consist merely in a restatement or explication of his position. However, in the course of his "reply," Rawls makes some important modifications to his view in response to Habermas's criticisms, and he also makes some telling criticisms of Habermas's discourse theory.

My aim in this chapter is threefold:

1. I will set out Rawls's criticisms of Habermas's discourse theory and appraise the arguments on either side (section 6.1).
2. I will set out and examine Rawls's modifications to his theory of political liberalism (section 6.2).
3. I will set out Rawls's rejoinders to those of Habermas's criticisms that are not merely based on misunderstanding and appraise the arguments on either side (section 6.3).[1]

6.1 RAWLS'S MAIN CRITICISM OF HABERMAS

Whereas Habermas reels off a number of criticisms in his short article "Reconciliation Through the Public Use of Reason," only some of which hit the mark, Rawls spends most of his time defending his own view and confines himself to making just one or two criticism of Habermas. The main one is, though, a deep and important criticism that goes to the heart of the dispute between their respective theories. This criticism also throws light on what Rawls considers to be the novel contribution of *Political Liberalism*: "Of the two main differences between Habermas's position and mine, the first is that his is comprehensive while mine is an account of the political and it is limited to that" (RH, 132/47). Again, he states that political liberalism is a doctrine that "falls under the category of the political" and "works entirely within that domain" (RH 133/47). Putting this point another way, he says that the political conception of justice proposed in *Political Liberalism* is "freestanding"; that is, it stands free from any one comprehensive doctrine or any group of comprehensive doctrines (in the exclusive sense). In other words, Rawls views Habermas's political theory, along with almost every other political theory in the long history of political thought, including many liberal theories and even parts of his own *A Theory of Justice*, as comprehensive, that is, as dependent on "comprehensive doctrines, religious, metaphysical, and moral" (RH, 133/47).

6.1.1 HABERMAS'S THEORY AS A COMPREHENSIVE DOCTRINE

To be more specific, Rawls criticizes Habermas's discourse theory for touching on subjects and resting on theories that range "far beyond political philosophy" (RH, 135/49): "Indeed the aim of his theory of communicative action is to give a general account of meaning, reference, and truth or validity both for theoretical reason and for the several forms of practical reason" (RH, 135/49). As evidence, he refers to a passage in *Between Facts and Norms* concerning the practice of argumentation and its ability to impose the reciprocal exchange of perspectives on all participants in discourse through ideal role-taking: "In this way Hegel's concrete universal is sublimated into a communicative structure purified from all substantial elements" (FG, 280; cited in RH, 136/50). Rawls concludes that "Habermas's doctrine . . . is one of logic in the broad Hegelian sense: a philosophical analysis of the presuppositions of rational discourse . . . which includes within itself all the allegedly substantial elements of religious and metaphysical doctrines" (RH, 137/51).

There seem to be three slightly different lines of criticism here:

1. Habermas's discourse theory is burdened with many controversial theoretical presuppositions.
2. Habermas's discourse theory presupposes what is akin to a secular metaphysical world view, namely that in the course of modernity, ethical, moral, and religious doctrines are gradually sublimated into procedures of communication.
3. Habermas's theory is metaphysical in the ordinary sense that it "presents an account of what there is" (RH, 130/51). Rawls contrasts this with his own philosophical and metaphysical quietism. His account is "political" only, and as such, he claims, it "leaves philosophy as it is" (RH, 134/48). His theory (unlike Habermas's) does not entail the rejection of controversial opposed philosophical theories such as naturalism or emotivism; indeed, it "leaves untouched all kinds of doctrines, religious, metaphysical, and moral" (RH, 135/49, 134/48).

So much for the textual interpretation. To appraise Rawls's objection, we need to analyze it more fully. As we have seen, Rawls uses the term "comprehensive metaphysical doctrine" as a wide and vague concept that covers three general cases. So we must first ask whether it is true that Habermas's theory is comprehensive in all three senses, that is, whether it depends on a religious, moral, and philosophical or metaphysical doctrine.

Obviously, as Rawls points out, and Habermas admits, discourse theory does depend on a whole raft of philosophical doctrines concerning truth, meaning, rationality, and so on, and some of these are indeed controversial.[2] This issue is the focus of Habermas's follow-up essay, which we will discuss in the next chapter.

In the case of moral doctrines, the answer is more complex. Certainly, Habermas's political theory presupposes discourse ethics, though Habermas denies that it depends on any particular extant substantive morality. As we have seen, Habermas defends a version of the doctrine of the autonomy of the political domain, and he claims that his theory of democratic legitimacy is "morally freestanding," as is the conception of legitimacy the theory reconstructs (BNR, 80; see also chapter 3, section 3.3.3). Habermas also denies the claim of natural law theory, that the authority of legitimate law is borrowed from the authority of an antecedent moral order. That said, he is a success theorist, in that he allows that there are some extant valid moral norms, and indeed his theory—for instance, the MPC—presupposes that there are. So it looks as though Habermas's political theory is "comprehensive" in that it presupposes both the truth of a particular moral theory and arguably also the existence of a substantive core morality.[3]

However, Habermas's theory does not presuppose the validity of any particular substantive *ethical* conceptions of the good life (in his sense of "ethics"). He explicitly denies that this is a possibility for a post-metaphysical theory under modern conditions. The only remnants of ethics in discourse theory are, according to Habermas, the "remnant of the good at the heart of the right" and the "dogmatic core" of the idea of public autonomy (BFN, 536–37; TIO, 28–29). But Habermas denies that these are full-blown ethical world views or conceptions of the good.

Finally, we must ask whether Habermas's discourse theory presupposes a religious doctrine. Rawls points to the fact that Habermas sees the communicative structure of modern forms of life as a sublimated form of ethical life and a secularized development of fellowship in a common religious tradition. Whether this counts as a religious doctrine depends on what is supposed to have happened in the course of sublimation and secularization. Habermas has a whole theory about this.[4] He would deny, and would have good grounds to deny, that this is merely a religious doctrine in disguise. Still, we should take on board Larmore's point that discourse theory (that is, all of Habermas's theory up to and including *Between Facts and Norms*) presupposes the truth of a secular world view by advancing a general theory about the obsolescence of religious and metaphysical narratives (Larmore 1995, 59). For Rawls, by contrast, secular world views are on a par with religious doctrines, so in presupposing a secular world view in his very rich theory of modernity, Habermas's theory can be seen to depend on something equivalent to a religious doctrine, a doctrine that is substantial, controversial, and open to reasonable disagreement.

6.1.2 HABERMAS'S THEORY AS A COMPREHENSIVE PHILOSOPHICAL DOCTRINE

We have resolved Rawls's complaint that Habermas's political theory is "comprehensive" into several different claims and seen that three apply. But in themselves, these claims do not bear out Rawls's objection. They would only do so if they presented a problem for Habermas. And when we ask whether it matters that they apply, we find that there is a significant ambiguity in Rawls's criticism.

Consider that Habermas's theory of democratic legitimacy takes many theoretical hostages to fortune. Theoretically that is bad, since it needlessly embroils Habermas's theory in controversies, for example, over the pragmatic theory of meaning and the associated conception of truth. It would be unwise for Habermas to structure his theory such that what he says about the concept of truth calls into question what he has to say about legitimacy, for example. But Rawls wants to say more than this. He claims that it is *practically* disadvantageous because it means that Habermas's conception of democratic legitimacy is not itself able to be the focus of a consensus of reasonable citizens, since it is not constructed only of ideas and values inherent in our common human reason. (At least, that is the rationale Rawls gives for presenting his own conception of justice as "political, not metaphysical," and for leaving philosophy as it is.)

Contrast this with two other cases. Suppose a political theory presupposes a comprehensive Kantian moral theory, in the sense of a repertoire of substantial duties and obligations and a reliable mechanism for determining them. Or, suppose a political conception of justice presupposes a Catholic doctrine of the sanctity of human life. A political theory that presupposed one or other of these doctrines would be objectionable in a completely different sense, as Andrew Lister points out:

> What is distinctive about religious views is that they are (a) fundamental to moral personality (intimately bound up with conceptions of moral

> obligation and integrity), and (b) inevitably the subject of reasonable controversy, in a democratic society (not only contested by reasonable people at present). The fact of current reasonable controversy by itself (about the dynamics of supply and demand, say) does not create the moral problem to which public reason is meant to be a solution. (Lister 2007, 13)

I take it that Lister's point here also applies to moral doctrines, or at least to some moral doctrines, such as a comprehensive Kantianism, for this doctrine, too, is fundamental to the moral personality of its adherents. At least, whether it does or not, Habermas assumes it does. Hence his qualified endorsement of Kohlberg's notion of a stage 6 moral consciousness. Lister's argument makes clear what is wrong with basing a political conception of justice on such comprehensive doctrines (religious or moral) and also shows that such considerations do not apply to most—or at least to many—philosophical and theoretical doctrines. And if Lister is right about this, which I think he is, it follows that most of the controversial theoretical presuppositions of Habermas's discourse theory do not in fact pose any of the *practical* moral and political problems that Rawls claims they do, problems he claims his own theory circumvents.

It is then crucial to differentiate between comprehensive *philosophical* and *metaphysical* doctrines—at least those that are comprehensive in the narrow sense of being needlessly controversial—and comprehensive *religious* and *moral* doctrines. Only the latter, when proposed as grounds for legislation, impugn the moral personality of others and jeopardize the freedom and equality of other reasonable citizens.

For Rawls's solution to what he takes to be the problem posed by attempts to formulate comprehensive political theories such as Habermas's under conditions of reasonable pluralism is quite drastic. It involves narrowly circumscribing the domain of the political, to which public reasons apply; imposing a very demanding moral duty of civility on citizens' actions and speech within that domain; and, if Quong is to be believed, disqualifying unreasonable citizens from the constituency of people to whom public justifications are owed. So even if one can accept that Rawls's drastic solution may be justified in ruling out legislation for the basic structure, or advocacy for such legislation, based on *religious* or *moral* grounds, the same consideration does not hold for all *philosophical* grounds.

The problem posed by the fact, undeniable as it is, that Habermas's theory takes needless theoretical hostages to fortune is not so serious as to demand such a drastic solution.

To that extent, Habermas's response to Rawls on this point is fully justified. He denies that a political theory can or should "'move entirely within the domain of the political' and 'leave philosophy as it is'" (MW, 92; see also RH, 47/93). This does not invalidate the criticism that discourse theory takes needless hostages to theoretical fortune: It does, and Rawls is correct to note this, for it is theoretically disadvantageous for Habermas's theory to do so. But it puts the objection into its proper place and gives it the appropriate weight.

Rawls's surviving point is this: Political theory that rests on controversial philosophical assumptions will be open to reasonable rejection. It thus won't be able to be the focus of a consensus of reasonable citizens and won't help to bring about stability for the right reasons. That might be damaging for a political theory like *Political Liberalism*, which has the explicit practical aim of advancing a political conception of justice that can be the focus of an overlapping consensus and that yields social stability on that basis. However, it is not obvious that the same point applies to Habermas's political theory, which does not have that practical aim. We will return to this point when we look at Habermas's response in the next chapter.

This brings us to another major area of disagreement between the two theorists, namely the relation, and the division of labor, between political theory and actual democratic politics. Rawls presents his theory as a contribution to practical reason. He assumes that political theory must answer to the canons of political justification. That is, the duty of civility and the requirements of public reason fall on him as the proponent of justice as fairness (his favored example of a political conception of justice), as the advocate of political liberalism, and as the author of the book of that name. And they apply every bit as much to Rawls the political theorist as they do to the speeches of citizens running for office, to senators involved in debates over legislation, and to judges adjudicating in a supreme court. Habermas, as we will see, denies this.[5] In his eyes, the task of political theorists is to put forward ideas, based on their expertise, to students and other experts in the field, or to any interested parties. They can do so on the basis of whatever theories they like, controversial or not, though the discipline of discourse and argumentation requires them, when called on, to defend the validity claims of their theories by argument.

6.1.3 HABERMAS'S THEORY AS A COMPREHENSIVE RELIGIOUS OR MORAL DOCTRINE

Let's briefly examine Rawls's objection that Habermas's discourse theory contains all the elements of a *religious* comprehensive doctrine in the guise of a substantive secular world view. I will be brief here because this issue resurfaces in chapter 8, where I examine Rawls's and Habermas's respective views on the public use of religious reason at greater length. For example, according to Rawls it would indeed be a problem if the claim to legitimacy of a law or government institution rested on a single secular world view that was not shared and hence was not acceptable to reasonable citizens in virtue of their sincere religious beliefs.

Given what he says in his work up to and including *Between Facts and Norms*, Habermas would certainly deny that his theory of modernity constituted a secular world view on a par with religious world views. Rather, it merely arranges certain facts about the political sociology of the modern age and puts these into the service of political theory. So, he would argue, this objection collapses back into the previous one. Insofar as Habermas's theory of democratic legitimacy does indeed rest on a controversial theory of modernity, it presents only such problems as any other theoretical controversy would, problems to be resolved through relevant discourse and argumentation.

What about the objection that Habermas's discourse theory rests on a comprehensive *moral* doctrine? One objection here is that *Between Facts and Norms* presupposes the truth of a controversial moral theory, namely his discourse ethics. Again, Habermas would reply that, should his discourse ethics be proven to be incorrect, one could in principle replace it with the correct, or a better, moral theory and make any necessary modifications to the theory. This is just another version of the first objection. The same is not true, however, of the charge that discourse theory rests on an *actually existing morality*. Now Habermas might offer the rejoinder that discourse theory relies only on the claim that there are some extant valid moral norms and that these constrain democratic legitimacy. However, in making such a defense, he opens himself up to another version of Rawls's objection—in my view, by far the most serious one—namely that the conception of democratic legitimacy advanced by Habermas's discourse theory rests on a substantive deontological morality (the one that discourse ethics reconstructs).

At this point, some of Habermas's avid defenders are apt to deny that discourse theory rests on a comprehensive moral doctrine on the grounds that the morality that it reconstructs is "procedural" and that discourse ethics entirely avoids substantial matters, delegating that task to participants in moral discourse. This move, however, is unconvincing for a number of reasons. First, as we saw in chapter 5, the procedures in Habermas's discourse theory are imbued with sublimated substance. Second, whatever discourse ethics might say, Habermas is a success theorist who allows that there are some extant valid moral norms or, as Baynes puts it, that there is a "core morality" (Baynes 2016, 169–70, 177). Without it, there could be no MPC, which is a central feature of Habermas's conception of legitimacy.

True, Habermas can still deny, with some justification, that his theory is "comprehensive" in the pejorative sense, the sense that Rawls holds to be inadmissible for a political conception. For, as we saw earlier, what marks out a doctrine as comprehensive in this pejorative sense is that it can be reasonably rejected, because it is subject to reasonable pluralism. But, according to Habermas (and also Larmore), the underlying core morality that discourse theory presupposes is exempt from reasonable rejection. If so, then the fact that Habermas's discourse theory presupposes the existence of a core morality need not pose a *practical* problem for the theory in the way Rawls supposes. That said, Habermas cannot make the same move with the "ethical harmonization requirement," which, as we saw in chapter 3, must be dropped or watered down if it is not to undermine Habermas's conception of legitimacy, in as much as Habermas accepts that ethical values and conceptions are subject to reasonable disagreement.

The real issue that divides the two thinkers here is not, in fact, whether there are substantive moral constraints on democratic legitimacy or whether the political conception of justice depends essentially on valid moral norms, for both thinkers accept that there are and that it does (even if both mean slightly different things by "legitimacy" and "political justice"). The dispute is about how to think of these constraints and of the status of the constraining moral norms. Habermas thinks of them as consisting in a general system of morality that is both interpersonal and institutional. Habermas repudiates what he calls the "ingrained prejudice" that morality pertains only to "social relationships for which one is personally responsible," whereas law and political justice (and not morality) pertain to "institutionally mediated spheres of interaction" (BFN, 108). Morality "crosses the boundaries between public and private" (BFN, 108). It flows into the political and legislative process through the channels of representative democracy and is given legal form by the human rights enshrined as basic rights in democratic constitutions. Rawls, by contrast, conceives these constraints as originating in the moral contents of the overlap of reasonable doctrines, which form a subdomain of the moral within the domain of the political. Beyond these, there are no substantive moral norms that are not subject to reasonable disagreement.

6.2 THE DEVELOPMENT OF RAWLS'S VIEWS ON JUSTIFICATION

The second important contribution of Rawls's "Reply to Habermas" is an important modification and clarification of Rawls's conception of public justification. In *Political Liberalism*, Rawls gives the political conception of justice a two-stage justification, in which the first step consists in a freestanding justification on the basis of the political values, and the second step assures that the conception is sufficiently stable by seeing whether it can be the focus of an overlapping consensus of reasonable citizens (PL, 64–65).[6] In his reply, by contrast, he specifies three kinds of justification of the political conception of justice.

The first stage consists of the freestanding, or *pro tanto*, justification. This means that it consists of "only political values," namely those contained in the overlap. At this stage, the political conception is checked for completeness by seeing whether these values can be ordered such that they answer "all, or nearly all, questions concerning constitutional essentials and basic justice" (RH, 142/56).

Unlike in *Political Liberalism*, Rawls makes clear that the idea of reasonable overlapping consensus is operative at the first stage:

> The . . . idea of consensus in political liberalism—the idea I call a reasonable overlapping consensus—is that the political conception of justice is worked out first as a freestanding view that can be justified *pro tanto* without looking to, or trying to fit, or even knowing what are, the existing comprehensive doctrines. (RH, 145/58)

This effectively rules out that Rawls holds what Quong calls the "common view" of political liberalism, according to which only the political conception itself, not the contents of the overlap (the political values) of which it is composed, is the focus of an overlapping consensus, and according to which the consensus of reasonable citizens comes into being only at the final stage of justification.[7] And it justifies my view that the "freestanding" justification, here called the *pro tanto* justification, indemnifies the political conception against reasonable rejection by cutting all comprehensive notions (that are not part of the overlap) out of the justificatory loop:

> It [a reasonable overlapping consensus] tries to put no obstacles in the path of all reasonable doctrines endorsing a political conception by eliminating from this conception any idea which goes beyond the political and which not all reasonable doctrines could reasonably be expected to endorse. (RH, 145/58)

At the second stage, all reasonable citizens as a members of civil society embed the political conception of justice in their own comprehensive doctrines. At this stage, which Habermas calls "full justification," whether other citizens can do the same, and if so how, is not considered. No particular weight is assigned to the political values in relation to the nonpolitical values. It is left up to the citizens to do this in the light of their comprehensive doctrines.

Finally, there is the third level, which Rawls calls "public justification." This label is somewhat misleading in that he does not hold (as Habermas thinks he should) that citizens jointly construct reasons for their political conception. Rather, the third level consists in their each finding out whether a certain social fact obtains, namely the fact that each reasonable citizen has successfully been able to embed the political conception in their comprehensive doctrine and hence that the political conception is the focus of a consensus among reasonable citizens. Rawls observes that at this stage, "citizens do not look into the contents of other doctrines"; thus, the "contents of those doctrines have no normative role in public justifications" (RH, 144/57). Although at this stage citizens are, then, inspecting other citizens' comprehensive doctrines as it were from outside (to see whether they have embedded the political conception as a module within them), the point is that citizens would assign normative weight to this social fact, once ascertained, since its emergence confirms that citizens can identify and endorse principles for fair cooperation while respecting their different reasonable comprehensive doctrines.

If this third level of public justification were all that was offered by way of justification for the political conception, it would invite the Forst–Habermas objection that political liberalism lacks "a common perspective on justice among citizens and a genuine moral consensus" and thus fails to meet the "validity requirement" essential to public justification in their eyes, namely that agreement is reached by all affected on the same thing for the same reasons (HRDP, 157).[8] Indeed, neither Rawls's stage 2 ("full" justification) nor his stage 3 ("public" justification) satisfies that stringent requirement. As we have seen, though, this condition is met, though not in the way Habermas and Forst envisage, by the first stage, to which Rawls admittedly does not give the name "public justification" but "*pro tanto*" or "freestanding" justification. And Rawls is not suggesting that stage 2 justifications or stage 3 justifications, severally or together, would be sufficient. In his view, all three kinds of justification must work together to ensure that the political conception is adequately (and morally) justified to all reasonable citizens and thus can secure "stability for the right reasons."

My hunch is that Habermas and Forst are partly thrown by Rawls's terminology. As I noted earlier, to call this third stage of justification "public justification" is misleading in several respects. It would have been more fitting to give this stage another label, reserving the term "public justification" for the entire three-stage process. For if the three stages have to be taken together as essential parts of one process, as I have argued they do, Habermas's and Forst's worries do not apply. Habermas's and Forst's suspicions may also be raised by the facts that at each stage, the process need not (though of course it may) be carried out in concert and that, in particular, the final stage, which Rawls calls "public justification," is achieved when all reasonable citizens have assured themselves of the existence of this social fact. In other words, all three stages of justification, and the entire process, are what Habermas would call "monological." This dismays theorists like Habermas and Forst, who insist that justification must be public in the sense that it excludes no one and is achieved by everyone jointly. We have seen, though, that their worry on this score is misplaced, because, as McMahon demonstrates (see chapter 5, section 5.1.2), there is no tenable distinction between monological and weakly dialogical procedures of justification in moral discourse, and the same goes for political discourse.

6.3 RAWLS'S RESPONSES TO HABERMAS'S VALID CRITICISMS

We are now in a position to appraise Rawls's responses to the surviving criticisms, namely the four valid criticisms Habermas makes in "Reconciliation Through the Public Use of Reason," which are presented here in ascending order of their importance, rather than in the order of their appearance:

First, Rawls cannot and should not maintain his own avowed "method of avoidance."

Second, Rawls falsely prioritizes liberal rights over the democratic process.

Third, Rawls's conception of the political is too narrow.

Fourth, Rawls says too little about democratic institutions and the institutionalization of democratic procedures.

6.3.1 RAWLS'S METHOD OF AVOIDANCE

I'll deal with this objection only briefly because I've already touched on how Rawls thinks his theory of political liberalism avoids "truth" and makes use of the idea of the reasonable, and because this is the topic of Habermas's reply to Rawls's "Reply to Habermas," " 'Reasonable' Versus

'True,'" which we will look at in the next chapter. That said, one aspect of Rawls's response calls for attention. Rawls claims that "political liberalism moves within the category of the political, and leaves philosophy as it is." Leaving philosophy as it is means that it "cannot argue its case by invoking any comprehensive doctrines, or by criticizing and rejecting them" (RH, 48). This is the animating presupposition of Rawls's criticism of Habermas's theory as being comprehensive. But this desideratum of theoretical abstinence is harder to achieve than it seems. Recall that one feature that unites any comprehensive philosophical doctrine is that it can be reasonably rejected. But Rawls's political liberalism makes all kinds of controversial philosophical assumptions, such as, to take just a few examples, that justification in political theory just is political justification (in Rawls's narrow sense of "political"), that political justification must do without truth, and that reasonable people accept the burdens of judgment, namely that their theories are open to reasonable disagreement. Indeed, one can say that the method of avoidance and its rationale are themselves controversial philosophical claims open to reasonable disagreement.

If that is right, then Habermas's suspicion that Rawls "cannot develop his theory in as freestanding a fashion as he would like" is justified. Rawls is, in spite of his best efforts, inevitably "drawn into long running and still unresolved debates" (RPUR, 131/45).

6.3.2 THE PRIORITY OF LIBERALISM AND THE OCCLUSION OF DEMOCRACY

Habermas's second objection is the most substantial. In fact, there are two parts to the objection. The first is directed at the formulation and justification of the principles of justice independently of the democratic process and at their external bearing on political actuality. The second concerns the institution of basic rights and liberties "beyond the reach of democratic legislation" (RPUR, 129/43).

The Democratic Process and the Principles of Justice

Through the device of the original position, and the four-stage sequence, which is supposed to be a model for political autonomy, the political theorist constructs and refines the principles of justice. But this is done without the participation of citizens and independently of democratic deliberation. These principles are then brought to bear externally on a liberal constitution, on which they confer legitimacy insofar as the constitution conforms to these principles.

Rawls's reply to this criticism is that the four-stage sequence is "neither an actual political process nor a purely theoretical one" (RH, 153/65; see also PL, 340). Rather, it is a theoretical framework that extends the idea of the original position and adapts it to the different contexts of application it will encounter in real life. The framework allows the principles arrived at in the original position to be sensitively applied, in the light of relevant information, in different contexts by delegates in a constitutional convention, legislators enacting laws, and judges interpreting the constitution. On Rawls's account, this work is not that of the political philosopher but that of "citizens in political office or civil society" (RH, 153/65). And though the task is guided by the ideal that the principles arrived at apply in perpetuity, this ideal is purely regulative. Philosophically speaking, all principles are subject to correction and amendment against considered judgments in reflective equilibrium. In other words, Rawls resists the claim that the principles of justice are merely theoretical constructions (constructed by the political philosopher). In my view, though, it is somewhat of a stretch for Rawls to claim that citizens or public officials would or will use these devices. Of course they might.[9] But Habermas is correct to note that, even in *Political Liberalism*, the work of formulating and justifying principles of justice is undertaken on behalf of the citizens by the political theorist. I don't see why Rawls does not just bite the bullet here, as, for example, Freeman does on his behalf:

> If reliance on standards of justice is necessary to resolve disputes of public reason, then the fact that citizens democratically rely on principles advocated by some known philosopher or statesman should not undermine anyone's political autonomy. (Freeman 2000, 409–10)

Rawls could argue with Freeman that all the political philosopher does is work up the political ideas and values, which are part of the common political culture and not themselves constructions, into a conception of justice and thus provide a freestanding or *pro tanto* justification of it at the first stage. In principle, though, anyone can fulfill that task who can correctly perceive the political ideas and values, work out their relations to one another, and establish their implications. It does not matter that such work is undertaken by the political philosopher rather than the citizen or public official. By contrast, the second stage—full justification—is something that all citizens, including the philosopher, must do for themselves. And the third stage can only be carried out once all citizens have successfully embedded the political conception of justice in their own comprehensive doctrines. The three-stage process partly consists in the work of all other reasonable citizens, as well as the work of the political philosopher. It is true that at no stage does this process *require* collective reasoning. At each stage, even stage 3, the justification can be done monologically. But as we saw earlier (see chapter 5, section 5.1.2), there is nothing objectionable about that. If the objection is that the principles are established by the philosopher working entirely on his or her own, without any input from other citizens, this is simply untrue as a claim about the whole three-stage process and applies strictly only to stage 1. Having said all this, without the political conception, none of this rather baroque procedure would be possible. It is the essential component. And the essential component is de facto the work of the political philosopher working alone, *even if* it need not be, and even though its component ideas are not. Rawls bites the bullet, but Habermas's objection stands.

What about the charge that the principles of justice are applied externally?[10]

Presumably, a principle applied externally to a political process is bad because the principle is likely irrelevant or inappropriate, or, worse, it may need to be imposed by force. These are the usual objections to external criticism. One can see how such an objection might run when directed at justice as fairness as set out in *A Theory of Justice*, interpreted according to the "standard blueprint" as proceeding from slender premises about rationality to substantial conclusions about social justice—although even there, the framing device of the four-stage sequence is designed to overcome such problems.

However, it is trickier to see how it applies to political liberalism, in which, as Rawls puts it, "at each stage the reasonable frames and subordinates the rational" (PL, 339). How might the objection apply to the argument of Rawls's later work?

Consider the following. The original position connects the basic liberties and their priority with principles of justice that are to set "fair terms of cooperation" (PL, 304). The parties in the original position, even though they represent reasonable citizens who enjoy "full autonomy," exhibit only "rational autonomy"; that is, they choose principles only according to their power of rationality and their capacity to choose, refine, and pursue a conception of the good. The reason the parties choose principles of justice merely on the basis of their rational autonomy is that in the original position, "the constraints of the reasonable are simply imposed from without" (PL, 306). Perhaps this admission lies behind Habermas's objection.

If so, it does not license Habermas's conclusion. For it is not the case with the citizens in society who affirm the principles chosen in the original position that the constraints of the reasonable are externally imposed on political actuality. Such citizens are *ex hypothesi* reasonable, and, according to Rawls, they exercise "full autonomy" insofar as they pursue their good in accordance with those principles. Nor does it follow from the fact that the constraints of the reasonable are externally imposed on the parties in the original position that the principles of justice chosen there must be externally imposed on the political process, with all the deleterious consequences that are supposed to follow. On the contrary, in *Political Liberalism*, the conception of justice is explicitly worked up from the values inherent in the political culture. And what marks these values out as "political" is not only their being "shared"—their falling into the overlap of reasonable doctrines—but also the fact that they are "very great ideas" and germane to a liberal constitutional democracy. The natural assumption, then, is that the principles worked up from such ideas will not be inappropriate or irrelevant or whatever. Insofar as such principles serve as standards of social criticism, that criticism is internal rather than external (Ron 2006).

This is actually what we should expect if we emphasize, as we should, the fact that the very idea of justice as fairness captures and explicates democratic values that allow citizens who live by them and by principles based on them to "face one another openly" as members of a "true community between persons in their common practices" (CP, 59). The substantive presuppositions of Rawls's view are laid out more clearly in *Political Liberalism* than in *A Theory of Justice*; in the former, Rawls specifically holds out an "ideal of democratic citizenship" and an ideal of public reason as the basis of such a democratic community (PL, 216).[11]

The Democratic Process and Liberal Rights

So much for the objection when directed at the principles of justice. How does the objection fare when directed at the individual rights that those principles are supposed to legitimate? Are such rights established "prior to all political will formation"? Does Rawls thereby fail to give equal weight and priority to private and public autonomy? Does his theory place a domain of liberties "beyond the reach of democratic self-legislation"? And do liberal rights impose external constraints on the democratic process? If this line of objection is not to push at an open door, it has to do more than target Rawls's liberalism. For, quite obviously, *Political Liberalism* is a theory of liberalism, though not a comprehensive one. Moreover, Rawls explicitly offers arguments in lecture VIII for the "Basic Liberties and their Priority" (PL, 289–371). And these arguments, Rawls acknowledges, are based on "a conception of the person that would be recognized as liberal," namely the idea of persons, both rational and reasonable, with the two moral powers and three higher-order interests (PL, 288, 370).[12] Similarly, the objection cannot be just that Rawls's theory assigns priority to basic rights and liberties, for that is what he sets out to do. The objection has to be that it does so in a way that fails to give due weight to democratic values, or the democratic process, and that it fails to achieve the balance between liberal rights and democratic values at which it aims (and which Habermas also aims to achieve through his co-originality thesis).

Rawls flatly rejects the claims that justice as fairness enshrines "basic liberties in a pre-political domain," that individual liberties place "prior restriction on the people's constituent will," and that it fails to give equal weight and priority to popular sovereignty and political autonomy (RH, 157–60/69–72). This whole line of objection, he argues, rests on a mistaken idea of the project of political liberalism: "Habermas thinks that in my view the liberties of the moderns are a kind of natural law, and therefore . . . they are external substantive ideas and so impose restrictions on the public will of the people" (RH, 159/71).

To evaluate the point of dispute here, we need to ask two questions about the priority of basic liberties that Rawls defends. First, what kind of priority is at issue? Second, how is that priority established?

In response to the first question, we can say that two kinds of priority are at issue. There is the axiological priority of liberty—the fact that liberty is a final value that cannot be traded off against any other value and can be restricted only for the sake of liberty itself (TJ, 266). And then there is the legal fact that the rights that preserve basic liberties are enshrined in the constitution, which is the highest law of the land.[13]

How is the axiological priority of basic liberty justified? The full answer is given in the very long final chapter of *Political Liberalism*. The short answer is that basic liberties and their priority are justified with reference to the liberal conception of the moral person (PL, 290) and the idea of society as a fair system of cooperation (RH, 167/78). In his "Reply to Habermas," Rawls gives a six-step summary of that argument. It suffices here to note that step 4 sets out a list of basic liberties compiled in two ways, "one historical, the other theoretical" (PL, 292–93; RH, 167/79). The historical way is to look at democratic constitutions, see which liberties they protect, and note which ones work well. The theoretical way is to consider which liberties are required for the adequate development of the two moral powers.

As for the constitutional status of individual rights, Rawls leaves this undetermined by the argument from the original position. Such matters are to be decided at the stage of constitutional convention, the second stage of the sequence of lifting the veil of ignorance, during which a constitution is adopted with a bill of rights and other provisions that protect basic liberties. Importantly, though, he points out that this "allows—but does not require—the basic liberties to be incorporated into the conventions and protected as constitutional" (RH, 157/70). It does not fix basic liberties in a pre-political domain. For any constitutional rule that restricts majority rule will flow from the will of the people expressed through procedures of ratifying and amending constitutions (RH, 158/70).

Habermas's objection targets (1) both the axiological and theoretical priority that justice as fairness grants to basic liberal rights and (2) the fact that they are granted constitutional status. Rawls responds to each point.

His response to the first point is to cite evidence directly to refute Habermas's claim. For example, he observes, "The liberties of private and public autonomy are given side by side and unranked in the first principle of justice" (RH, 164/76). Further, Rawls notes that all the arguments from the original position and the four-stage sequence are open to amendment in reflective equilibrium, a process that can, though it need not, be undertaken collectively. Finally, Rawls could also, though he does not, invoke the substantial ideal of democracy presupposed by the original position, namely a true community of citizens who can face one another openly and who have an equal share in the coercive power they exercise as citizens over each other (noted in chapter 5, section 5.3.1).

Rawls's response to the second point is that the constitution and the institutions in which citizens in civil society find themselves are not the product of the political theorist but the bequest of history—"the work of past generations." This does raise questions about how each new generation of citizens can see these as the expression of their sovereign will, but that is not just a question for him to answer, and it is nothing specifically to do with *Political Liberalism*. Besides, as Rawls notes, constitutions are subject to the democratic procedures of ratification and amendment, and though they restrict majority rule, they do not do so externally to the democratic process (RH, 159/70).

The only piece of direct textual evidence adduced by Habermas to support his objection is Rawls's claim that "the role of political liberties is . . . largely instrumental in preserving the other liberties" (RPUR, 129/43). This is supposed to bear out the objection that, in Rawls's view, "the private sphere enjoys priority" and "a domain of liberties is withdrawn . . . from the reach of democratic legislation" (RPUR, 129/43). But that is not in fact what Rawls says in the passage cited. Habermas misquotes Rawls, omitting a crucial qualifier. Rawls is canvassing the views of, among others, Berlin and Constant, who maintain that in the modern world, in comparison with the ancient world, the political liberties are of less intrinsic value to citizens than civil liberties such as the freedoms of thought and conscience. If so, then the role of the political liberties is, Rawls writes, "*perhaps* largely instrumental in preserving the other liberties" (PL, 299, my emphasis). Even if this is so, claims Rawls, they must still count as basic liberties, and enjoy priority, because they are essential to the preservation of the other basic liberties (PL, 299). This of course does not rule out that the political liberties may also be of intrinsic value. Indeed, it shows that a range of considerations drives the argument for the priority of liberty. And one of these is that if it can be shown that some liberties enjoy priority, and that other liberties are necessary to their preservation, then these other liberties also enjoy priority.

Rawls offers two more general responses to Habermas's criticism that he prioritizes liberal rights over the democratic process and fails to give equal weight and priority to both.

The first response is to draw attention to similarities between their views that suggest that they both hold, albeit in different ways, that private and public (political) autonomy have equal weight and priority. Their theories both have a two-stage construction.[14] Both thinkers demonstrate an internal connection between private and public autonomy: Habermas through his reconstructive functional account, and Rawls through his construction of justice as fairness as a political construction (RH, 168/80). Most strikingly of all, he suggests that the parties in the original position are answering exactly the same fundamental question as that which guides Habermas's discourse theory of law: "Which rights must free and equal persons mutually accord one another if they wish to regulate their coexistence by the legitimate means of positive and coercive law?" (RH, 163/75; RPUR, 43/130) Rawls suggests that even in the original position, the liberties of the moderns and of the ancients (private and public autonomy, to use Habermas's terms) are co-original.

Rawls also claims that the four-stage sequence is compatible with citizens discussing "questions of political principles and social policy" and that "the idea of a just society is something also to be worked toward" (RH, 154/67). To that extent, Habermas's worry that citizens cannot understand the process of constitutionalization or the realization of basic rights as an "open," "incomplete," and "ongoing" process in the civic life of their society is misplaced (RPUR, 128/42).

The second response is to offer a counter-critique of Habermas—one that Rawls is not alone in offering—namely that Habermas, though he officially insists on the equal weight and priority of private and public (political) autonomy, in fact grants priority to the latter. Rawls quotes a sentence in *Between Facts and Norms* in which Habermas claims that "the sought for internal connection between popular sovereignty and human rights lies in the normative content of the very *mode of exercising political autonomy*" (BFN, 103; RH, 169/80–81). The objection is good, but here again the evidence does not support it. In that passage, Habermas is making the point that the content of the general will is given not only by what is decided on, but also by the internal discipline of the discourse, namely the degree to which the arguments conform to the rules of discourse. Rawls's objection would be better targeted at Habermas's strategy of deriving unsaturated basic rights as functional prerequisites of democratic discourse.

This point of the dispute is hard to arbitrate. There is a significant difference of emphasis between the two theories. One way to put it is that although the history and the institutions of democracy are always in the background of *Political Liberalism*, they generally remain in the background. Rawls offers a democratic theory of liberalism that focuses on its underlying principles and values, whereas Habermas gives a sociologically much richer account of liberal democracy, with a greater focus on its institutions.

Quong's Defense

At this juncture, it is interesting to briefly consider Quong's robust rebuttal of Habermas's claim that Rawls wrongly prioritizes philosophically derived liberal principles over the democratic autonomy of actual citizens. For it is easier to see how Habermas's objection applies to Quong's more starkly liberal conception of political liberalism than to Rawls's more complex and nuanced account. Quong offers two counterarguments:

> First, certain fundamental liberal rights and principles—for example, free speech and freedom of religion—are beyond reasonable dispute, and so incorporating such rights and principles into the content of public reason does nothing to unreasonably threaten democratic autonomy. . . . Second, as Rawls has emphasized, the content of public reason is not fixed by one specific conception, but rather it can include any conception of justice within a broadly liberal family, and so there is ample scope for each citizen to exercise his or her democratic autonomy by advocating for the conception of justice he or she thinks best. (Quong 2004, 267)

The first point just restates, rather than answers, the problem Habermas raises. Why are liberal rights and principles "beyond reasonable dispute"? He would have been better off pointing out that no constitutional basic right is beyond amendment, provided the correct procedures are followed.

The second fares no better. It offers as an answer an intensified version of what worries Habermas in the first place. Quong claims that democratic autonomy is sufficiently exercised in deliberations about which of the various liberal conceptions of justice is best. Not only that, it is deliberation only among the reasonable, as Rawls defines this; and he defines it such that reasonable persons are apt to be not only public spirited, but also tolerant of others who disagree. That does, however, imply that many of our fellow citizens are unreasonable, including those who, for example, don't accept the burdens of judgment. Quong's view of public reason thus has the significant disadvantage of excluding a large section of the citizenry from the constituency of democratic deliberation (Quong 2011, 290–314). On Quong's account, unreasonable citizens are the resident aliens of deliberative democracy: They are granted the protection of the laws they live under, but they may not contribute to the legislative process.

6.3.3 THE NARROWNESS OBJECTION

Despite the full and carefully argued responses that Rawls gives to Habermas's objections regarding liberal rights versus popular sovereignty (see chapter 5, section 5.3.3), I don't think he gets off the hook entirely. There is a certain plausibility to the claim that Rawls's *Political Liberalism* fails to give equal weight and priority to democracy and liberal rights. And this objection gains in plausibility when linked to Habermas's other objections. In "Reconciliation Through the Public Use of Reason," section III (B), Habermas objects that Rawls conceives the political domain too narrowly and that, accordingly, he imposes restrictions on the scope of public reason that are too severe.

In chapter 5, I established that, although the evidence in *Political Liberalism* is somewhat mixed, Rawls appears to settle on the narrow view of the political domain and hence of the scope of public reason's application. Whether he does so with good justification is moot. Scanlon attributes the narrow view to Rawls and defends it on the grounds that the basic structure and constitutional essentials enjoy a kind of priority in as much as special considerations apply to the basic structure such that, "if these institutions have the right sort of justification, then this justification also supports legislation enacted through the procedures they define" (Scanlon 2003, 163). However, Scanlon's point does not so much defend the narrow conception as smudge the line between narrow and broad. For although he claims that constitutional essentials and matters of basic justice should be justified by public reason, the public justifications that apply directly to the political domain narrowly construed therefore apply indirectly to political matters more broadly.[15] This might be right, but, as Quong argues, it does not show why matters of ordinary legislation *should not* be supported by principles of public reason directly, as he and Larmore claim they should (Quong 2004, 236–37).

Rawls's favored answer to this question is that a political conception of justice needs to be complete, namely arranged so that the values in it "answer all or nearly all" the questions that arise in respect of it (PL, 225). Scanlon agrees and argues that this can be the case only on the narrow view of the scope of public reason: "It does not, however, seem plausible that a political conception—which must refrain from taking sides on issues on which reasonable comprehensive views may disagree—could provide the basis for answering all questions that arise in the course of legislation" (Scanlon 2003, 163).

Quong has a good reply to this, which is that there is no a priori (nor even a halfway reliable) way to know that a matter of ordinary legislation—whether to build a new road or subsidize an opera house—will be amenable to resolution through public reason: "Indeed, the best way to determine whether it is the case is by engaging in a public debate where we try to adhere to the norms of public reason" (Quong 2004, 243). I think Habermas can make a more direct and powerful response: On what basis does Rawls assume that a political conception of justice must be complete? It ought not to be merely a *theoretical* desideratum. That would go against the practical grain of *Political Liberalism* and arguably offend against the method of avoidance. So there should be a good practical reason why the political conception must be complete. What is it? Rawls does not say. Neither do his defenders. They assume that if it is not complete, it is not practicable.

Aside from the question of whether Rawls has adequate justification for holding the narrow view of the political and of the domain of application of the principles of public reason, there is the further question of what is wrong with the narrow view of the domain of the political and the scope of public reason.

Habermas's argument that Rawls's narrow construal of the political domain and the scope of public reason means that too many matters of "ordinary legislation," matters in need of coercive regulation, are thus exempted from the requirements of public reason is on the mark. By Rawls's own reckoning, this makes it extremely difficult for citizens to achieve full autonomy in the sense of acting on "principles which it is reasonable to expect each to accept" such that they can "face one another openly" as members of a true community. Only in a narrowly circumscribed domain of social life will that be the case. Habermas's worry is that Rawls's theory, in offering a very narrow and demanding theory of public reason instead of a theory of democracy that examines how democratic institutions actually work, places too many issues "outside the bounds of democratic deliberation and discussion."

6.3.4 THE INSTITUTIONAL DEFICIT OF RAWLS'S *POLITICAL LIBERALISM*

The narrowness objection brings us to the final aspect of Habermas's criticism of Rawls, which is carried over from the criticism he makes in *Between Facts and Norms* and which animates all of the specific criticisms he levels at Rawls in the exchange. There, he argued that Rawls's theory is "unrealistic," since it focuses too much on the normative basis of legitimacy and too little on the legal and institutional basis of the production of legitimate law. His very slender theory of public reason answers to a single practical problem: how laws can gain buy-in from all citizens under conditions of reasonable pluralism. Rawls's answer takes the form of a moral theory of democratic citizenship. And he almost completely neglects to explain how institutions are supposed to embed and facilitate the "public use of reason," or democratic discourse, and fails to offer a proper analysis of existing democratic institutions and their implicit norms. He does not show how political norms and democratic values penetrate and gain traction within the "harder material of institutions and action systems" (BFN, 64). Habermas's theory has a broader range and different foci and is designed to answer his guiding question of how an essentially bureaucratic procedure of majority voting can give rise to legitimate laws, which achieve adequate buy-in from all citizens because they had a say in the wider legislative process. Habermas's theory may well, though, as Rawls claims, put more emphasis on democracy than on liberalism in the end, rather than achieve an equal balance. That is in part because Habermas's theory of the "public use of reason" is embedded in a much richer, more sociologically informed theory of democratic institutions.

7

"'REASONABLE' VERSUS 'TRUE'": HABERMAS'S REPLY TO RAWLS'S "REPLY"

7.1 THE DILEMMA OF REASONABLENESS

Habermas was understandably a little dissatisfied with his contribution to the 1995 exchange.[1] Doubtless, as an early reviewer of a long and difficult book and with a relatively small word count to work with, he had by far the more difficult task of the two disputants. Thus, in 1996, he produced a long and considered response to Rawls's "Reply to Habermas" entitled "'Reasonable' Versus 'True,' or the Morality of Worldviews" (MW, 92–113; TIO 75–105). The basic strategy of the second article is similar to the strategy adopted in the first. He wants to impale Rawls on one horn of a dilemma; let's call it the "dilemma of reasonableness." Either Rawls's notion of "reasonableness" is "too weak to characterize the mode of validity of an intersubjectively recognized conception of political justice, or . . . what is practically reasonable is indistinguishable from what is morally right" (MW, 94).

By the time he writes the second article, Habermas has abandoned several of the misconceptions that prevented a similar strategy from succeeding in the first article. Indeed, the second essay shows that all of Rawls's careful restatements, clarifications, and refinements to his position in "Reply to Habermas" had given Habermas a fuller, more nuanced appreciation of *Political Liberalism*.

For example, Habermas completely drops the claim that Rawls's justification of the political conception is merely instrumental; indeed, he barely mentions the question of stability. For the first time, he introduces a systematic distinction between "justice in general" (by which he means justice-qua-morality) and "political justice"[2]: "Since moral judgments are only concerned with questions of justice in general, political justice must be specified in terms of the medium of law" (MW, 111; TIO, 98). And in the second essay, Habermas has a much fuller and more accurate grasp of what Rawls means by the "reasonableness" of doctrines, and of citizens. For example, he observes that the attribute "reasonable" refers to "the attitude of people who are (a) willing to propose, agree upon, and abide by fair terms of social cooperation between free and equal citizens and (b) capable of recognizing the burdens of judgment" (MW, 102). He also gives due acknowledgment to the fact that, according to Rawls, political values are indeed moral values and that the political conception of justice is a moral conception, though he continues, as we will see, to find it puzzling how Rawls can make such a claim.

Some of Habermas's puzzlement arises from certain quirks of his interpretation that carry over from his earlier view:

1. He continues to make the assumption underlying the serendipity objection, namely that the overlap is merely "felicitous," a "lucky convergence" of the moral components of reasonable world views (MW, 94, 99).
2. He continues to propound the "common view" according to which consensus between citizens is forged only at the third stage of justification, Rawls's "public" justification: "Only at the final stage . . . do we take the other citizens into account" (MW, 104).

This implies, of course, that the first stage, the "freestanding," *pro tanto* justification, such as the argument from the original position, does not involve consensus and does not take other citizens into account:

> Before an overlapping consensus is established [at stage 3] there is no public, intersubjectively shared perspective from which the citizens could make . . . impartial judgments. The citizens are denied the 'moral point of view' from which they could develop and justify a political conception in joint public deliberation.[3]

This was, as we saw in the previous chapter, one of the assumptions underlying Habermas's claim in the first essay that Rawls's justification lacked "cognitive meaning" and hence, in Forst's words, "a genuine moral consensus" (see chapter 6, section 6.2). Recall that a genuine moral consensus in Habermas's (and Forst's) eyes is one that arises when all affected participate in public discussion and converge on a norm that all affected can accept for the same reasons (and so meets the validity requirement). In other words, throughout the second article, Habermas continues to draw what I have previously argued is an invidious comparison with discourse ethics (MW, 101, 105).

Although Habermas no longer objects that Rawls's justification of the political conception is merely instrumental or functional, he continues to claim that the *only* moral justifications Rawls offers are ones that come from each person's comprehensive doctrine and that are based on "private, nonpublic reasons" (MW, 100). In this, Habermas claims, Rawls's political theory is still more Hobbesian than Kantian, but for the fact that the different reasons are moral reasons, rather than merely prudential or instrumental reasons (MW, 100). As such, Habermas likens Rawls's conception of public justification to a "compromise" agreement that falls short of a genuine moral consensus because it fails the validity requirement. To be sure, Habermas has a somewhat peculiar notion of a compromise, one that does not necessarily involve one or both parties ceding their interests for the sake of agreement but merely involves them agreeing to something for different reasons.[4]

Habermas describes stage 3 as the "radicalization of a still incomplete ego-centric universalization procedure" (MW, 104). On such a view, Habermas claims, "everyone must accept the same conception . . . for her own nonpublic reasons, and each must at the same time satisfy herself that all others also accept it" (MW, 105). It is true, according to Rawls, that this stage 3 justificatory procedure of "mutual observation" involves no mutual insight into the substantive content of the doctrines and that it can be, though need not be, performed entirely monologically. "Public" justification involves observing, as it were from the outside, whether citizens can agree upon a political conception of justice. What is not true, though, is that this observation is itself a nonpublic reason. The ascertaining of this social fact (that each can accept the political conception of justice for his or her own nonpublic reasons, and that each knows that everyone else can, too) is a kind of public reason. It is no less public than any other observable fact, for example that everyone around the dining table, each from his or her own perspective, can see that there are two bottles of wine on the table and can ascertain that everyone can see that. To conclude then, as Habermas does, that the whole three-stage design "lacks a perspective of impartial judgment and a public use of reason in the strict sense" is to misrepresent what is supposed to be going on both at stage 1 and at stage 3—and to think that stage 2, "full justification," is doing the entire justificatory work (MW, 105).

Now Habermas is faced with a puzzle, however. How can Rawls construct an adequate public justification, comprising a genuine moral consensus, on the basis of nonpublic reasoning carried out by each person monologically? This would not be puzzling were Habermas not making the invidious comparison with moral discourse and were he not making the tendentious assumption that a genuine moral consensus has to be strongly dialogical, that is, actually carried out collectively by all concerned (see chapter 5, section 5.1.2).

Nor would it be puzzling if Habermas allowed that both *pro tanto* justification (stage 1) and public justification (stage 3) meet the validity requirement that everyone can reach agreement on a principle (or a conception of justice) for the same reasons, albeit in a slightly weaker sense than the one Habermas has uppermost in his mind owing to the invidious comparison. But then, allowing that would undermine his dialectical strategy of trying to force Rawls into the dilemma of reasonableness. So in spite of Habermas's better understanding of Rawls's notion of reasonableness, his strategy of trying to pin Rawls on the dilemma of reasonableness is not convincing.

7.2 HABERMAS'S SECOND SET OF OBJECTIONS

Fortunately for Habermas, this is not the only line of argument he offers in his reply to Rawls's "Reply." There are several more, which we will look at in turn.

7.2.1 AGAINST THE METHOD OF AVOIDANCE

Here again, Habermas develops his objection to Rawls's method of avoidance. He denies that "political theory can itself move entirely within the domain of the political and steer clear of stubborn philosophical controversies" (MW, 93). Political theory cannot avoid making theoretical assumptions that some reasonable people will doubt. Here is a case in point. In *Political Liberalism*, Rawls offers a moral psychology that he claims, rather puzzlingly, to be "philosophical, not psychological" (PL, 86). The puzzle is partly resolved when one reads that the psychology he has in mind, which is supposedly "not psychological," would better be termed "political, not psychological," in the sense that it is based not on "the science of human nature" but on "a certain political conception of the person and an ideal of citizenship" (PL, 87). But the puzzle is only partly resolved, because the point of his moral psychology, as shown, for example, in part III of *A Theory of Justice*, is to demonstrate the stability of his conception of justice by means of what Thomas Baldwin has called an "intimate explanatory relationship between moral and natural psychology" (Baldwin 2008, 252). In *Political Liberalism*, Rawls thinks he must forgo such a rich explanatory account of moral psychology in order not to make any assumptions that depend on a possibly controversial account of natural psychology; however, rather suspiciously, his "philosophical, not psychological" conception of moral psychology in the later work remains fairly similar to that of the earlier one. But that's not the worry. The worry is that if Rawls is to demonstrate the stability of justice as fairness, even when construed as a political conception, he needs to show substantive explanatory connections between a politically slimmed-down moral psychology and natural human psychology. Baldwin claims, "Stability requires that under normal circumstances it is in our interests to be moral, and our interests are rooted in our natural psychology" (Baldwin 2008, 252). That seems, however, to be the position in Rawls's argument from congruence, from which he rows back in *Political Liberalism*. What the latter requires is not an argument that shows that acting justly is in the interests of individual citizens so much as that reasonable citizens are minded and ready to act according to the political conception of justice, whatever their comprehensive doctrine. Stability is ensured to the extent that the political conception has wide uptake (since it is embedded in each person's comprehensive doctrine) and that this is public knowledge. But even thus construed, the goal of stability "for the right reasons" requires that explanatory relations obtain between Rawls's political conception of the person and natural human psychology, and, to that extent, Baldwin's underlying point holds good.

I offer Baldwin's account of Rawls's moral psychology as just one example, among others, that bears out Habermas's suspicion that Rawls is not able to offer a theory that is "political, not metaphysical" in all respects. That said, political theory can, Habermas claims, avoid getting entangled in fruitless and theoretically undesirable metaphysical debates (MW, 93; TIO, 77). It is true that when Habermas makes that claim, he has in mind a very different view of metaphysics than Rawls; for example, that his own political theory claims to be true and assumes background theories that also claim to be true, like discourse ethics, is not, he thinks, metaphysical in any objectionable sense. The truth claims will have to be borne out in the relevant discourses and arguments. If they are defeated, alternatives will have to be proposed. There is nothing either morally objectionable or politically impracticable about that. This point escapes Wolterstorff, who, in raising Larmore's objection that Habermas's conception of post-metaphysical philosophy amounts to a world view, points to Habermas's underlying anthropology as evidence that his post-metaphysical philosophy is not "free of ontology," as it claims to be (HR, 110). However, post-metaphysical philosophy in Habermas's sense does not imply that it has no ontological commitments, but rather that it is, among other things, ontologically parsimonious and restricted in scope.[5]

Habermas makes a second claim about Rawls's method of avoidance, namely that a political theory cannot but make moral claims, claims that are not to be "relegated to the black box of comprehensive doctrines" (MW, 112) of which political philosophy dare not speak. He acknowledges that Rawls considers discourse ethics and the actually existing morality it reconstructs to be comprehensive moral and philosophical doctrines. But for his part, he denies that they are. Morality, as Habermas construes it, is more than a world view and quite distinct from ethical conceptions of the good. And it is, he maintains, operative in the legal and political systems, in civil society and in the broader political culture of democracy.

That said, Habermas's own discourse theory is supposed to refrain from making substantial normative or critical judgments on the basis of moral norms. It must, he claims, prescind from matters of substance and limit itself to "clarifying the moral point of view and the criteria for democratic legitimacy" in a way that "does not anticipate their content" (Forst 2011, 157). Whether Habermas actually lives up to this requirement in either discourse ethics or *Between Facts and Norms* is a moot point.

7.2.2 AGAINST PATERNALISM

This brings us to Habermas's second line of criticisms, which is that Rawls's project is guilty of paternalism. This is much the same objection as the externalism objection he levels in *Between Facts and Norms*.[6] One specific charge is that Rawls "lays down a complete design for the well-ordered society" and the implied contrast is his own theory, which supposedly "restricts itself to clarifying the implications of the legal institutionalization of procedures" of democracy (MW, 108). The claim is that Rawls anticipates the results that should be made by citizens invoking such procedures. Although Habermas claims that political philosophy *must* make *critical* judgments on the basis of a political conception of justice, rather than "merely accept established convictions," he still insists that the philosopher must not "construct such a conception out of whole cloth and hold it up to a society as a norm" (MW, 109).

Once again, Rawls's justice as fairness is the target. There is no problem with Habermas's construing justice as fairness (or any other political conception of justice) as a "norm" against which society is judged. It certainly is that. However, it is problematic to claim that justice as fairness represents a "complete design for the well-ordered society." Perhaps here, Habermas is thinking of the various implications of the difference principle. Nonetheless, a principle is one thing; a complete design for society is another.

As a matter of fact, because Rawls's political conception of justice is a normative moral conception, it is far easier to see how his theory can be *critical* of society and of actual political traditions than it is Habermas's, which supposedly restricts itself to "explicating" the moral point of view and the legal institutionalization of democratic procedures. Doesn't this very restriction mean that discourse theory remains in the final analysis "explicatory" rather than critical? For discourse theory cannot forge substantive normative criticisms of democratic society by merely clarifying its procedures. It can reconstruct those procedures correctly or otherwise, and it can, Habermas claims, even find confirmation of the correctness "in a perspective which it encounters in society itself, namely the moral point of view from which modern societies are criticized by their own social movements" (MW, 110). To my mind, that still means that the theory remains explicative or reconstructive, while normative criticisms remain the prerogative of citizens. If that is right, it means that something like the descriptivist critique that Hedrick aims exclusively at Rawls's theory, rather than at Habermas's, can with more justification be turned against Habermas. The rationale for leveling the descriptivist critique at Rawls was that the political conception is worked up from values inherent in the political culture and thus won't reach beyond the existing institutions (Hedrick 2010, 26–33). That does not follow. It is fanciful to think that the two principles of justice merely describe the basic structure of U.S. liberal democracy. No actually existing liberal or social democracy comes close to realizing the ideals of justice as fairness, though some countries have certainly come closer to an approximation than others.

(Note also that the descriptivist critique of Rawls cuts in the opposite direction to the externalism critique. If the fact that the political conception of justice is worked up from political values in the existing culture is supposed to blunt its critical edge, it can hardly also be claimed that the political conception of justice is an external or transcendent standard and that, like all such standards, it results in paternalism or elitism. So this means that, if Hedrick levels the descriptivist critique of Rawls, he ought not, at the same time, to join Habermas in affirming the externalist critique.)

Another assumption behind Habermas's paternalism charge is that at the first stage of justification, it is the "professional" philosopher who works out a "freestanding conception of justice" (MW, 109). Habermas believes that this grants to the expert philosopher too great a role in constraining the democratic procedure and leaves too little up to the actual citizens who invoke it (see chapter 6, section 6.3.2). However, the difference between their two positions may not be as stark as Habermas presents it. In his view, the political theorist merely reconstructs the principles implicit in practices that participants or citizens invoke all the time in their everyday lives, by means of which they themselves decide what is morally and political "right," whereas Rawls hands over to citizens a ready-made conception of political justice.

But if that conception of justice really is worked up from values belonging to the political culture, and which reasonable citizens already hold in common, then what is it that is lost to democracy if such a conception is, as it were, handed to citizens already constructed? For Freeman, the answer is that nothing much is lost if democratic citizens rely on principles advocated by the philosopher to resolve disputes concerning political justice (see chapter 6, section 6.3.2). Strictly speaking, though, something is lost to democratic citizenship, namely the work of constructing the political conception that is undertaken on behalf of citizens by the political philosopher, though not the materials of construction, namely the political values and ideas, as these already belong to the common political culture. Recall that Rawls contends—in my view, somewhat implausibly—that this is work that citizens can do for themselves (RH, 153/6). What about the work of clarification and reconstruction undertaken by the social theorist in Habermas's view? Well, in his view, such work neither adds nor subtracts from the democratic process (or from moral practice), since the democratic and moral procedures of everyday life are not in need of clarification by the philosopher. Such work is a theoretical contribution by the theorist to social and political theory, in which it has its proper place.

To my mind, the charge of paternalism disguises an underlying methodological difference between the two theorists about whether political theory is fundamentally part of politics or is a theoretical discipline that has politics as its object. Given Rawls's position, and given that the political philosopher undertakes much of the work of theory construction—for example working up a political conception of justice—then Freeman had better be right: Such work can be done by the philosopher and need not be done by citizens themselves.

7.2.3 THE POLITICAL PRIORITY OF PUBLIC REASONS

The third criticism Habermas makes targets what he sees as Rawls's failure to establish the priority of political (public) reasons over nonpolitical (nonpublic) reasons. Habermas contends that the priority of public reasons is supposed to follow "from the reasonableness of citizens," but he denies that it does, and claims that Rawls "simply asserts" that the political values are "very great" and establishes their priority by fiat. As a matter of interpretation, this is questionable. As Habermas notes himself, "reasonable" citizens are willing to propose and abide by fair terms of cooperation with their fellow citizens, which alone gives them reason to prioritize public reasons in their political advocacy (MW, 102). Perhaps Habermas thinks it too much to expect one's fellow citizens to be "reasonable" in that sense, or perhaps he is suspicious of the very way in which the reasonableness of citizens is defined, such as to make the case that reasonable citizens are disposed to honor the requirements of equality and reciprocity.

Habermas claims that the "expectation of reasonableness" and the priority of public reason have to be "imposed" on world views and that such priority is a "requirement of practical reason," indeed a moral requirement (MW, 107). He appears to think that the priority of public over nonpublic reasons is an application of the priority of morality over ethics and enlists Forst for support on this point (MW, 107n). As we have seen, others such as Larmore have made similar claims. But neither Forst nor Larmore makes such a strong claim about the autonomy of the political. Neither denies, as Habermas does, that the authority of legitimate law depends not at all on the authority of morality. Habermas would thus be better off arguing that the priority of public over nonpublic reasons is a requirement of practical reason rooted in the discursive and communicative conditions of political life, which is the line of argument of both *The Theory of Communicative Action* and discourse ethics. Alternatively, he would be better off arguing, along the lines of *Between Facts and Norms*, that the priority of public over nonpublic reasons is a necessary condition of the legal institutionalization of democracy and an implication of the medium of law. Instead, he claims that the priority of public reasons is grounded in "the moral point of view"; that is, it is a legal application of the priority of morality over ethics (MW, 107). Still, that Habermas does not present a clinching alternative argument for the priority of public reason does not invalidate his objection. What does not exist, he contends, is a subset of moral values that are, as it were, already ready for politics, exhibiting a priority that reasonable citizens recognize and affirm over all comprehensive values (exclusively conceived) and nonpublic reasons.

7.2.4 THE PRIORITY OF LIBERTY OVER DEMOCRACY

The final objection Habermas levels in his second essay is another version of his objection in "Reconciliation Through the Public Use of Reason," that is, that Rawls prioritizes individual rights and liberties over the democratic process. In the final analysis, he claims, "public autonomy appears in the first instance as a means for realizing private autonomy" (MW, 113). That seems right, to the extent that Rawls's political liberalism is, in the end, a liberalism. Political justice, Rawls writes, "draws the limit, and the good shows the point" (PL, 174). By contrast, Habermas's "Kantian republicanism" is in the final analysis a republicanism, the guiding insight of which is that "in an age of completely secularized politics, the rule of law cannot be had or maintained without radical democracy" (BFN, xlii).[7] One worry one might have about Habermas's theory is that, as a republican theory, it presupposes an unrealistic degree of political participation, though the worry is somewhat mitigated by Habermas's contrastingly broad conception of the political, which encompasses civil society. As such, it is not that Habermas envisages modern citizens hurrying to the assemblies, as Rousseau did. Assuming that the political system is responsive to civil society in the way Habermas thinks it should be, when it functions properly, merely inhabiting civil society, with its untrammeled flows of discourse and communication, is a form of indirect political participation. This consideration allays the objection put by Onora O'Neill that "deliberation and dialogue may offer an attractive . . . model for organizing the affairs of small associations, but are not feasible at great or even medium scale" (O'Neill 2015, 141). In large modern societies, "inclusive deliberation about public affairs is difficult, if not impossible."[8]

This concludes our discussion of the exchange. Though Habermas's reply to Rawls's "Reply" was not published in the *Journal of Philosophy*, it belongs, temporally and thematically, to the exchange, and gave Habermas the opportunity to elaborate and refine his earlier criticisms on the basis of a better appreciation of the argument and central ideas of *Political Liberalism*. We will review and evaluate the arguments on both sides in the concluding chapter. As is clear already, though, Habermas aims many more criticisms at Rawls than Rawls aims at Habermas. That is because as the exchange eventually panned out, it took the shape of Habermas's developing various objections to *Political Liberalism* and Rawls, in the main, defending his theory against them. This same one-sidedness is also in evidence in the debate over religion and public reason that forms the legacy of their dispute, though one reason for that is that, by the time Habermas penned his first criticisms of Rawls's ideas on religion and public reason, Rawls had already sadly passed away. It is to these works we now turn.

IV

THE LEGACY OF THE HABERMAS–RAWLS DISPUTE

8

RELIGION WITHIN THE BOUNDS OF PUBLIC REASON ALONE

The Habermas–Rawls exchange that we have examined in the last three chapters is, at bottom, as Habermas writes and Rawls acknowledges, a "family" dispute. The same cannot be said with such confidence about their respective works of political theory in general, what I have called the "dispute" as distinct from the "exchange." There is considerable disagreement among commentators over the family to which both Rawls and Habermas are supposed to belong. One of the better answers to this question is that the family in question is the family of public justification accounts of political legitimacy in democratic constitutional states. Habermas's dispute with Rawls about the role of religious reasons in the political public sphere, though it postdates the exchange by a decade or so, belongs to this family. This is one rationale for including a chapter on the topic.

Although Rawls was not a participant in it, his ideas about the role of religious reasons in the political public sphere were the catalyst for the debate, which Habermas joined relatively late in the day. Supporters and critics of both Rawls and Habermas subsequently contributed to the discussion on one side or the other. This means that, as with the early debate, the dialectic between Rawls and Habermas is indirect and rather complex.

In brief, the history of the debate between Habermas and Rawls on religion and public reason looks like this. In the late 1980s and early

1990s, a vigorous debate arose among political and legal theorists about the moral and constitutional implications of the principle of the separation of church and state. Arguments that Rawls makes in *Political Liberalism* about the duty of civility were taken up, interpreted, and endorsed by Robert Audi on the one hand and criticized by Nicholas Wolterstorff and Paul Weithman on the other. Briefly put, the objections are that Rawls's duty of civility places unfair burdens on religious citizens and wrongly impugns their identity as citizens of faith.[1] Rawls must have thought those criticisms valid, because in 1997, largely in response to them, he came up with a revision of his position in "The Idea of Public Reason Revisited," a response that he called "the proviso" (PL, 453). (We'll look at this development in more detail later on.) Habermas's participation in the debate does not begin until 2005. He takes it upon himself to show why these criticisms, which he believes apply with full force to the theories Rawls advances in *Political Liberalism* and "The Idea of Public Reason Revisited," do not also apply to his own view, which he calls the "institutional translation proviso." The label appears to suggest that Habermas's view is a modified version of Rawls's "proviso," and this is how the majority of commentators have seen things. They have assumed that Habermas's "proviso" is similar to Rawls's and focused their attention accordingly on the question of whether it adequately answers the objections brought against Rawls's "proviso."[2] Those who come down on the side of Rawls's critics think that Habermas's theory falls prey to exactly the same objections as Rawls's, whereas Rawls's defenders, who deny that the objections apply to him, find little to recommend Habermas's modified "proviso." In my eyes, the initial assumption that the two positions are similar is mistaken. Habermas's theory is in several significant respects quite distinct from Rawls's. The similarities are more superficial than real, and the differences are crucial.[3] As for the objections, for various reasons, I believe that they apply neither to Rawls's nor to Habermas's theory and that Habermas gets himself into considerable difficulty by trying to answer them.

In this chapter, I'll first set out Rawls's position (section 8.1) and the objections to it (section 8.2). Then I'll set out Habermas's position and examine how he attempts to deal with the objections (section 8.3). Finally, I'll attempt an overall assessment of the two theories (section 8.4).

8.1 RAWLS ON PUBLIC REASON

The central ideas of Rawls's idea of public reason in *Political Liberalism* are the "liberal principle of legitimacy" and the duty of civility. Recall that the first states, "Our use of political power is . . . proper only when . . . exercised in accordance with a constitution the essentials of which all citizens . . . may reasonably be expected to endorse in the light of principles and ideals acceptable to their common human reason" (PL, 137). Rawls holds that this principle implies the duty of civility, namely the duty "to explain to one another on those fundamental questions how the principles and policies they advocate and vote for can be supported by the political values of public reason" (PL, 217).

What does it mean to explain to others that the principles and policies one advocates "can be supported by the political values of public reason"? The answer is that they must be able to be supported by the values and ideas that fall within the overlapping consensus of all reasonable comprehensive doctrines and that, as such, form the normative common ground of all reasonable citizens. Recall that the political ideas and values are a subset of those that happen to fall within the overlap among reasonable comprehensive doctrines and are thus part of a common stock of ideas and values held by all reasonable citizens.[4] They include the values of justice, equal political liberty, fair equality of opportunity, and economic reciprocity. They form the component ideas of the political conception of justice, which is an arrangement of them into a theory designed to answer virtually all questions asked of it.[5] A justification is political (or "public") when it appeals only to the values that fall within the overlap and to no values or ideas that don't and, in that sense, is shared by all reasonable citizens.

Now recall the relation of modularity between the political conception of justice and reasonable comprehensive doctrines (PL, 12, 145, 387). This is important because, as we saw in chapter 4 (section 4.3.3), there is an ambiguity in the way Rawls uses the term "comprehensive doctrine." One can think of a reasonable comprehensive doctrine as being merely compatible with the political conception of justice, considered apart from the module, and as including it and thus being congruent with it. The full sense of "reasonable comprehensive doctrine" should be one that includes the module, because otherwise the doctrine is neither "reasonable" nor "comprehensive" in Rawls's sense of those terms. So there are inclusive and exclusive senses of the notion "reasonable comprehensive doctrine," and Rawls uses now one, and now the other.[6] The relevance of this ambiguity is that most religious reasons are comprehensive in the exclusive sense; that is, they are not political and not public.[7]

Several questions arise in respect of the duty of civility:

1. What kind of duty is it? It is a duty of citizenship. And Rawls says that it is "a moral, not a legal, duty" (PL, 217), though it is part of a political morality, not a general moral theory of right conduct (PL, xv). Hence, it is not enforceable by law.
2. On whom does it fall? Rawls says that it falls mainly on judges, especially Supreme Court judges, but also on "government officials," "legislators," and "candidates for public office" (PL, 443).[8] However, importantly, it also falls on citizens (PL, 217).[9]
3. In which contexts does the duty of civility apply? Rawls's answer is that it applies in political contexts. These are contexts in which citizens advocate indirectly or directly for policies that require coercive legislation. Political contexts, though, include the ballot box, at which citizens vote (PL, 216).
4. To what matters does it apply? According to Rawls, it applies to "constitutional essentials and matters of basic justice." The duty of civility does not apply in the—correspondingly broad—background culture.
5. To what is it a duty? What actions does it enjoin or prohibit? According to Christopher Eberle, it imposes two demands. As a *principle of pursuit*, the duty of civility requires citizens (and public officials) in the public political realm to attempt to find and offer public justifications for their favored coercive laws or policies. As a *doctrine of restraint*, the duty of civility imposes the obligation to restrain from offering reasons that are comprehensive in the exclusive sense and hence nonpublic and nonpolitical (Eberle 2002, 68).[10]

8.1.1 RAWLS AND "THE PROVISO"

In *Political Liberalism*, rather than an absolute prohibition on comprehensive reasons, Rawls initially endorses a permissive view that nonpublic, thus comprehensive, reasons can be offered by citizens in the course of political advocacy if done "in ways that strengthen the ideal of public reason itself" (PL, 247, 247n). Later, in "The Idea of Public Reason Revisited," he makes the additional claim that "reasonable comprehensive doctrines may be introduced in public political discussion at any time, provided that in due course proper political reasons—and not reasons given solely by comprehensive doctrines—are presented, sufficient to support whatever the comprehensive doctrines are introduced to support" (PL, 462; l). He calls this view "the proviso."

Rawls's main concern with "the proviso" is to emphasize how much scope there is for the use of religious reasons in political discussion in the background culture, if not the political forum proper, and to emphasize the role of comprehensive doctrines as the "vital social basis" of the political conception (PL, 463). For "the proviso" contains no injunction on individual citizens themselves to exercise *restraint* even in the political forum here and now, and the duty to *pursue* public justifications can now be deferred into the future and devolved onto others.[11]

Rawls's "proviso" raises many questions that we must set aside here. Is restraint now enjoined at all? If so, at what point? Is it called for once citizens have made a good-faith attempt to provide a public justification and have failed? How far into the future can the obligation be deferred? On whom does the duty now fall? His somewhat unsatisfactory answer to these questions is that "the details of how to satisfy this proviso must be worked out in practice," though he insists that it must be satisfied "in good faith" (PL, 462).

Let's briefly recall what is at stake in the Rawlsian idea of public reason that underlies the duty of civility.

First, there are the moral (as opposed to the legal or constitutional) implications of the First Amendment and what is usually called the "principle of the separation of church and state." This is related to what Rawls considers to be the appropriate basis of the legitimacy of law in a liberal constitutional democracy under conditions of reasonable pluralism (PL, xl–xli, 385–89). Beyond stability and legitimacy, what is at stake is the very ideal of good citizenship for a liberal constitutional democracy under conditions of reasonable pluralism. Rawls always remained faithful to his early vision of a well-ordered society, according to which

> persons engaged in a fair or just practice can face one another openly and support their respective positions [that is, when advocating for coercive legislation] by reference to principles which it is reasonable to expect each to accept. Only if such acknowledgment is possible can there be a true community . . . otherwise their relation will appear to them as founded to some extent on force. (CP, 59; see also A. S. Laden 2011, 140)

8.2 WOLTERSTORFF'S AND WEITHMAN'S OBJECTIONS TO THE DUTY OF CIVILITY

In the 1990s, Rawls's idea of the duty of civility came under attack from various religious critics of liberalism, Nicholas Wolterstorff and Paul Weithman central among them.[12] To be accurate, it is not only Rawls who came under fire, but also, and arguably more centrally, Robert Audi, who argues for what he calls the "principle of secular rationale," namely that "one should not advocate or support any law or public policy that restricts human conduct unless one has and is willing to offer adequate secular reasons for this advocacy or support" (Audi 1989, 279; 1993, 691). According to Audi, citizens have a moral obligation to offer secular justifications (construed in accordance with the principle of secular rationale) for laws or public policy.[13] Audi denies that citizens in the public square have the right to offer *religious* reasons alone for their favored coercive policy or law. That is a slightly different position from that of Rawls, who denies that citizens are morally permitted to offer *nonpublic* reasons when in the public political forum in political contexts as set out earlier. That said, Audi argues that Rawls is on his side to the extent that most secular reasons (as Audi construes them) count as public reasons in Rawls's view, whereas almost all religious reasons (as Audi construes them) would count for Rawls as nonpublic, comprehensive reasons in the *exclusive* sense.[14]

Wolterstorff and Weithman both argue, contra Rawls, that religious citizens may adduce solely religious (in Rawls's sense, comprehensive) reasons for their political views. Thus, they deny that there is a duty of civility: In their view, there is no obligation to pursue public justification or to exercise restraint if public justification fails. Wolterstorff writes,

> It belongs to the religious convictions of a good many religious people that they ought to base their decisions concerning fundamental issues of justice on their religious convictions. . . . If they have a choice, they will make their decisions about constitutional essentials and matters of basic justice on the basis of their religious convictions, and make their decisions on more peripheral matters on other grounds—exactly the opposite of what Rawls lays down. (Audi and Wolterstorff 1996, 105)[15]

There is more than one objection in play here. In what follows, I shall canvass only two: the split-identity objection and the unfairness, or asymmetry, objection, since these are the ones that are widely discussed in the literature concerning Rawls and Habermas on public reason.

The split-identity objection is that the duty of civility obligates religious citizens to embrace an identity that is not really theirs and thus impugns their integrity. It is widely held to apply to Rawls. Michael J. Perry, for example, argues that "one's basic moral/religious convictions are (partly) self-constitutive and are therefore a principal ground . . . of political deliberation and choice. To 'bracket' such convictions is therefore to bracket—to annihilate—essential aspects of one's very self" (Perry 1988, 181–82; see also Yates 2007, 883). A related version of the objection is that the duty of civility obliges religious citizens (but not secular ones) to become disingenuous in their political advocacy by adducing reasons for their favored laws and policies that they do not actually endorse and by not adducing reasons that they do endorse (Lafont 2007, 246; Skorupski 2017, 189).

The unfairness objection is that the psychological, cognitive, and normative burdens imposed by the duty of civility fall unequally on religious and secular citizens. The former, but not the latter, are obliged to make a good-faith attempt to pursue public justifications to supplement, or to substitute for, their religiously held views, when advocating for coercive legislation. If that pursuit fails, they, but not their secular counterparts, are required to exercise restraint. This is allegedly unfair to religious citizens and supposedly contravenes the basic moral-political idea that citizens are free and equal. Finally, it is claimed that the said unfairness undermines the duty of civility.

8.2.1 RAWLS DEFENDED FROM THE OBJECTIONS

I believe these two objections are misplaced when considered as objections to Rawls. Some of the reasons why this is so have been well aired. One riposte, made by defenders of Rawls, is that the duty of civility imposes the obligation to pursue public justifications only in the public political domain narrowly construed, and not in the background culture broadly construed, in which religious citizens can adduce comprehensive reasons and neither the principle of pursuit nor the doctrine of restraint applies (Loobuyck and Rummens 2011, 140). Against this, it should be noted that political contexts include the ballot box, at which citizens vote (PL, 216).

A second riposte is that Rawls's theory does not operate with the distinction between religious and secular reasons but between comprehensive (nonpublic) and political (public) reasons, and the latter distinction is not the same as the religious–secular distinction, because some secular reasons are comprehensive, and some religious reasons are political.[16]

Both observations are well taken. However, the point at issue is not only whether Wolterstorff's objection rests on a correct interpretation of Rawls, but also whether it engages the position under discussion. Most religious reasons are comprehensive in the exclusive sense, and many, perhaps most, secular reasons are not. Wolterstorff could easily modulate the objection slightly to say that the duty of civility unfairly affects, and impugns, the integrity of, if not all, then most religious citizens in the public forum when engaged in political action, whereas it applies to comparatively few secular citizens. So these standard Rawlsian replies are welcome clarifications but not clinching counterarguments.

In my view, there are much more powerful and direct ripostes to both objections. Call these the knock-down arguments. Here is the knock-down reply to the split-identity objection. Recall that, in Rawls's account, the political conception of justice is a module that slots into all reasonable comprehensive doctrines. It is worked up from political values and ideals in the public political culture that are part of our "common human reason." Furthermore, the political conception of justice (or the family of such conceptions) has the power to shape and bend reasonable comprehensive doctrines toward it (PL, 246 & 144). All of this implies that the moral identities of reasonable citizens are complex and dynamic and that they centrally involve a commitment to the political values.[17] This is a general point that Rawls, among others, recognizes. Thus, it is not plausible to claim that the moral obligation to pursue a public justification on the basis of such values impugns, undermines, or, at the limit, destroys the religious identities of reasonable citizens. That would be true only if the political values were opposed to, and not part of, their identities as citizens.

Of course it may be, as Rawls later allows in discussion with Habermas, that in some circumstances, the values of a comprehensive doctrine (exclusively conceived) might outweigh the values of the political conception of justice where these come into conflict, though given the power of the political conception to shape comprehensive doctrines over time, and given the weight and gravity of the political values, such cases will be rare. Even so, talk of splitting or destroying the identity of religious persons is overblown. In such cases, the duty of civility, as a principle of pursuit, asks religious citizens to express, and act on, one very important part of their self-identity, namely their moral-political identity, which they share with other reasonable citizens, rather than another, namely their comprehensive identity, which they don't. Citizens in liberal democratic states are generally shaped not by a closed, homogenous culture but by a complex and differentiated one composed of many subcultures, and their complex and internally differentiated identities reflect this. To claim that they are not is to fall back on a simplistic and anthropologically outdated idea of identity (Mautner 2013, 24).[18] We should conclude, then, that the duty of civility as a principle of pursuit does not impugn the identities of religious citizens in any reprehensible way.

What about the duty of civility insofar as it implies a doctrine of restraint? The duty of civility requires that where the conflict between the political conception of justice and a citizen's religious values is such that the citizen cannot make a good-faith attempt at public political justification, or where that attempt fails, then they should exercise self-restraint. Although this duty is no doubt very demanding, it does not actually endanger the identity of religious citizens. There are many situations in which reasons of tact, or mere prudence, are normally sufficient to prevent someone who, say, holds that homosexuality is impermissible on religious grounds from stating or acting on their conviction. Such reasons are just a normal way of avoiding conflict and smoothing out interaction with one's fellow citizens and pose no threat to their identity.[19] It appears, then, that the split-identity objection does not invalidate Rawls's duty of civility.

So much for the split-identity objection. What about the unfairness objection? Is it *unfair* to ask religious citizens to pursue public justifications and, where these fail, to exercise restraint? Again, there is a knock-down counterargument. The moral requirements of public reason apply to all citizens and thus fall equally on the religious and nonreligious alike. It is true that the *burden* of compliance with this duty may well weigh more heavily on religious citizens when the reasons they endorse are comprehensive and nonpublic. For in the public political realm, they will have to make an extra effort to find public reasons (in addition to their religious, nonpublic reasons) for their favored laws and policies, or to show restraint, should no public reasons be found. This will not be so for most of their secular fellow citizens.

Crucially, though, the requirement to pursue public justifications is not unfair. It is, in my view, rather the good luck of secular citizens if most of their (secular) reasons for their favored policies are already public reasons and the bad luck of religious citizens if, unlike their secular counterparts, the reasons they endorse are religious and nonpublic, and they are therefore required to pursue public justifications instead or, failing that, to show restraint.

It is, after all, similar in the domain of morality. It seems to be true that the burden of meeting any moral obligation (that is, the psychological difficulty of complying with it) falls more heavily on enkratic citizens, who do not "instinctively" want to be good but know they ought to be, than on good citizens for whom it is second nature to be good. The fact, if it is one, that virtue is more of a burden to enkratic citizens than to good citizens, since they have to override their contrary inclinations in order to be virtuous, does not undermine the moral obligation to be good.[20] Nor do enkratic persons have any right to be compensated just because, unlike good people, they find it more burdensome to pursue the good. In the realm of politics, then, religious citizens who feel they ought to base their political decisions and advocacy on their nonpublic religious reasons are analogous to enkratic agents in the moral sphere. Living in a mainly secular society, their religious character and inclinations are their political misfortune but do not give rise to any inequality or unfairness for which either Rawls, or his theory, can rightfully be held responsible or that needs to be rectified.

8.3 HABERMAS'S "INSTITUTIONAL TRANSLATION PROVISO"

In a paper entitled "Religion in the Public Sphere: Cognitive Presuppositions for the 'Public Use of Reason' by Religious and Secular Citizens" (BNR, 114–47), Habermas sets out his response to Rawls's idea of public reason, and in particular to "the proviso." In a deliberate allusion to Rawls's modified position, Habermas labels his own position the "institutional translation proviso":

> Every citizen must know and accept that only secular reasons count beyond the institutional threshold that divides the informal public sphere from parliaments, courts, ministries, and administrations. But all that is required here is the epistemic ability to consider one's own faith reflexively from the outside and to relate it to the secular view. Religious citizens can well recognize this "institutional translation proviso" without having to split their identity into a public part and a private part the moment they participate in public discourses. They should therefore be allowed to express and justify their convictions in a religious language even when they cannot find secular "translations" for them. (BNR, 130)

As I claimed, Habermas's use of the label "proviso" encourages many commentators to treat it as a minor modification of Rawls's position, but in reality, his theory is significantly different.

8.3.1 THE DISTINCTIVENESS OF HABERMAS'S THEORY AND ITS BACKGROUND IN *BETWEEN FACTS AND NORMS*

To understand the distinctiveness of Habermas's position, one needs to recall the theory of democracy in *Between Facts and Norms* from which it stems. Habermas's conception of democracy has two interlocking components: a hard institutional core—the political system geared to taking decisions (which he also calls the "formal public sphere")—embedded in, and surrounded by, a soft social periphery, namely "civil society" (or the "informal public sphere"), in which "wild" and "anarchic" flows of communication and discourse circulate (BFN, 187). Public opinion and political will crystallize in the flows of moral, ethical, and theoretical discourse circulating in the informal public sphere. As Habermas puts it, the flows of communication and discourse in civil society "besiege the political system, without, however, intending to conquer it" (BFN, 487). By that means, public reasons flow into the political system and "program" it in the common interest of citizens. Legitimate laws then issue as outputs from the political system and are apt to elicit compliance from most citizens, since they understand and accept the reasons for them.

Note that Habermas's distinction between formal and informal public spheres does not map nicely on to Rawls's central distinctions: between the political conception of justice and the reasonable comprehensive doctrines (exclusively conceived), and between the background culture of society and the political domain, or the "public political forum" (PL, 244, 433).[21] Why? Because Habermas's formal public sphere (the political system) is more than a "political conception" of justice: It is an institutional reality. While its counterpart, the informal public sphere (civil society) is, in Habermas's view, part of the political domain proper, albeit distinct from the political system (for example, parliament) that lies at its center, the background culture, in Rawls's view, is no part of the political domain proper and hence is not governed by principles of public reason. So although each theorist distinguishes between civil society and the state, they have very different conceptions of their respective roles and relations.

The Institutional Component

Like the theory of democracy that undergirds it, Habermas's "institutional translation proviso" has two interlocking components that correspond to the formal and informal public spheres. Let us turn to the first of these.

According to Habermas, the political system (the state) is entirely secular. The principle of the separation of church and state means that in the political system, "only secular reasons count" (BNR, 126, 130–31).[22] This does not imply that no religious reasons can be adduced and discussed in the formal public sphere—in parliament and assemblies—but that no religious reasons may enter into the process of drafting, laying down, and enacting legislation. Speakers of parliaments, he notes, have the power "to strike religious positions or justifications from the official transcript" (BNR, 131).

In a modern democratic state, government officials are tasked with providing secular justifications for laws. This is a legal requirement with an institutional basis.[23] More broadly, it is a "functional requirement of social integration," since it enables the production of legitimate law. It forms a filter between the informal and formal public spheres that keeps religious reasons out, and lets secular reasons in, thus acting as a semipermeable barrier between church—or religious discourses in civil society—and state (EFP, 79; RPS, 10). The institutional filter has two effects. On the one hand, it keeps all religious reasons and religious arguments out of the political (parliamentary) system. On the other, it allows citizens in civil society, which is still part of the political domain proper in Habermas's view, to freely adduce religious arguments, now or in the future, in open discussion and in any context, including that of political advocacy.

Habermas's thesis that in the political system only secular reasons count is not just an empirical claim. He justifies the claim as follows. Secular reasons, on Habermas's understanding of the term "secular," form a kind of neutral common ground on which a background consensus between people of all faiths and persuasions can arise. They do not "expand the perspective" of one community, namely the secular one, but "push for mutual perspective taking so that different communities can develop a more inclusive perspective by transcending their own universe of discourse" (PRPS, 66). Religious reasons, as Habermas understands them, don't have that character and thus cannot form the basis of a consensus.

The reasons Habermas thinks citizens in the public sphere should be free from any obligation to pursue public justifications for their views, or to exercise restraint should that pursuit fail, flow from his conception of democratic legitimacy.

First, in the context of Habermas's wider theory of democratic legitimacy, given that the state protects the "basic right" of religious citizens to free expression and worship, it cannot, he claims—on pain of being in conflict with itself—at the same time "expect all citizens in addition to justify their political positions independently of their religious convictions or world views" (BNR, 128).[24] Indeed, the conflict runs so deep that it constitutes a fracture at the very heart of what Habermas sees as the communicative infrastructure of modern society, which is structured according to rules of discourse, one of which is that "everyone is allowed to introduce any assertion whatsoever into the discourse."[25]

Second, according to Habermas's earlier discourse theory, religious world views and arguments are conceived as ethical discourses that make validity claims to authenticity (not truth) and hence make possible authentic ways of life (BFN, 108–109; JA, 1–15) On this view, it makes sense for a secular state to allow religious arguments to circulate in civil society in order to facilitate a variety of authentic ways of life.

The third reason is related to the second. Habermas's theory of legitimacy includes the "ethical harmonization requirement," namely that for a law to be legitimate, it must resonate with the ethical world views of all of its citizens (BFN, 99).[26] No law could meet such a requirement if there were a standing moral obligation on religious citizens to refrain from voicing their religious arguments. Such an obligation would hinder the production of legitimate law. So, according to Habermas, the state's interest in protecting the freedom of religious expression, fostering authentic ways of life, and producing legitimate law as the basis of civic life speaks against the requirement to adduce only secular arguments and to refrain from offering religious ones.

The first (the institutional) component of Habermas's "institutional translation proviso" shows that Habermas's conception of public reason differs from Rawls's "proviso" in several decisive respects:

1. In spite of the label Habermas attaches to it, it is not a "proviso." Rawls's proviso consists in a moral permission, subject to a condition, a moral requirement on individuals to pursue public justification in good faith and, in the event that public justification fails, to show restraint. None of this applies to Habermas's theory. It is a legal, not a moral, requirement with an institutional basis. If one replaces the label "proviso" with the more accurate term "institutional filter," it becomes clear that what is at issue here is not a conditional permission. To be sure, some of Habermas's statements suggest that the institutional filter constitutes a proviso; for example, he writes of religious citizens, "They may express themselves in a religious idiom only on the condition that they recognize the institutional translation proviso" (BNR, 130). But this claim is misleading, since once the filter is in place, it fulfills its task whether or not citizens recognize and accept it, not provided that they do. If by "recognize," Habermas means "comply with" rather than "willingly endorse," the condition is always met.
2. Whereas Rawls's theory obliges citizens to provide public justifications for their favored coercive laws and to refrain from offering religious ones (or at least some such obligation falls on some citizens at some point in the process), Habermas's theory grants religious citizens unconditional freedom to adduce whatever reasons they want, religious or not, in support of their favored laws in the informal public sphere (and arguably even in the formal public sphere, although of course these will be struck from the official transcript).
3. According to Habermas's theory, the "requirement" to provide secular translations of religious reasons for coercive laws is structural and institutional, not moral. This freedom is guaranteed by a legal and administrative arrangement—the institutional filter—that has the status of a social fact. Morality plays no role.
4. In Habermas's theory, the "requirement" to provide secular translations of religious reasons falls *exclusively* on government officials, not on the religious citizens themselves or on their fellow citizens.

5. Finally, on Habermas's view, what is required is the translation of religious arguments into generally accessible—which, in his eyes, means "secular"—language.[27]

Some people have criticized Habermas's assumption that secular reasons are generally accessible whereas religious reasons are not (Cooke 2006; Chambers 2010; Waldron 2010; Skorupski 2017). Kevin Vallier has argued that, understood as the requirement that reasons be intelligible to all, the general accessibility requirement is so lax as to permit most religious reasons, whereas understood as the requirement that reasons be acceptable to all, it will hardly ever be satisfied (Vallier 2011, 386–87). Anja Hennig uses the examples of the Vatican's opposition to laws permitting abortion, assisted fertilization, and gay marriage to show that, for strategic reasons, many religious agitators present arguments for positions they hold on religious grounds in secular language (Hennig 2015, 100). This is supposed to show that Habermas's translation requirement is too weak for the purpose he assigns it. No doubt Habermas's assumption that religious arguments are not intelligible to all, whereas secular arguments are, is questionable. However, in itself, this is an ineffective objection to Habermas, whose position is that translating an argument into secular language is a *necessary*, but not *sufficient*, condition of its being a public justification. Once reasons are formulated in secular language, they must still be taken up into discourse if they are to count as good reasons. As such, they must be amenable to "rationally motivated consensus." Thus, Habermas's translation requirement has to work in concert with the principle of democracy as an acceptability requirement.[28] They are jointly necessary conditions of legitimacy.

There is overwhelming evidence, then, to show that Habermas's filter is quite unlike Rawls's "proviso." It is not only different in the respects outlined here, but it is also not a "proviso," strictly speaking.[29] So the common view that Habermas's position is similar to Rawls's is prima facie untenable.

So much for the institutional component of Habermas's theory of public reason. As it stands, it lacks detail. Yet it is, in my view, the load-bearing component of Habermas's idea of public reason, and the one that gives the most clear-cut answers to the two objections that worry him: the split-identity and the asymmetry/unfairness objections. It answers them, however, by showing that neither applies, since with the filter in place, citizens are unconditionally free—legally and morally permitted—to adduce religious reasons in civil society and in the political system.

That said, although it is the crucial and most distinctive part of Habermas's theory, it has not been the focus of critical attention. Why? Part of the answer is that, as Hugh Baxter observes, Habermas has failed "to acknowledge explicitly that he has in effect fully repudiated the Rawls/Audi view that citizens must place special restrictions on their use of religious reasons in public political discourse" (Baxter 2011, 208). Beyond that, Habermas himself appears dissatisfied with this view. He thinks that more needs to be said if the theory is to answer Wolterstorff's objections convincingly, and so he puts the onus on the second component of the theory to do so. And this is what has attracted most critical attention.

Habermas also has qualms about the strictly secularist understanding of the political system, and though he is not prepared to jettison it, he thinks it needs both softening and modifying. Furthermore, he now rejects a central tenet of his theory of modernization as too Weberian (RR, 79, 141). That theory construed modernization as a process in the course of which religious meaning is gradually separated out into scientific truth claims and universal moral claims, and in which religious and traditional authorities are gradually replaced by procedures of communication and discourse. Since about 2001, however, instead of seeing religion as a social binding force destined to wither away, he has identified social and functional reasons for the persistence of religion in modern societies whose capacity to generate their own normative resources has declined.[30] In post-secular societies, religions play an indispensable role in replenishing the fast-depleting values and meanings of the lifeworld. Thus, citizens in civil society cannot afford to turn a deaf ear to religious discourse containing "possibly undiscovered treasures" and "possible truth contents" (BNR, 241; FHN, 143) that must not remain buried, even if they need to be translated into secular terms if they are to be understood and affirmed by all citizens (BNR, 131).[31] At the same time, Habermas also stops conceiving religious world views entirely under the category of ethical discourses, which, according to discourse ethics, unlike theoretical and moral discourse, lack "cognitive meaning" since they make claims to authenticity rather than truth.[32] Now, by contrast, he sees religious discourses as also being repositories of possible truth contents and hence important sources of "cognitive content" (BNR, 245).

Hence, in the second interlocking component of his conception of public reason, Habermas sets himself a very tricky threefold task: to modify and attenuate the strict secularism of his earlier modernization theory in a way that remains compatible with his secularist understanding of the state (that is, "political system" or "formal public sphere"), while demonstrably and definitively answering Wolterstorff's and Weithman's objections to Rawls's "proviso."

The Societal Component

The second component of Habermas's "institutional translation proviso" concerns the "informal public sphere," or "civil society." The subtitle of his article "Religion in the Public Sphere" announces it as an account of "the cognitive presuppositions of the 'public use of reason' by religious and secular citizens" (BNR, 114). Habermas contends that the cognitive content of the religious contributions that citizens of faith make in the informal public sphere "can enter into the institutionalized practice of deliberation and decision-making only when the necessary translation already occurs in the pre-parliamentary domain, i.e., in the political public sphere itself" (BNR, 131).[33] This shunts the translation requirement (to provide good justifications for laws and policies and to formulate them in generally accessible language) into the informal public sphere and shifts the burden of meeting it onto citizens, religious and secular. One might think that this brings Habermas closer to Rawls's "proviso." However, Habermas does not construe the fulfillment of his so-called translation proviso as compliance by individual citizens with their moral obligations but as the achievement of broader modernization processes that more or less require religious and secular citizens, conscious of the persistence of a plurality of religious and secular world views, to take a reflexive stance toward their own world views. In other words, the institutional translation filter can work as it should only if the socialization and modernization processes taking place in civil society meet it halfway.

Of course, he no longer sees such modernization processes as mono-dimensional secularization processes that dissolve and replace religious traditions. Under post-secular conditions, modernization takes the form of two "complementary learning processes" that place cognitive burdens, albeit of different stripes, on both religious and secular citizens.[34]

As regards the former, religious believers, claims Habermas, must reflexively acknowledge three social facts of post-secular society:

1. the existence, and legitimate standing, of other faiths
2. the epistemic standing of modern science as an institutionalized monopoly on knowledge
3. the normative principles of the liberal democratic order: egalitarian law and universalistic morality (BNR, 136–37)

According to Habermas, religious citizens have been forced to become reflexive and to process "cognitive dissonances" that arise from the challenge posed to their self-understanding by these three social facts. By contrast, "enlightened secular citizens" are spared such "cognitive dissonances" inasmuch as their secular world view is not similarly challenged by these three social facts of modern society (BNR, 138). This is not to claim that no cognitive burdens fall on any secular citizens or that they experience no cognitive dissonance at all. All secular citizens are required to facilitate the translation process, and some, namely the subgroup Habermas calls "secularists," are required to abandon their narrow secularist outlook in favor a "politically agnostic" view of religion; that is, they must open their minds to the possibility "that contributions formulated in religious language could have a rational content" (BNR, 5, 140).[35]

8.3.2 DOES HABERMAS'S THEORY ANSWER WOLTERSTORFF'S OBJECTIONS?

So does Habermas's account of "the cognitive presuppositions of the 'public use of reason' " answer Wolterstorff's objections? If so, how? Do the alleged cognitive requirements of democratic citizenship in post-secular society force religious citizens to split their identities? Habermas's given answer is no.[36] This is not only because no moral obligation falls on religious citizens to exercise restraint owing to the institutional filter, but also because citizens in modern, post-secular society are reflexively well-adjusted to the social facts of post-secular society, or, as he calls them, "modern conditions of life to which there are no alternatives" (BNR, 138). I believe he is right about this. As I argued earlier in regard to Rawls, the requirement to pursue public—which, in Habermas's case, means secular—justifications should present no threat to the identities of modern democratic citizens.

Second, are the cognitive demands of citizenship in post-secular society asymmetrical, and must religious citizens therefore shoulder unfair burdens if they are to meet the requirements of public reason? Habermas concedes this question is still "open" (BNR, 138).[37] However, his attempt to close it is unclear. Some of his statements suggest that his considered answer is no. For example, he claims "the recognition by secular citizens that they live in a post-secular society" requires "a change of mentality that is *no less cognitively exacting* than the adaptation of religious consciousness to the challenges of an environment that is becoming progressively more secular" (BNR, 139, my emphasis).[38] Most commentators take this as his considered view, and he has been much criticized on this point.[39] Other statements of his, though, seem to suggest that his answer is yes. For instance, he states that the cognitive burdens experienced by religious citizens are appreciably greater and that their secular fellow citizens are "spared similar cognitive dissonances" (BNR, 138). Secular citizens find it fairly easy to reasonably disagree with each other and with their religious compatriots. Religious citizens who believe they have the one true faith, by contrast, bear a "heavier burden" in accommodating reasonable pluralism (BNR, 309). If these two sets of statements are not to be taken as contradictory, his overall position must be something like the following: The cognitive burdens that public reason imposes *do not* fall *equally* on religious and secular citizens. The former bear the heavier burden, but some burden falls on secular citizens nonetheless. Finally, Habermas notes that although "the expectation of tolerance" is not neutral between believers and unbelievers, this "does not reflect an injustice per se," pressing the very point I earlier claimed Rawls and he should make against Wolterstorff (BNR, 309).

As a matter of note, most of Habermas's critics, including Wolterstorff, remain unconvinced by the two knock-down counterarguments I've presented: (1) that modern religious citizens have complex identities that are not threatened by the requirement to formulate political justifications in secular terms and (2) that an asymmetry in the distribution of cognitive burdens does not in itself amount to an unfairness. These critics are also unpersuaded by Habermas's own elaborate, if also slightly fuzzy, responses. In spite of the fact that the "institutional translation proviso" is designed explicitly to address their objections, they still criticize it for *imposing* asymmetrical and hence *unfair* demands on religious citizens.[40]

However, there is third, somewhat more complex but nonetheless, I think, decisive, counterargument to be made. For there is something egregiously wrong with this whole line of criticism of Habermas, which rests on a basic misunderstanding of the kind of theory he is proposing. Habermas's theoretical approach since the early 1980s has been one of "rational reconstruction."[41] His theories reconstruct norms and principles implicit in social practices. Examples are principles (D) and (U) and the principle of democracy. His account of the cognitive presuppositions of democratic citizenship is of similar ilk, though even the requirements are not explicitly formulated as principles. It follows that neither he nor his theory *imposes* or *assigns* any cognitive burdens; they merely (reconstructively) register them. Habermas is not in the business of making public policy recommendations.[42] Nor is he doing normative theory that imposes moral demands and gives citizens reasons for action. He is thus quite unlike Rawls, who is doing a kind of normative theory. Indeed, the differences are starker, for Rawls's arguments are themselves justified on the basis of the political values alone, thus satisfying the principles of public reason. Rawls himself, in justifying his idea of public reason, obeys the duty of civility. He writes, as a political philosopher, from the perspective of a citizen offering fellow citizens first- and second-personal reasons for action.

Not Habermas. He makes a strict distinction between the perspective of the theorist and that of a citizen. Qua theorist, he offers philosophical and social-theoretical justifications for his theory and prescinds from making normative demands on citizens, which, in his eyes, would be to adopt the perspective of a participant.[43] This is why, I surmise, he replies to his critics that the cognitive attitudes required by the complementary learning processes of modernity "cannot be prescribed by political theory" (HR, 373).[44] The many critics who take Habermas's conception of public reason to be a modification of Rawls's "proviso" fail to see this important difference. Once we factor it in, we see not only that the asymmetries that Habermas's theory reconstructs do not constitute an unfairness but that, even if they did, it would not be one for which either Habermas or his theory was responsible. His *theory* is to be faulted, insofar as it is to be faulted, for the incorrectness of his account of the cognitive presuppositions of democratic citizenship.

To be sure, Habermas encourages this misunderstanding of his position by using terminology that makes it look more similar to Rawls's than it is, and by being unclear about the normative status of the requirements of public reason. The second point deserves elaboration. On occasion, Habermas attempts clarifications but does not succeed in throwing much light on the crucial questions of whether his *theory* is normative political theory, and, if so, what kind of normative claims it makes.[45] Does it, for example, impose moral or ethical demands on citizens, and, if so, how do these relate to the "cognitive requirements" of public reason that his theory reconstructs? On the one hand, Habermas says things like the "duty [*die Pflicht*] to make public use of one's reason can be fulfilled only under certain cognitive preconditions" (BNR, 136; ZNR, 142), which makes it look like the requirements of public reason are indeed moral requirements. Such a view is also implied by his claim that "epistemic obligations follow from the demand that they must show each other mutual respect [*gegenseitiger Achtung*]" (BNR, 4; ZNR, 11). On the other hand, Habermas frequently talks of a "democratic civic ethos" [*demokratische Staatsbürgerethos*] (BNR, 139; ZNR, 145), suggesting that its demands are "ethical" as distinct from moral.[46]

The trouble is that the requirements in question *cannot* be moral ones, for that would flatly contradict his argument in *Between Facts and Norms* and the main lines of his critique of Rawls for proposing an account of political legitimacy based on the normative authority of an antecedently given moral order.[47] Nor, however, can the requirements be "ethical," in Habermas's technical sense of the term "ethics." For by his own lights, ethical world views form a plurality of rival and sometimes discrepant comprehensive doctrines. An ethical requirement would apply to all citizens only if they shared a common ethos or conception of the good. But Habermas denies this. Take for instance his considered response to Böckenförde's thesis, which is to deny that the liberal democratic state has pre-political foundations in an overarching ethical (or religious) world view (BNR, 101).[48] So despite Habermas's incautious talk of morality and ethics (which indeed makes it look as though Habermas's conception of public reason is a normative ideal theory like Rawls's), the cognitive requirements of democratic citizenship cannot, on his view, be straightforward moral or ethical demands.

If this line of argument is correct, we can now put the methodological differences between Rawls's and Habermas's approaches to public reason in stark outline. To the devout Catholic who wants to ban physician-assisted suicide on the grounds of the sanctity of human life, and to the Israeli settler who tries to justify settlements on the West Bank on grounds of the Bible or Torah, Rawls says, both as citizen and political theorist, that one ought not to argue on such grounds. It violates the duty of civility and vitiates the possibility of living in a "true community" in which citizens "can face one another openly" (CP, 59). As a theorist, Habermas can say no such thing but merely observe that liberal democratic states function better—that is, they are better at producing legitimate law and thereby achieving social integration—when they permit legislation to be written only in secular language and justified only on secular grounds, adding that some religious content can nonetheless be rescued and made safe for democracy by translation.

8.3.3 HABERMAS AND THE UNFAIRNESS OBJECTION

I have offered three arguments to show why Habermas does not have to worry about the split-identity or unfairness objections. I've shown that neither objection applies to the first component of Habermas's theory, which, though lacking in detail, is fine as it stands. I've offered knock-down counterarguments to the objections. And I've shown that consideration of Habermas's method of rational reconstruction immunizes him from both criticisms as they are usually made.

Yet, curiously, Habermas continues to be worried, especially by the unfairness charge. Why? Perhaps he pays so much attention to the unfairness charge because he is worried that the version of the liberal democratic state that his theory reconstructs violates the ideal that the state should be neutral between competing world views—an ideal to which he subscribes—because it allows only secular reasons in the formal public sphere. But if that were the underlying worry, why does Habermas not relax the requirement that in the political system, "only secular reasons count"? Why does he instead stick to a conception of the formal public sphere that is in fact biased against religious arguments, and hitch it to an account of modernization processes under post-secular conditions that itself introduces a peculiar bias against secularists, requiring them not merely to participate in the collective effort to translate religious arguments into secular language, but also to abandon their scientific naturalism in favor of "political agnosticism" toward religion (BNR, 5, 131, 140, 241)?

Critics have argued that such a requirement is not only "peculiar" and "surprising"—I guess because it is aimed not at atheists in general but at scientific naturalists who are atheists—but also unfair and illiberal (Lafont 2007, 248; Yates 2007, 887).[49] However, in the light of the methodological considerations I have outlined, we should be careful not to blame Habermas and his theory for imposing this requirement: The requirements of modernization are what they are. The pertinent question is whether Habermas's account of the requirements of modernization is correct.

In my view, it is not. For none of the various arguments Habermas offers to support the peculiar thesis is convincing. He offers four lines of argument for the view, but none is fully developed.

The first is that the freedom of religious expression guaranteed by the liberal state "only makes sense if all citizens can be reasonably expected not to exclude the possibility that these contributions may have cognitive substance" (BNR, 139). That conclusion conflicts with the assumptions of Habermas's own discourse theory. Curtailing freedom of expression would violate what Habermas takes to be the communicative and discursive infrastructure of modern society, for such a requirement violates the rules of discourse that guarantee equal participation and freedom of expression.[50] Furthermore, as we have seen, for Habermas, religious discourses as ethical discourses make authentic ways of life possible. Not only is that good per se, but it is also essential to the process of generating legitimate law (BFN, 99, 155).[51] Neither the free flow of ethical discourse nor the production of legitimate law requires that secular citizens adopt a "politically agnostic" stance toward the possible truth of religion and participate in the translation of religious reasons into secular ones.[52]

The second argument is that but for the cognitive requirement on secularists and secular citizens, the possible truth of religion and a vital source of social meaning would be lost. But lost to whom? In Habermas's view, religious citizens are free to offer religious reasons in "civil society." Moreover, he believes that post-secular society is characterized by the persistence of religions. So contrary to the Weberian assumptions of his earlier theory, religion is not on the wane. This undermines his contention that the cognitive content of religion threatens to be lost unless successfully translated into secular arguments that make their way into law. It is not lost so much as confined to civil society. Besides, as several commentators have pointed out, and Habermas has himself acknowledged, success in translating religious arguments into secular language is hard to achieve.[53] So it is odd to claim that this is the *only* way that the cognitive and moral content of religious discourse can be preserved.

The third argument is that to cling to secularism is to fail to treat one's religious fellow citizens as equal partners in democratic discourse. Lafont counters rightly that although there may well be a civic duty on the part of secular citizens, if they are to respect their fellow citizens as equals, it only requires "democratic citizens to provide one another reasons that everyone can reasonably accept for the legislative decisions with which all must comply" (Lafont 2007, 250). It by no means implies that secularists must give up their scientistically motivated atheism in favor of "political agnosticism." I agree with Lafont that this feature of Habermas's approach, which is designed to avoid what he thinks would be "an unfair exclusion of religions from the public sphere" (FHN, 109), looks arbitrary, given that the point of the institutional filter was to allow all citizens to make any argument whatsoever, religious or not, in the informal public sphere (Lafont 2007, 248). Why should secularist arguments now be excluded from civil society?[54] Moreover, as I argued earlier, such an exclusion violates the pragmatic presuppositions of discourse, the very point of which is to ensure the inclusion of all voices and to ensure that all agents participate in discourse on an equal footing.[55]

The fourth argument Habermas offers is that, on pain of experiencing cognitive dissonance, secularist citizens, too, must overcome "their rigid and exclusive secular understanding" by opening their minds to the possible truth contents of religion and being willing participants in the process of sacred-to-secular translation (BNR, 138–39). Habermas's approach here is his usual one of rational reconstruction, which is supposed to work alongside the natural and social sciences and to be open to empirical confirmation. As a matter of fact, Habermas rarely refers to any empirical studies. However, he does make frequent use of the idea of "cognitive dissonance" from behavioral science. Now, Leon Festinger's classical theory of cognitive dissonance says that when two elements of knowledge conflict, the knower will experience pressure to reduce or eliminate the dissonance (Festinger 1985, 3). People can do this in various ways. One way is to change a cognitive element by modifying one's actions or views. But there are other ways; for example, one might add a new cognitive element that reconciles the conflicting elements or mitigates the conflict. Or, if one has control over it, one can change one's social or physical environment so that the reality to which the cognitive element responds is altered (Festinger 1985, 19).

Classical cognitive dissonance theory offers support to some of Habermas's claims. A religious believer's faith might well provoke dissonance because it conflicts with the results of natural science. Since the institutionalized authority of natural science is a comparatively permanent and pervasive feature of modern life, and is consequently difficult to deny or ignore, it is easier for religious citizens to reduce dissonance by "reconstructing articles of faith," as Habermas maintains (BNR, 138).[56]

It is quite different with "secularists," though, since their views are already consonant with secular culture (FHN, 108–109). They may well, like Richard Dawkins, view all religion as a kind of delusion, deny that citizens of faith are reasonable, and experience no dissonance (Dawkins 2006). However, if the persistence of religion and of secularists' interactions with citizens of faith indeed cause them to experience cognitive dissonance, secularists have options open to them that are foreclosed to religious citizens. They can comparatively easily change their social environment by not engaging with religion at all, thereby avoiding having their nonreligious or anti-religious views challenged.[57] Or they can add other cognitive elements, by, say, reading Marx, Freud, or Nietzsche on religion in addition to their diet of scientific naturalism and thus reduce dissonance by engaging with theories which dismiss the claims of religious consciousness. The point here is that cognitive dissonance theory—the only empirical theory to which Habermas refers—offers little to no support to Habermas's conclusion that secularists *must* "overcome their rigid and exclusive secularist self-understanding" in favor of "political agnosticism."

In sum, Habermas ends up with a view of the cognitive requirements of citizenship under post-secular social conditions, the normative status of which is unclear and which is peculiar and ultimately implausible in what it says is the requirement of "secularists" to abandon their scientific naturalism in favor of "political agnosticism." This peculiar thesis is unsupported by argument, and even by the very theories—of cognitive dissonance—that Habermas adduces in defense of it. Worse still, such a requirement would itself violate the rules of discourse, which guarantee equal participation and freedom of expression to all participants in discourse.[58] Surely the requirements of modernization cannot directly conflict with the communicative and discursive deep structure of modern society as Habermas has hitherto conceived it.

8.4 A FINAL ASSESSMENT OF RAWLS AND HABERMAS ON RELIGION AND PUBLIC REASON

Let's conclude by assessing the strengths and weaknesses of both positions. This is no easy task, because each theory is only sketched out and lacks important detail.

In Rawls, there is, in the final analysis, a *moral* duty on citizens to pursue public justifications for coercive legislation about matters of basic justice and essential constitutional matters and, where that justification fails, to show restraint by not adducing arguments based exclusively on nonpublic reasons. But once Rawls adds his "proviso," it is hard to say on whom that moral duty falls. For example, when and how can it be determined that the attempt to replace comprehensive or religious justification with public justification has failed, such that restraint should be exercised? It is hard to say. Rawls's statement that "the details of how to satisfy this proviso must be worked out in practice" is really just hand-waving (PL, 462).

Rawls's "proviso" appears to have come about from consideration of, among other examples, Martin Luther King Jr.'s campaign for civil rights. As a matter of fact, King argued against racial segregation both on the grounds of Christian values and on constitutional grounds, but, as Rawls notes, had he argued exclusively on the basis of Christian values, his speeches would still have satisfied the "proviso" because "these doctrines supported basic constitutional values . . . and . . . reasonable conceptions of political justice" (PL, 464).[59] It is not clear what it is about the example of Martin Luther King Jr. that warrants the shift from Rawls's initial idea of the requirements of public reason, which excluded all religious (comprehensive) reasons, to the much more permissive "proviso," since, though King argued explicitly against racial segregation on the basis of Christian values, he did not do so exclusively.[60] The shift is justified, if at all, because it permits more exclusively religious (or comprehensive) arguments into the public political forum. But it introduced a great deal of indeterminacy about what was to be morally permitted by the requirements of public reason, and what not.

That said, the major flaw in Rawls's theory is that it devolves so much onto the moral duty of individual citizens, for morality is a notoriously unreliable basis for political society. What if the civic-mindedness of citizens is simply not strong enough for them to follow the call of the duty of civility? What if it is all too easily overridden by comprehensive (nonpolitical) reasons? At best, the "true community" is not realized, and legislation appears as an external imposition on a significant number of citizens. At worst, theocracy and illiberality threaten in the event that religion-based legislation results and is imposed on nonreligious citizens.

The same cannot be said of Habermas's theory. In one respect, it is even more permissive than Rawls's, since it grants virtually unconditional permission to religious citizens to voice religious arguments in civil society (which is, in Habermas's view, part of the broad political domain). However, in another respect, it is far less permissive. Whatever happens in civil society, the institutional filter remains in place and acts like a backstop in case of a failure or erosion of the civic duty of public reason. Overall, I think this makes the idea of the secular state that Habermas's theory defends more robust than the one that Rawls defends. Habermas's theory entrusts more to the design of institutions and less to individual moral duty.

That said, Habermas's theory is lacking important detail about the crucial mechanism of the institutional translation filter. Who are the officials entrusted with the task of sacred-to-secular translation? How are they to carry their task out? How are they to distinguish between religious and nonreligious reasons? He does not say enough on these points. What he does say, namely that religious reasons are characterized by their "reference to the dogmatic authority of an inviolable core of infallible revealed truths" (BNR, 129) is not particularly helpful. Somewhere, there is an official with a red pen striking references to religion and scripture from the transcript of parliamentary debates. That official needs to know what to erase and why.

Habermas is also, in my view, far too optimistic about the possibility of finding secular equivalents for religious arguments. But if the translation task proves difficult or impossible, then nothing really changes, for in the political sphere, as he puts it, "only secular reasons count." In the worst-case scenario, religious citizens are permitted a say in the democratic procedure, but their voices simply won't be heard, or will be heard but won't be acted upon, because the political system speaks a different (secular) language.

Of course, this is to assume that the institutional component of Habermas's theory is where the action is. However, that seems a fair assumption. Whether religious and secular citizens in civil society succeed in finding good translations for religious arguments, and in feeding them into the political process—first in the informal and then in the formal public sphere—remains an independent variable in the theory. They may, or they may not. The institutional filter, by contrast, remains a fixed point. However, if one accepts Habermas's argument about the cognitive requirements on religious and secular citizens in the informal public sphere (which I do not), it turns out that public reason makes the peculiar prohibition on secularists asserting their scientistically or naturalistically based atheism and enjoins them to adopt political agnosticism instead. That is quite the reverse of the permissiveness and liberality shown toward religious citizens.

Overall, the civil society component of Habermas's theory exhibits the typical indeterminacies of discourse theory. Habermas never successfully makes clear what the normative status of the requirements of democratic citizenship is. Are the cognitive requirements of democratic citizenship under post-secular social conditions moral or ethical requirements? As I argued earlier, there are good reasons to think they can be neither. Of course, one can say that they are "just" political requirements, or requirements of democratic citizenship, but given that democratic discourse is supposed to put all kinds of reasons (moral, ethical, and pragmatic) into play, two questions arise: How much moral or ethical weight do they carry? And, if they carry any at all, how do they carry it without threatening the autonomy of the political system in exactly the same way for which Habermas criticizes Rawls, natural law theory, and civic republicanism?

Habermas never attempts to derive, or to reconstruct, these normative demands on citizens as functional requirements of the democratic system, as he does, say, with the system of rights in *Between Facts and Norms*. That would be an obvious move for him to make. (Though in one respect, it is good that he does not, because that would be to slide from the sideways-on perspective of the expert social theorist, who rationally reconstructs the principles and features of democratic practices, to the participant's perspective of citizens facing one another.) Consequently, Habermas, and his reconstructive theory, have nothing directly to say to the Catholic who lobbies parliament to abolish or ban physician-assisted suicide on religious grounds or to Israeli settlers who offer the Torah as grounds for occupying disputed territories. At best, his theory can lead indirectly to the advice that such arguments are politically otiose in a secular state and that democracy works better (that is, is better at producing legitimate laws) when such arguments are translated into secular terms and can be tested in discourse and fed into the political system.

The same complaint cannot, however, be leveled at Rawls. He is very clear that the requirements of public reason have normative, moral weight because they flow ultimately from the moral ideas and values inherent in the political culture. It is true that this assumes the existence of an isolable, readily identifiable subset of moral ideas, namely the political values, an assumption that Habermas, for his part, finds dubious. Nonetheless, Rawls and his theory of political liberalism can say to these citizens that they ought not to use such arguments as the exclusive grounds for the laws or policies they advocate. He can say, in addition, that if they succeed in realizing their legislative and policy aims on religious grounds, they will eventually destroy the "true community" in which citizens can "face one another openly" and the political good that is congruent with their civic duty. The "ought" of public reason has moral, political, and prudential normative weight.

That said, the very same assumption that affords Rawls this normative perspective, namely the assumption that justification in political theory just is political justification, forbids him from offering any sideways-on philosophical, sociological, or theoretical justifications for political liberalism and his attendant conception of public reason. For Rawls's theory is supposed to remain within the domain of the political and leave these other theories where they are. The chief difference is that Rawls offers a normatively heavy, but sociologically light, theory of public reason, whereas Habermas advances a rich explanatory theory that is, to the extent that its normative status is clear at all, normatively light.

CONCLUSION

As the argument of this book has shown, the Habermas–Rawls debate, its origins in the young Habermas's work and the early debate, its maturation in Habermas's and Rawls's respective mature works of political philosophy, *Between Facts and Norms* and *Political Liberalism*, the eventual exchange of the mid-1990s, and the debate on religion and public reason a decade later present a dynamic complex of arguments stained through by various interpretations and misinterpretations. The misinterpretations affect not just the two disputants but also many critics and commentators on the dispute and thus shape its effective history. Given how difficult it can be in philosophy to adjudicate a debate on a well-defined issue, with fixed positions on either side, keeping track of the arguments in the case of the Habermas–Rawls debate, let alone keeping score, is even trickier.

The obvious place to begin is with Rawls's argument against Habermas—for Rawls aims only one fundamental objection at Habermas's theory, which is typically right on the mark—that Habermas's discourse theory of law and democracy is comprehensive, whereas his is "an account of the political and limited to that" (RH, 132/47). In the introduction, I noted that more needs to be said about the various respects in which Habermas's theory can be rightly said to be comprehensive, and about what the alleged problem with this is. I have argued that there are two objections at play depending on whether the comprehensive doctrine imputed to Habermas is philosophical or moral.

That Habermas's discourse theory has a lot of associated background theory on which it depends, and is thus a comprehensive philosophical doctrine, is not in dispute. And no doubt this is objectionable, since it means Habermas's theory gets embroiled in needless controversies. Against that, I have argued, pace Rawls, that this poses no moral, practical, or political problem. Rawls thinks it does, but only because he assumes that political theory must answer to the strict demands of public reason, because justification in political theory is just political justification. But this assumption is itself, as Habermas counters, theoretically controversial. Moreover, that Rawls is unable to cut his theory entirely free from all such debates is some indication that the demand itself may be misplaced, although it remains the case that it is philosophically desirable to avoid taking hostages to theoretical fortune.

The objection that Habermas's discourse theory depends on a comprehensive moral doctrine is also true. It presupposes the truth of discourse ethics; that is, it presupposes that discourse ethics is the correct moral theory, and it presupposes the existence of the actually existing Kantian-pragmatic morality that is its object. The consequences are different and, in some respects, more serious for Habermas. They are serious not for the reasons Rawls gives, that is, because these presuppositions threaten the self-understanding of citizens who reasonably disagree with them and because the theory cannot support an overlapping consensus. They are serious because in Habermas's own conception of the autonomy of the political realm, legitimate law (and the political system in general) is and should be, as he claims, "morally freestanding" (BNR, 80, 262–63). It should be morally freestanding, Habermas claims, because in a constitutional democratic state, the authority of legitimate law does not depend on the authority of an antecedently given moral order. This is the rationale for his "logical genesis" of basic rights as functional requirements of the democratic process and his thesis that the principle of democracy is "derived" from the discourse principle and the form of law, independently of principle (U).

There is another criticism that Rawls does not press against Habermas as much as I think he should, although it is implied by Rawls's approach. This is the objection that Habermas, in spite of all his criticism of Rawls's approach for being too external and too philosophical, does not succeed in making the normative weight and status of his own theory clear, where Rawls does.

The basic difficulty here is that Habermas's approach, which is to offer a theory that is reconstructive and explanatory, although it engages the normative stances and ethical self-understanding of citizens in its reconstructions and explanations, does not allow Habermas as a theorist to base criticisms of the social and political order he reconstructs on those norms and values. Discourse ethics, Habermas maintains, limits itself to the clarification of the moral point of view. The discourse theory of law limits itself to explication of the conditions under which democratic procedures and discourse are legally institutionalized and administratively realized. Yet Habermas insists that his rational reconstructions provide "a critical standard against which actual practices—the opaque and perplexing reality of the constitutional state—can be assessed." (The German original has "can be assessed" [*beurteilt*], whereas the English translation has "could be evaluated" [BFN, 5; FG, 20]). But unless the standard is a normative one, such as a valid moral norm, the assessment it yields will not be normative. This does not affect *Between Facts and Norms* so much, for its characteristic approach of reconstructing the democratic process, and laying out the conditions of the production of legitimate law, affords Habermas a perspective from which he can explain how a democratic constitutional state functions when it functions as it should. But it leaves his theory of public reason without anything directly to say to the Catholic believers who oppose physician-assisted suicide on religious grounds.

Let me turn now to Habermas's criticisms of Rawls. Among various lines of criticism Habermas develops, three stand out as very productive.

First, Rawls does not say enough about the legal and institutional basis of democracy. The nearest he comes to offering a theory of democracy is his idea of public reason, and, as we have seen, that theory makes public justification ultimately a matter of individual civic morality.

This is closely related to a second line of criticism, which is that Rawls fails to do justice to the autonomy of the political realm. Of course, Rawls claims that *Political Liberalism* does just this, but it does so, Habermas argues, only by presupposing a domain of political values readily identifiable as political that are acceptable to all reasonable citizens and ready to serve as the sole basis of the political association of reasonable citizens.

In Habermas's eyes, the basis of our political lives together consists in democratic practice and procedures, the basic rights that these procedures presuppose, civil society as a source of communication and discourse, the political and legal systems, and the legitimate laws that flow as outputs from the legislative process.

The third productive line of criticism is that Rawls's conception of the political (and politics) is too narrow. The political, on Rawls's conception of it, becomes almost a term of art, an ideal of good conduct among reasonable citizens that bears little relation to the messier and more extensive business of normal politics. And this is true both at the bottom, where a handful of shared values, readily identifiable and ready for democratic politics, is supposed to provide the slender basis of the common life of reasonable citizens, and at the top, where public justifications are owed only for laws concerning matters of basic justice and constitutional essentials.

Fourth, Rawls can rightly say that his political conception of justice is anchored in real life because it is worked up from values inherent in the political culture and thus can be the focus of a consensus of the reasonable. Habermas, for his part, contends that his theory is realistic because it reconstructs and explicates norms and principles implicit in actual democratic procedures and because it focuses on the conditions of their legal institutionalization. Habermas can also fairly claim that his theory is more realistic to the extent that it is supported by empirical theories such as social theory and the sociology of law.[1]

Fifth, Habermas criticizes Rawls for failing to give due priority to the democratic process, in relation to liberal rights and freedoms, and to the conception of political justice. One aspect of this criticism is that Rawls leaves up to the philosopher—who works up a political conception of justice from the political values—what should be left to citizens.[2]

Finally, while writing this book, I was conscious that although I have said something about "why Habermas and Rawls," I have not really said anything about "why Habermas" and "why Rawls." Rather, I have assumed that the works of the two philosophers and their importance in contemporary politics, political philosophy, and social theory speak for themselves. Moreover, I have assumed that whoever values political justice and democratic legitimacy will be interested in what these two giants of political philosophy have to say on the matters. I hope readers will forgive me for that. Yet in the course of writing this book, it hardly escaped my notice that our current political actuality is moving ever further away from the moral and political vision of democracy that Habermas and Rawls championed. And this is not only due to spiraling inequality, the fracturing of political consensus, and the shift to the political extremes. Something even more precious is in jeopardy.

One of the greatest writers of the former Czechoslovakia, Bohumil Hrabal, wrote a book of short stories with the title *An Ad for a House I Do Not Wish to Live In Any Longer*, a line taken from a poem by the exiled Czechoslovakian poet Viola Fišerová. The house in question was a metaphor for postwar Czechoslovakia. A passage in the preface has stayed with me since I first read it:

> During this period, I was living with people who felt or knew that every era carries in its womb a child in whom one may not only place one's hopes, but through whom and with whom it is possible to go on living. They were people who had not forgotten the fundamental house rules of human coexistence and who were heroes if only because they had not succumbed to semantic confusion, but were able to call things and events by their real names, and recognize them for what they were.[3]

This passage can be taken out of context and applied to our own time.[4] Nowadays, it appears, as it did in Hrabal's time, though for different reasons, that the political elite not only live in different houses from those of the rest of us; they inhabit a different reality altogether. Never has it been more important to recall and to respect the fundamental house rules of human coexistence and to be prepared to call things and events by their proper names. Of course, there are many citizens, and many political philosophers among them, who have done this and continue to do so, but none more conscientiously than Habermas and Rawls.

NOTES

INTRODUCTION

1. Rawls to Habermas, June 8, 1992.
2. Morgenbesser to Rawls, July 31, 1991.
3. "OP" stands for "original position." See the discussion in chapter 2. For an explication of principle (U), see chapter 1, section 1.2.3.
4. See Rawls's 1993 seminars, Public Reason I and II. A reading list for these seminars indicates that Rawls knew Habermas's *Moral Consciousness and Communicative Action* and *Justification and Application* well and, among the secondary literature, had read the discussions of discourse ethics in McCarthy (1978), Baynes (1992), and the not-yet-published Rehg (1994).
5. Wolff stops short of making the judgment that the debate is an "embarrassing failure," but his report that others have come to that conclusion is accurate.
6. A rational reconstruction is an attempt to formulate and explicate norms or principles that are implicit in an existing practice of speech or argument. For a more detailed discussion, see chapter 1, section 1.2.9.
7. That said, some deny that thinking of Rawls as a Kantian is justified or helpful (Höffe 1984). Dreben writes, "Kant's talk about practical reason is useless for understanding Rawls" (Dreben 2003, 340; see also O'Neill 2015). And others maintain, interestingly, that the Hegelianism of both Habermas and Rawls is more salient than their Kantianism (Hedrick 2010; Gledhill 2011). Such claims have to be carefully handled, however, in the light of Rawls's criticism that Habermas's theory is "Hegelian" in the sense that it presupposes too many controversial philosophical doctrines (RH, 137/51). See also chapter 6, section 6.1.1.

8. See also Habermas to Rawls, November 20, 1992: "Our exchange moves anyway within the confines of a family quarrel."
9. Throughout this book, I refer to two sets of page numbers in RH and RPUR (see abbreviations list in frontmatter). The first page number is from the original 1995 publication in the *Journal of Philosophy*, and the second is from HRDP 2011: *Habermas and Rawls: Disputing the Political* (London: Routledge, 2011).
10. See, for example, Specter (2010, 209). In my heterodox view, very many of Habermas's critics conveniently tend to ignore the degree to which the apparently more radical Marxism of his mentors in Frankfurt, Adorno and Horkheimer, was always closely tied to the safety net of liberal democracy and the rule of law.
11. "To say that a law is a legitimate law is not to say that all reasonable citizens agree with it. That is why legitimacy is such a complex and interesting notion in political philosophy. What you really have to worry about in a liberal constitutional democracy is how, when a law is appropriately passed, it is binding on all citizens, even on those citizens who reasonably can differ with it. That is the problem of stability for the right reasons" (Dreben 2003, 326–27).
12. See chapter 2, particularly section 2.7.
13. In what follows, I use the term "discourse theory" as a deliberately broad term covering all of Habermas's work from *The Theory of Communicative Action* onward. By "discourse ethics," I refer only to Habermas's moral theory as set out in his various essays on the topic.

1. TWO NONRIVAL THEORIES OF JUSTICE

1. See Mulhall and Swift 1992, Freeman 2007, and Pogge 2007.
2. Munoz-Dardé 1998, 335–36.
3. Freeman 1996.
4. See O'Neill 2015, 74–75.
5. This point is due to Richard Brandt (see Scanlon 2003, 146).
6. Scanlon 2003, 144.
7. Though Rawls does not use the terms "narrow" and "wide" in *A Theory of Justice*, he later comes to the view that wide reflective equilibrium is "plainly the most important concept" (JFAR, 31).
8. This line of thinking was picked up and developed by David Gauthier (1986) in *Morals by Agreement*.
9. Most of what is included in *Justification and Application* appeared originally in *Erläuterungen zur Diskursethik*. I believe that Habermas's and Rawls's theories of justice are not, when properly understood, rival conceptions of justice at all, but two very different kinds of theory about two quite different, if not entirely unrelated, notions of justice. To my mind, these differences have not been sufficiently appreciated.
10. I have cited this from Rehg 1994, 62.
11. Habermas quotes Alexy 1983, 169, translated in Benhabib and Dallmayr 1995, 166.

12. In this manner, Habermas differentiates his approach of "weak transcendentalism" from Kant's transcendental deduction of the moral law (MCCA, 95–96).
13. In the English translation of *The Inclusion of the Other*, the biconditional "iff" is not formulated. Compare with the original, which states "*genau dann . . . wenn*" (DEA, 60). Still, this version of the principle is clearer than the one given in *Moral Consciousness and Communicative Action* (MCCA, 65).
14. One commentator argues that principle (U), just like the rules of discourse, is not in need of justification because it is an inescapable presupposition of the practice of argumentation. See Heath 2011a and 2014.
15. Habermas's reference to discourse ethics here alludes to the 1983 manuscript of *Moralbewusstsein und kommunikatives Handeln*, 53ff., which at the time was in press.
16. On this, see Ott 1996 and Lumer 1997.
17. In such societies, mature moral agents are assumed to have reached Kohlberg's stage 6 of moral consciousness. Habermas refers to these as "post-conventional" societies. See section 1.2.8 for a discussion of Kohlberg and the post-conventional level of moral consciousness.
18. Habermas also claims that premise 2 consists in the participants' knowledge of "what it means to discuss hypothetically whether norms of action should be adopted" (MCCA, 92, 198).
19. See Gunnarsson 2000, 97–99, and Finlayson 2000a.
20. See Finlayson 2000a and criticisms in Ott 1996, Lumer 1997, and Steinhoff 2009.
21. This gives rise to the suspicion that the rules of discourse, as Habermas reconstructs them, may not be universal across all types of discourse since they are so heavily moralized.
22. There is a good question, which Habermas does not address, about the extent to which "giving consideration" here is compatible with weighing interests against each other, disregarding some interests in favor of others or discounting them entirely.
23. "The moral problem is one which involves certain conflicting interests. All of those interests which are involved in conflict must be considered" (Mead 1967, 386).
24. Habermas has always been worried about positing outlandish metaphysical entities as the truth-makers for moral statements (see MCCA, 56, 62, 68, 76). Indeed he still is. For example, he claims that "it is to be doubted whether there are 'facts' to which moral statements 'fit' or 'correspond' in the same way as descriptive statements" (RW, 185 [WR, 55]).
25. Habermas is resistant to being labeled a noncognitivist, for he does not want discourse ethics to be lumped in with various early noncognitivist moral theories, for example, Ayer's and Stevenson's emotivism, with which it has little in common (see Ayer 1936; Stevenson 1979). That said, Habermas has more in common with the noncognitivist projectivist or expressivist theories of, say, Blackburn and Gibbard than he thinks (see Gibbard 1990; Blackburn 1993). He frequently adopts their characteristic talk of "projection" and "project"; for instance, he uses "*der Entwurf, einer ideal entworfenen sozialen Welt*" to describe the nature of the moral world as opposed to the natural one

(RW, 198ff.; see also DEA, 50; VE, 144). One should bear in mind, though, that Habermas's use of the word "project" is neo-Heideggerian and phenomenological rather than neo-Humean and empiricist.

26. "Thus we open up a conceptual space in which the concept of normative rightness, here in particular moral validity, can be housed. The rightness of moral norms (and of general normative utterances) . . . can then be understood in analogy to truth" (SE, 91).
27. Letter to the author, April 30, 2004.
28. I have my doubts about this because of the fact that (on most theories of truth) truth outstrips justifiability, whereas rightness in Habermas's account of it consists only in (idealized) justifiability (see Finlayson 2005).
29. This looks to be very close (almost equivalent) to the discourse principle (D), which Habermas formulates as follows: "Only those norms can claim validity that could meet with the acceptance of all concerned in practical discourse" (BFN, 107; DEA, 59; FG, 138; MCCA, 66).
30. See section 1.2.3.
31. See Finlayson 2000b.
32. It is not as easy as Habermas and McCarthy suggest to spell out exactly where the difference between dialogical and monological agreement lies. Indeed, it is not obvious that there is a tenable distinction between "dialogical" and "monological" moral theories. Nevertheless, in spite of such criticism, Habermas continues to maintain that dialogical approaches are distinct from and superior to monological approaches.
33. "The moral problem is one which involves certain conflicting interests. All of those interests which are involved in conflict must be considered" (Mead 1967, 386).
34. Kohlberg worked in the tradition of the genetic structuralism of Jean Piaget, whose 1932 work, *The Moral Judgment of the Child*, was significantly influenced by the moral philosophy of Immanuel Kant (see also MCCA, 8).
35. Such formal criteria define judgments and reasoning as involving "a moral point of view" or as being "principled" (where moral principles are distinguished from concrete moral rules and laws). "The veil of ignorance exemplifies not only the formalist idea of universalizability, but the formalist idea of Hare and others that a moral judgment must be reversible, that we must be willing to live with our judgment or decision when we trade places with others in the situation being judged" (Kohlberg 1981, 197; see also 201; for Kohlberg's criteria of adequacy, see Kohlberg 1981, 134–35).
36. However, he continues for ease of reference to use "discourse ethics" as the proper name for the theory (JA, 1).
37. Compare with Rawls, who in *A Theory of Justice* has a variety of notions of the good that contrast with a notion of the right constituted by the principles of justice. These include (1) goodness as rationality, (2) primary social goods, (3) permissible comprehensive doctrines of the good, (4) the idea of political virtues, and (5) the good of the well-ordered political society (CP, 449).
38. For a highly informative account of Habermas's engagement with Gehlen, to which my brief summary owes much, see Pensky 2008, 211–35.

2. HABERMAS'S EARLY CRITICISMS OF RAWLS

1. Although some of the main ideas had been sketched out in part III of *Legitimation Crisis*, they had not yet been disentangled from Habermas's theory of political legitimacy and in that respect did not yet count as a discourse ethics or moral theory proper.
2. See Finlayson 2013 for a critical analysis of the common interpretation of Habermas's critical social theory.
3. See also Daniels 2003 and Scanlon 2003.
4. In a way, this is not a clear-cut example since human rights are political and legal entities, not just moral ones. However, as I will show in chapter 3, Habermas thinks that human rights have a fully moral content and that they are the legal and institutional embodiment of valid moral norms.
5. Rawls's notes on part III of his 1986 graduate seminars on this topic show that he was wondering what this criticism actually amounted to as he took up some challenges from communitarian critics.
6. Though it was influential, it seems not to have influenced Rawls. In the original version of *Political Liberalism*, there is only one passing reference to Michael Sandel (PL, 27n). Moreover, Rawls explicitly denies that changes in the later chapters of *Political Liberalism* were motivated by criticism from communitarians (PL, xvii). However, Sandel's objection was influential in that it provoked robust defenses of Rawls by his followers and shaped what I'm calling the "early debate."
7. Sandel represents Rawls's point thus: "What matters above all are not the ends we choose, but our capacity to choose them" (Sandel 1984, 86).
8. "It is as though the unencumbered self had begun to come true—less liberated than disempowered, entangled in a network of obligations unassociated with any act of will, and yet unmediated by those common identifications . . . that would make them tolerable" (Sandel 1984, 94).
9. That this is what Rawls thinks can be seen from his remark that "much of the objection to the conception of the person and the idea of human nature springs from not seeing the idea of the original position as a device of representation" (PL, xxiv; see also Pettit 2005).
10. The first claim is also unoriginal. In 1976, Ernst-Wolfgang Böckenförde, to take just one prominent example from the German context, argued that "the liberal secularized state is nourished by presuppositions it cannot itself guarantee," namely Christian morality. For Habermas's response, see BNR, 101; DS, 21–47; and Gordon 2013.
11. See chapter 1, section 1.1.6.
12. See discussion in the introduction.
13. See also Putnam 2002 and Habermas's response in Habermas 2000.
14. In my view, neither Taylor nor Sandel pays enough attention to the fact that, while discourse ethics is a broadly Kantian general moral theory, Rawls's is not, despite certain comments that suggest it is. However, since discourse ethics is a moral theory, Taylor's critique poses a serious threat. For the relevance of this misinterpretation, see section 2.5.
15. *In a Different Voice* was published the same year as Michael Sandel's *Liberalism and the Limits of Justice*.

16. "In sum, stage 3 notions fit best the institutions of family and friendship that can be grounded on concrete, positive interpersonal relationships" (Kohlberg 1981, 150; see also 118, 148–50, 215, 410).
17. In a later essay, Gilligan explicitly argues that what she calls an "ethic of care" is "fundamentally incompatible" with an "ethic of justice"—a conclusion, incidentally, not supported by the evidence presented in her earlier study (Gilligan 1986, 238; Thompson 1998, 53).
18. She might be claiming that both the theory and what it is a theory of (namely a conception of morality and a set of moral practices) are incomplete. Still, in the first view, the incompleteness is a fault in the theory, whereas in the second, it is a fault in the practice that is the object of the theory.
19. Another feature of the feminist critique is the attempt to harness deconstruction and post-structuralism for social and political purposes. For example, Iris Marion Young argues that the Kantian attempt to ground ethics and politics on ideals of impartiality and universality gives rise to a whole series of related exclusions of "particularity," "difference," "desire," and "affectivity and the body" (Young 1987, 60–69).
20. I'll confine myself to a discussion of Benhabib's "classic" article "The Generalized and the Concrete Other: The Kohlberg–Gilligan Controversy and Feminist Theory" because it has been so influential on the field. See Maihofer 1998, 386.
21. Philosophically speaking, "abstract" means disengaged, dispersed, or separate, but it can also refer to something's being derived by a mental process. "Concrete" literally means grown together, cohesive, or compounded and figuratively means definite and actual.
22. Marx's notion of "real abstraction" and Weber's notion of "value generalization" are two examples of real social processes of generalization.
23. Hegel captures this idea when he explains why the beautiful days of Greek art are past: "The reflective culture of our life today makes it a necessity for us, in respect of our will no less than our judgment, to adhere to general points of view, and to regulate particular matters according to them so that general forms, laws, duties, rights, [and] maxims are what have validity as grounds of determination and are the chief regulative force" (Hegel 1993, 12).
24. Recall that not only had Kohlberg read and appropriated Mead's work, but also explicitly based his conception of stage 6 on Rawls's device of choosers in the original position behind the veil of ignorance.
25. By "contemporary moral theory," Benhabib means the theories ranked by Kohlberg at stage 6: Kant's ethics, Rawls's theory of justice, and discourse ethics.
26. Somewhat later, Rawls responded to this objection to justice as fairness by pointing out that gender oppression and exclusions that matter can be revealed and criticized by his principles of justice. Everything here turns on whether the domestic sphere falls within the basic structure (PL, 466–71). If the private and domestic sphere exists outside the basic structure, then, since women perform a disproportionate share of domestic labor, justice as fairness neglects women's interests. Rawls would be vulnerable to this criticism. If, on the other hand, the domestic and family sphere is not excluded from the basic structure, then the principles of justice apply there, too, and provide a relevant standard of criticism.

27. The friendly reception of Habermas's discourse ethics within feminist social theory can be gauged from the contributions to three important volumes: Benhabib and Cornell 1987, Benhabib 1992, and Meehan 1995. For a useful survey of the feminist reception of discourse ethics, see Meehan 2000.
28. This is linked to the charge of "epistemological blindness to the concrete other" (Benhabib 1992, 164–65).
29. This strongly resembles Sandel's rejection of the "unencumbered" self.
30. According to Rawls, and more recently Okin, this is exactly what the veil of ignorance requires the occupants of the original position to do. Since they do not know whose shoes they will occupy once the veil of ignorance is lifted, they have to find principles of justice that can be welcomed from the point of view of every other concrete, flesh-and-blood citizen (Okin 1989a, 101; Okin 1989b, 248).
31. Discourse ethics sets out to do exactly what Benhabib claims only her "interactive universalism" can do, namely "recognize the dignity of the generalized other through an acknowledgement of the moral identity of the concrete other" (Benhabib 1992, 164).
32. In discourse ethics, this can be seen in his attempt to capture the moral standpoint in a single principle: (U).
33. Exponents of what I call, following Rehg, "the political reading," include Benhabib (1994, 27), Cohen and Arato (1992, 231), Ferrara (1985, 45–74), Heller (1985, 5–17), Reese-Schäfer (1994), and Wellmer (1991, 193).
34. Rehg is sympathetic to the "political reading" but shies away from endorsing it himself.
35. Recently, Baynes has claimed that the discourse theory of law is "a sophisticated version of consent theory" (Baynes 2016, 135). One could say just the same about discourse ethics. This demonstrates the same point, namely that it looks more like a political theory (of legitimacy) than a normative moral theory.
36. That said, G. H. von Wright is one modern moral theorist who contends that the principle of justice (as he construes it) is "the cornerstone of the idea of morality" (von Wright, 1963, ch. 10).

3. HABERMAS'S *BETWEEN FACTS AND NORMS*

1. See chapter 2, section 2.1.
2. See Finlayson 2014 on the features and alleged virtues of immanent critique.
3. For an analysis of Rawls's idea of an "overlapping consensus of reasonable doctrines" and Habermas's understanding of this idea, see chapter 4, section 4.3.1.
4. Hedrick situates Habermas in a long line of critics of Rawls including, among others, Kurt Baier (1989), G. A. Cohen (2008), Jean Hampton (1989), Chandran Kukathas and Philip Pettit (1990), and Joseph Raz (1990) (Hedrick 2010, 201n16).
5. This is closer to the critique urged by commentators such as Borman (2011).
6. See Hugh Baxter's discussion of the structure (Baxter 2011).
7. See the discussion of the principle of democracy in section 3.3.3.
8. See the discussion of Habermas's sociology of religion in chapter 8.

9. In 1976, E. W. Böckenförde formulated a dictum about the foundations of the modern state that was to become a reference point for political theory in Germany thereafter: "The liberal, secularized state is nourished by presuppositions that it cannot itself guarantee" (Böckenförde 1976). Habermas always denied that the modern state must be embedded in a single ethical world view, such as Christian morality. That said, he has modified his answer to Böckenförde's dictum, as his early Weberian secularist theory of modernization has given way to a post-secular view that sees religions as indispensable sources of social meaning; see chapter 8. His skepticism toward Böckenförde's thesis can be seen from the fact that the title of his essay "Pre-political Foundations of the Constitutional State?" ends in a question mark (BNR, 101). For more on Böckenförde and Habermas's engagement with him, see Gordon 2013 and Holst and Molander 2015.
10. However, one must not forget the validity that is operative within the laws' facticity. Laws are authoritative also *because they have been properly enacted in accordance with legally enshrined decision procedures*. This confers legitimacy on them. That said, though Habermas inherits this point from Niklas Luhmann's systems theory, he wants to avoid what he thinks of as Luhmann's mistake, which is to claim that conformity with the relevant decision procedure is necessary and sufficient for validity, a view which collapses the very distinction between facticity and validity. See BFN, 48–51, and Luhmann 2001, 31–34.
11. See also TIO, 257.
12. Later on, he makes an equivalent claim: that "legal norms . . . claim to be in accord with moral norms [*Moralnormen*]; that is, not to violate them" (BFN, 155; see also FG, 193).
13. Baynes, indeed, makes it stronger still by claiming that the public political culture must contain a moral component—the "core morality"—and thereby satisfy the validity requirement: "Citizens must simultaneously both presuppose and strive to articulate a basic political consensus . . . focused on the idea of a core morality that all citizens can endorse as valid for the same (publicly available) reasons" (Baynes 2016, 179).
14. For more on this question, see Finlayson 2016.
15. Habermas writes, "I understand 'action norms' as temporally, socially, and substantively generalized behavioural expectations" (BFN, 107).
16. One cannot help noticing that in these five schemas, Habermas's "logical genesis" of rights broadly mirrors the "Whiggish" historical order in which the historical sociologist T. H. Marshall, in his seminal lectures *Citizenship and Social Class*, claimed that civil, political, and social rights were won by working men in the course of the eighteenth, nineteenth, and twentieth centuries. The first three are rights to liberty, association, and legal protection. The fourth category comprises rights to political participation, and the fifth comprises material and social rights (Marshall 1992).
17. See Larmore 1995, Cohen 1999, Forst 1999, and Rummens 2006.
18. One can see this in a passage from Weber, cited by Habermas, where Weber claims that the most stable and effective legal order is one that has "the prestige of 'legitimacy' " (Weber 1978, 31, cited in BFN 68).

19. "From a normative point of view this corresponds to the assumption that moral and civic autonomy are co-original, and can be explained with the help of a parsimonious discourse principle that merely expresses the meaning of post-traditional requirements of justification" (BFN, 107).
20. Compare with Rousseau, who famously wrote in *Du Contrat Sociale*, "Dans un cité bien conduit *chacun* vole aux assemblées" (In a well-run city all citizens hasten to the assmblies). Rousseau 1964, 429.
21. Habermas claims that overall, "Kant suggests more of a liberal reading of political autonomy, Rousseau a republican reading" (BFN, 100). I tend to think that Kant is more of a republican and closer to Rousseau than Habermas does. But Habermas is right to point out that the contract in Kant's view is merely a regulative idea that serves as a hypothetical test of legitimacy.
22. This is the point he wants to make against Luhmann. See section 3.3.3.
23. Habermas also refers to the informal public sphere as "civil society," which marks it as a nongovernmental part of the political process.
24. For much the same reason, Baxter suggests that in Habermas's theory, the endorsement of democratic procedures of argumentation and legislation takes the place of the endorsement of substantive outcomes of those procedures. If being both subject and author of the law is implied by the latter, then a legitimate law would be an impossibility, or at most a rarity (Baxter 2011, 100). But the main thrust of Habermas's theory is that because citizens can (and do) endorse the democratic procedures, they can also endorse their outcomes; that is, they can assent to the latter as justified, and they are justified to the extent that democratic procedures of legislation channel public reasons into the decision-making process.
25. The best discussion of this phenomenon as it appears in the context of Habermas's theory of law is provided by Baxter (2011, 33–35).
26. "Government by law is designed to spell out the system of rights in terms of a constitutional order in which the legal medium can become effective as a power transformer that reinforces the weakly integrating currents of a communicatively structured lifeworld" (BFN, 176). Power, in the form of bureaucracy, makes administrative decisions that enter the legal process and end up as legitimate law.

4. RAWLS'S *POLITICAL LIBERALISM*

1. "The diversity of reasonable comprehensive religious, philosophical, and moral doctrines found in modern democratic societies is . . . a permanent feature of the public culture" (PL, 36).
2. "Pluralism is a doctrine about the nature of a value. It asserts that the form of moral concern, as well as the forms of self-realization, are in the end not one, but many. It stands opposed therefore to religious and metaphysical conceptions of a single source of value" (Larmore 1996, 167).

3. I say "true or correct" because someone might hold a philosophical doctrine that includes a noncognitivist account of morality and denies that any moral view is true.
4. The term "reasonable" has no entry in the index of *A Theory of Justice*, indicating that it is not a term of art. Compare the indices of *Justice as Fairness: A Restatement* and *Political Liberalism*, in which the term "reasonable" has more entries than the term "rational" (JFAR, 212; PL, 513–14).
5. That said, we must not assume that reasonableness is therefore dialogical in Habermas's sense.
6. Nevertheless, the reasonable can be public in scope or reach (that is, the universal applicability of the results of reasoning) without needing also to be public in participation, that is, in the way in which the results are reached.
7. For example, see Enoch 2015, 12.
8. I find this a puzzling claim. On the one hand, my first thought is that if we allow that Plato's *Republic*, Aristotle's *Politics*, and Hobbes's *Leviathan* (not to mention Durkheim and Weber) belong to the history of moral philosophy, then the claim is not true. If we do not allow this but claim instead that these and other figures belong to the history of political philosophy, then Rawls's claim about moral philosophy is entirely unsurprising.
9. According to Rawls in *Political Liberalism*, a well-ordered society is one in which everyone accepts and knows that others accept the same conception of justice and in which the basic structure of the society is known to satisfy that conception and citizens have a normally effective sense of justice; that is, they are willing to propose and abide by fair terms, provided others do likewise (PL, 35).
10. If it is only, or primarily, the argument from congruence that rests on comprehensive premises, as, for example, Samuel Freeman, Gerald Gaus, and Paul Weithman argue, then it follows that *A Theory of Justice* and *Political Liberalism* can appropriately be seen as part of the same project (Freeman 2003; Weithman 2010; Gaus 2013).
11. On the difference between the 1993 and the 1996 paperback versions of *Political Liberalism*, see Dreben 2003 and Gaus 2013.
12. Essentially, I agree with Dreben (2003) that legitimacy (rather than justice) is the central guiding concept in *Political Liberalism*.
13. It has been objected that the metaphor of the Venn diagram encourages the mistaken view that comprehensive doctrines are extant sets of propositions and that the liberal comes along and picks out the intersection set. It has also been objected that the metaphor neglects to consider the intrinsic significance and priority of the political values and makes the political conception look too contingent. Note, however, that these objections do not apply to my interpretation. First, the political values have to meet criteria other than just falling in the overlap. Second, I distinguish between the political values, as the existing content of the political conception of justice, and the political conception itself, which is an arrangement of those values into the theory. The latter, a module that can fit into any comprehensive doctrine, may require a rearrangement of the other comprehensive ideas. See section 4.3.3.

14. For example, when discussing the exclusion of the religious reasons, Philip L. Quinn interprets Rawls thus: "Comprehensive doctrines lie outside the limits of public reasons" (Quinn 1995, 43). See my discussion of the distinction between the exclusive and inclusive senses of "comprehensive doctrine" in section 4.3.3.
15. Quine 1952, 41.
16. Rawls does not make such a distinction. However, I believe that such a distinction is implicit in Rawls's position and can be helpful in distinguishing between his theory and Habermas's.
17. Rawls does not, but could, adduce the passage from Weber in support of his view that Habermas cites in *Between Facts and Norms* (BFN, 68).
18. On this distinction, see chapter 6, section 6.1.2.
19. Rawls has the exclusive sense in mind when he writes that nonpublic, thus comprehensive, reasons can be offered by citizens in the course of political advocacy if done "in ways that strengthen the ideal of public reason itself" (PL, 247n; see also xlii, l, 46, 386).
20. Rawls has the inclusive sense in mind when he claims that a "reasonable and effective political conception may bend comprehensive doctrines toward itself" (PL, 144, 246).
21. Otherwise, to "accept" and to "affirm" are the same. Throughout *Political Liberalism*, Rawls talks about citizens affirming their comprehensive doctrines, not just the political conception. Thanks to A. R. Booth for this point.
22. Hedrick writes that Rawls "believes that a freestanding theory must be substantive: it culls beliefs about political justice, which are validated within privately held ethical world views, and works them up into a conception that could be the object of an overlapping consensus" (Hedrick 2010, 83). Hedrick here uncritically accepts many of Habermas's misconceptions. For one thing, "comprehensive doctrines" for Rawls are not equivalent to ethical world views. More seriously, the consensus of shared substantive political ideas already exists in the overlap of reasonable comprehensive doctrines and makes possible (and likely) a consensus of reasonable citizens on a political conception worked up from those ideas. Finally, it is not true that a conception of justice is validated *only* privately. As Rawls later goes on to explain, "full justification" is not the only kind on offer. Hedrick's criticism of *Political Liberalism* as involving "a one-way dependence of the public on the private" is vitiated because it is premised on these various misconceptions of Rawls's position (Hedrick 2010, 84).
23. On this, see Coicaud, 2002.
24. In *Political Liberalism*, Rawls assumes that neither congruence with the nonpolitical values of unreasonable citizens nor their agreement is a necessary condition of political legitimacy, though it is of course desirable.
25. See the discussion of Luhmann's theory of legitimation by procedure in chapter 3.
26. Whether this would count as legitimacy in Weber's sense is not clear. According to Amanda Greene, if political domination is based merely on fear of sanctions and lacks an associated belief in the validity of power, it is not legitimate. So the question for Weber would be, does compliance with law based on a *modus vivendi* include or exclude a belief in the validity of power on the part of the compliant (Greene, forthcoming)?

27. For a detailed analysis of the "realist" criticism of *Political Liberalism*, see Gledhill 2012.
28. In making this distinction, I follow Ciszewski (2016, 83–85).
29. "Public reason in PL is the reasoning of legislators, executives (presidents, for example), and judges (especially those of a supreme court, if there is one). It includes also the reasoning of candidates in political elections and of party leaders and others who work in their campaigns, as well as the reasoning of citizens when they vote on constitutional essentials and matters of basic justice" (RH, 140/53n13; PL, 382).
30. We will look at Rawls's conception of public reason in more detail and more critically in chapter 8.
31. So do Freeman (1996) and Scanlon (2003).
32. This is Ciszewski's judgment, and I believe it is correct (Ciszewski 2016, 90).
33. Laden 2011, 144.
34. In an interview with Eduardo Mendieta, Habermas observes how far the world order is from abstract principles of global justice: "Just imagine for a moment that the G7 nations assumed global responsibility, and unified themselves through policies that met John Rawls's (contractualistically grounded) second principle of justice" (RR, 165). It is true that in this example Habermas is specifically talking about global distributive justice, but the argument applies also to domestic political justice.

5. HABERMAS'S "RECONCILIATION THROUGH THE PUBLIC USE OF REASON"

1. I include, where relevant, remarks from the follow-up article that appeared in *The Inclusion of the Other*, " 'Reasonable' Versus 'True.' " However, since that article also includes some novel claims, and positions different from those in the earlier article, I'll devote an excursus to this at the end of part III.
2. "Our exchange moves anyway within the confines of a family quarrel" (Habermas to Rawls, November 20, 1992).
3. See Burton Dreben's account of *Political Liberalism* (Dreben 2003, 320).
4. See JA, 113–33; JS, 220; and MCCA, 119–33.
5. Note how closely this resembles the communitarian and feminist objections to the detached, rational, self-interested idea of the person assumed by the original position. See Sandel 1982 and Taylor 1985.
6. To be precise, judgments of right and wrong are not binary in that way, since an action that is not wrong is not thereby right, for it may be permitted rather than enjoined.
7. The textual evidence here is slender. McMahon adduces passages from Rehg that endorse strong dialogicality (Rehg 1991, 40–43 Rehg 1994, 62–75; McMahon 2000, 515): "Until all can agree on what the relevant reasons require, each must suspend judgment" (McMahon 2000, 521). Habermas endorses Rehg's interpretation (BFN, 109n38; JA, 32n18) and does talk of discourse involving a "jointly and publicly reached consensus" (MW, 101).
8. Rawls describes this ancillary difference as obtaining between Habermas's device of representation, namely "the ideal speech situation," and his own device of representation, "the original position" (PL, 132).

9. See chapter 2, section 2.5. Much of the literature up to the present date has focused on the contrast between the original position and principle (U). A representative sample of the commentators who endorse the interpretation I reject includes Benhabib (1992), McCarthy (1994), Moon (1995), Gutmann and Thompson (1996), McMahon (2002), Michelman (2002, 398), Skinner et al. (2002), Nussbaum (2003), and Bankovsky (2012). In my view, this focus of inquiry is misplaced.
10. It is the consensus view in the literature that Habermas and Rawls failed to understand each another. It is most trenchantly expressed by Christopher McMahon (2002) and was the near-unanimous view of a panel of Cambridge political philosophers including Onora O'Neill and Andrew Kuper (Skinner et al. 2002). More recently, Joseph Heath has remarked on the "relatively low level of philosophical engagement between the two thinkers" (Heath 2011a, 117), and A. S. Laden has claimed that Rawls and Habermas "end up talking past one another" (Laden 2011, 135). Jonathan Wolff (2008) describes the debate as "an exchange that other readers have felt to be a somewhat embarrassing failure of two of the greatest contemporary minds to meet." Habermas has also been frank enough to acknowledge that initially he did not grasp the "true significance" of *Political Liberalism* (Reply 2, 284).
11. See chapter 1, section 1.2.5.
12. Indeed, it is suggested by his remark that from their various perspectives, reasonable citizens will judge that "political values are very great values to be realized in the framework of their political and social existence" (RH, 147/168). He does not state that these values enjoy special political significance because they happen to be shared, although that is also true.
13. Habermas claims that Forst helped him to come to grips with Rawls's theory: "I relied on his advice on first reading the unpublished manuscript of Political Liberalism" (HRDP, 295). So I'm assuming that Forst is not only reporting Habermas's view here, but to some extent also endorsing it.
14. To show how adhesive this interpretation is, in Habermas's mind, observe the claims about Rawls's *Political Liberalism* that Habermas makes in 2010 in a review of Rawls's bachelor of arts thesis, *A Brief Inquiry Into the Meaning of Sin and Faith*. Here, Habermas repeats two claims: (1) that the freestanding justification of the political conception of justice in *Political Liberalism* is "supposedly independent of moral beliefs" and (2) that Rawls vacillates between a justification of the political conception that is merely instrumental in securing stability and one that is intrinsic and grounds its validity (Habermas 2010, 451–52).
15. Or, "close to true in the sense that it is endorsed by a true doctrine" (PL, 153n19).
16. Habermas's remark comparing the modesty of his approach with that of Rawls at the end of "Reconciliation Through the Public Use of Reason" has been the subject of much discussion (Hedrick 2010, 77, 90–99; Forst 2011, 156; Gledhill 2011, 198).
17. One might object that the method of reflective equilibrium involves checking that these principles conform to our considered intuitions about justice. This might, as Tim Carter put it to me, be seen as an external check on the choice of principles of justice, although considered intuitions are not quite an "independent criterion for the right result." And although they are separate from the principles, they are not external to the whole procedure, or to the result of that procedure, especially if the original position is seen as a

vehicle for bringing the principles into reflective equilibrium. Still, the fact that reflective equilibrium is central to Rawls's endeavor indicates that Rawls's arguments in *A Theory of Justice* and *Political Liberalism* are not straightforward examples of pure procedural justice.

18. Habermas also claims in an interview with Michael Haller (cited chapter 3, section 3.1.2.) that, by contrast with Rawls and Nozick, he does not "design the norms of a well-ordered society on the drafting table" (PF, 101).
19. The example is complicated in the sense that human rights are not only moral but also legal and political entities.
20. See chapter 1, section 1.2.1.
21. Hedrick remarks that the contrast Habermas draws is not one between Rawls's substantive theory of political justice and Habermas's strictly procedural theory, but rather one between a substantive theory of justice for political society and a theory of democracy and law that is procedural: "A theory of political justice, in Rawls's sense, is a theory that advances substantive principles; a theory of law and democracy, in Habermas's sense, is not. Law and democracy are, instead, the normative structures and procedures that make possible the practice of rational and collective self-governance" (Hedrick 2010, 83).
22. See Flynn's response to this criticism (Flynn 2003, 440–42). See also Baynes 2016, 169–70, 177, and in response, Finlayson 2017.
23. "The *performative meaning* of this practice, which is merely set forth and explicated in constitutional principles and the system of rights, already contains as a doctrinal core the (Rousseauian–Kantian) idea of the self-legislation of voluntarily associated citizens who are both free and equal. This idea is not 'formal' in the sense of being 'value-free.' However, it can be fully developed in the course of constitution-making processes that are not based on the previous choice of substantive values, but rather on democratic procedures" (Rosenfeld and Arato 1998, 406).
24. That said, Samuel Freeman's claim that Rawls and Habermas do not disagree in holding that some ultimate standards are needed when cultural values conflict, that matters need to be resolved in legitimate ways, and that nothing will do except "substantive principles of justice and other moral norms" is too simplistic (Freeman 2000, 409). They do disagree. For Habermas, only the democratic procedure (and its inputs from moral discourse) can legitimately regulate such disputes between democratic citizens in the absence of shared ethical or cultural values; it is just that the procedure is richer in substance than Habermas makes out.
25. On the importance of the idea that public reasons constitute a political relation in which citizens can face each other openly, see Laden 2011, 135–53.
26. If that is right, then Hedrick's claim that the descriptivist critique applies to Rawls but not to Habermas, which is a rearticulation of Habermas's "internal criticism of Rawls," is moot (Hedrick 2010, 33).
27. That Habermas interprets Rawls in this way is shown by his complaint against Rawls that "the concept of practical reason cannot be drained of moral substance and morality cannot be relegated to the black box of comprehensive doctrines" (MW, 112).

28. David Enoch agrees, though he makes this claim about public reason accounts of legitimacy in general (Enoch 2015, 24).
29. Until the last word, this reads like a correct description of Rawls's project and its intentions. The objection, then, must turn on the pejorative sense of a constraint that operates *externally*. Generally, what is supposed to be bad about external constraints is that they are assumed to be irrelevant, or inappropriate, or imposed by force on a recalcitrant object. But Habermas seems to have in mind a more weighty objection. We shall return to this in chapter 6, section 6.3.2, in which I analyze Rawls's reply.
30. See chapter 1, section 1.1.6.
31. See chapter 4, section 4.3.4.
32. Habermas explicitly refers to Rawls's Tanner lectures, "The Basic Liberties and Their Priority," which formed the basis of chapter 8 of *Political Liberalism* (RPUR, 128/42n24). This line of criticism is an extended version of the external criticism of Rawls in *Between Facts and Norms*, which also targets the "two-stage" justification (see chapter 3, section 3.1). However it draws out what Habermas considers to be the concrete political implications of that criticism.
33. In "Reply to Habermas," Rawls sketches an argument that "connects the basic liberties into a fully adequate scheme of the two kinds of liberties" in six steps. The argument from the original position is the final step (RH, 167/79).
34. Rawls, who considers this difference between their two theories as of secondary importance, deals somewhat cursorily with it in Reply 1 (3) (RH, 139–40/52–3).
35. It may seem unfair and cavalier of me to dismiss all of Habermas's objections regarding the design of the original position (section 5.1) and most regarding the idea of the overlapping consensus (section 5.2). In my defense, first, I'll repeat my assessment that "Reconciliation Through the Public Use of Reason" shoots out a whole array of criticisms, many of which were carried over from the early debate and only a few of which apply to *Political Liberalism* and thus to the exchange and the dispute. Second, I note that my judgment here of which of Habermas's criticisms are valid and important coincides with that of Rawls, who devotes the majority of his long "Reply to Habermas" (sections III–V) to answering the objections Habermas sets out regarding private and public autonomy (section 5.3).

6. RAWLS'S "REPLY TO HABERMAS"

1. Sections 6.1, 6.2, and 6.3 of this chapter thus mirror the order of exposition in "Reply to Habermas," namely sections I, II, and III–V, respectively.
2. See Habermas's remarks (MW, 93; TIO, 77).
3. On the role of the "core morality" in Habermas, see Baynes 2016 and Finlayson 2017.
4. On this, see Rees 2018, 21–45. For an account of Habermas's view of the role of religion in modernization, and in secular and post-secular society, see chapter 8.
5. See section 6.3.
6. This is the "common view" of *Political Liberalism* that forms the object of Quong's critique. See chapter 4, section 4.3.4.

7. Quong does not actually claim that Rawls holds the widespread view. There is an important passage in *Political Liberalism* that suggests that he does not, in which he claims that he is looking to see whether "the fundamental idea of society as a fair system of cooperation" can be the "focus of a reasonable overlapping consensus" (PL, 39–40). If this is his view, he cannot think that such a consensus is sought only at the final stage of justification, nor can he believe that only the political conception of justice can be the focus of a reasonable overlapping consensus, and not the fundamental ideas and values of which it is an arrangement.
8. Recall Habermas's validity requirement: "Anything valid should also be capable of public justification. Valid statements deserve the acceptance of everyone for the same reasons" (MW, 101; TIO, 86). Hedrick's in many ways fine-grained and well-informed discussion of this question is marred by the same mistaken interpretation of public justification in *Political Liberalism*: "Even in the ideal case, in which the semantic content of the principles of justice is fixed by a fairly explicit consensus, there is an important sense in which the conception is not shared: It is embedded in the various comprehensive doctrines of citizens" (Hedrick 2010, 164). Hedrick tows the Forst–Habermas line. Forst continues to hold this interpretation in later reflections on the Habermas–Rawls debate. However, this interpretation neglects to take into account the fact that the conception of justice, namely the two principles and what follows from them, is justified *pro tanto* on the basis of the shared values in the overlap. Hedrick also subscribes to Habermas's view that the overlap is contingent, a "fortunate confluence in the political culture rather than being established by rational discourse between citizens" (Hedrick 2010, 164). But we have seen that this is mistaken. It is not that political values are constituted as political just by virtue of their being serendipitously included in every reasonable doctrine. Rather, they are included in every such doctrine because they are very great moral values that are also germane to a liberal democratic constitution. Who is to know how much the centrality of these ideas to the political culture is down to "the rational discourse between citizens," to mere luck, to ideology, or to imposition by political violence? None of these can be ruled out. And besides, the question of how these ideas were established is different from the question of what maintains them in existence, which may well be the fact that they continue to command the approval of reasonable citizens.
9. By way of comparison, it is interesting that, as Michelman notes, it is hard to say whether Rawls's theory has had any influence at all on American constitutional law (Michelman 2002, 408–10).
10. Recall Habermas's charge that Rawls devised "the basic norms of a well-ordered society on the drafting table" (PF, 101).
11. "Democracy involves . . . a political relationship between citizens within the basic structure . . . it implies further an equal share in the coercive political power that citizens exercise over one another" (PL, 217).
12. This is Rawls's reply to Hart's objection that the priority of liberty in justice as fairness rests on a comprehensive conception of the liberal person as a public-spirited citizen who prizes political activity and service to others above all other goods. This, Hart claims, is at odds with the line of argument in *A Theory of Justice* that the priority of liberty purports to rest "on interests, not ideals" (Hart 1973, 555).

13. Michelman points out that there is no congruence between the set of ultimate values that cannot be traded off against any other and what is included under "constitutional essentials" and hence regulated by constitutional higher law. Indeed, there is a two-way incongruence. Some politically decidable matters (for example, securing a fully adequate scheme of basic liberties) are covered by the priority of liberty, an ultimate value immune against trade-off yet not covered by constitutional law, whereas other matters that are covered by constitutional (higher) law do not involve the priority of liberty (for example, formal equality of opportunity) (Michelman 2002 402–403).
14. Recall that Habermas claims that the "two-stage character" of Rawls's theory is the root of its failure to give due weight and priority to political autonomy (RPUR, 128–29/41–43.)
15. Michelman defends a similar view to Scanlon: "A hypothetical–contractual standard of political justification can only be meant for application to constitutional laws—a restricted set of laws that fundamentally shape, organize, and limit the country's law-making system. Constitutional contractarian political justification depends on the view that your finding the constitution acceptably in line with reasons that apply to you, considering your interests, commits you to acceptance of the daily run of lawmakings that issue properly from the constituted system, regardless of whether each and every one of them does or should elicit your agreement" (Michelman 2002, 396).

7. "'REASONABLE' VERSUS 'TRUE'": HABERMAS'S REPLY TO RAWLS'S "REPLY"

1. I take it that this is why Habermas insisted on having his second essay, "'Reasonable' Versus 'True,' or the Morality of Worldviews," published alongside "Reconciliation Through the Public Use of Reason" in both the French and English reproductions of his exchange with Rawls.
2. On this, see Finlayson 2018.
3. This is a serious misapprehension because the original position is an account of the moral point of view in regard of matters of political justice, and the point of it is to achieve impartiality in the choice of principles by eliminating bias.
4. For more on this, see Finlayson 2000b.
5. Insofar as it works alongside the natural sciences, and takes the perspective of common sense, post-metaphysical philosophy cannot avoid all ontological commitments. See chapter 1, section 1.2.9.
6. See chapter 4, section 4.4. He also makes the paternalism charge about natural law theory, because it sets external moral restrictions on the democratic process (HRDP, 296).
7. For an excellent account of radical democracy in *Between Facts and Norms*, see Grodnick 2005.
8. O'Neill cites Andrew Kuper (2006) and Ingrid Volkmer (2014) for support. Insofar as the objection is aimed at Rawls, his answer is that public reason can be public in reach, even if it does not involve actual, universally inclusive, joint deliberations. Habermas's position on this issue is harder to parse, as can be seen from discourse ethics. Moral agents

must take part in an actual discourse, but in doing so they participate in argumentation that involves pragmatic idealizations—ideal role-taking—the aim of which is to reach agreement on norms that all affected can accept. That, in turn, involves advocatory discourses with universal reach but does not require that every moral agent must actually participate in the joint deliberations. So far as democracy is concerned, his view is that at the lower limit democratic participation means just that, in civil society, one's opinions (say, in moral matters) are formed discursively, through interaction with others, and, as such, they are swept up in the vortex of idealization and formed in accordance with universal norms.

8. RELIGION WITHIN THE BOUNDS OF PUBLIC REASON ALONE

1. We will examine these objections in more detail later on.
2. Peter E. Gordon, among others, claims that Habermas "continues to insist on the Rawlsian proviso" and that "the idea of a translation proviso . . . is borrowed from the later Rawls" (Gordon 2013, 175, 193). Boettcher claims that the two positions, in spite of differences, end up "not so different" (Boettcher 2009, 216). Baynes writes, "Though Habermas has expressed some sympathies for the asymmetrical burdens this imposes on a religious believer, he has essentially endorsed the same position" (Baynes 2014, 500). Ferrara claims they "offer a similar recipe with an important variation" (Ferrara 2009, 82).
3. Two rare dissenters, who argue for the distinctiveness of Habermas's position, are Hugh Baxter and Adil Usturali. See Baxter 2011, 208, and Usturali 2017, 567.
4. The political ideas form a subset of the overlapping ideas, which meet further criteria: They are moral ideas that are "not easily overridden" and are apt to support a viable democratic constitution (PL, 139, 217).
5. Rawls claims that the political conception of justice should be complete in that it gives public answers to "all, or to nearly all, questions involving the constitutional essentials and basic questions of justice (PL, 207, 225, 454).
6. Rawls has the inclusive sense in mind when he claims that a "reasonable and effective political conception may bend comprehensive doctrines toward itself" (PL, 144, 246). He has the exclusive sense in mind when he writes that nonpublic, thus comprehensive, reasons can be offered by citizens in the course of political advocacy if done "in ways that strengthen the ideal of public reason itself" (PL, 247; see also l, 46, 386).
7. Rawls's distinction between comprehensive and political (public) reasons does not sit flush with the distinction between religious and secular reasons, because some secular doctrines are "comprehensive" in the exclusive sense, and thus nonpolitical, whereas some religious reasons are also political (PL, 459). That said, even for Rawls, in broad terms, most religious reasons will be nonpublic and most secular reasons will be public.
8. I've cited the passage from Rawls's "The Idea of Public Reason Revisited," but the same thought is expressed in *Political Liberalism* (217ff).
9. Citizens, Rawls claims in a later essay, "are to think of themselves as legislators" (PL, 445).

10. Though Eberle claims that this is Rawls's view, he denies that the duty of civility implies a doctrine of restraint (Eberle 2002, 75).
11. However, Jeremy Waldron (2010) sees the difference as being that Rawls puts the onus on the religious citizen to provide proper public justifications, whereas Habermas sees public reason as requiring "two-way translation." In my view, though Rawls is perhaps less clear, there is no salient difference between the two on this point.
12. Perry 1988; Audi and Wolterstorff 1996; Weithman 2002; see also Yates 2007.
13. There are some other important differences. For example, Audi has a broad conception of the political domain and thus of the domain of application of "the principle of secular rationale." It applies to contexts of deliberation, which, I take it, means it is linked to decision-making, political advocacy, and contexts of justification in which citizens give reasons to one another—or the state gives reasons to citizens—for the laws that restrict their freedom (Audi 1993; Audi and Wolterstorff 1996).
14. "A secular reason is roughly one whose normative force does not evidentially depend on the existence of God or on theological considerations, or on the pronouncements of a person or institution qua religious authority" (Audi 1993, 692; for evidence that Audi thinks Rawls is on his side, see Audi and Wolterstorff 1996, 135).
15. Here is Weithman's version: "Citizens of a liberal democracy may offer arguments in public political debate which depend upon reasons drawn from their comprehensive moral views, including their religious views, without making them good by appeal to other arguments—provided they believe that their government would be justified in adopting the measures they favor and are prepared to indicate what they think would justify the adoption of the measures" (Weithman 2002, 3).
16. For an example of a secular but comprehensive view, see Dawkins 2006. Religious but political doctrines are harder to find, but Rawls give examples of works by the Catholic thinkers John Finnis and Jacques Maritain (PL, 452).
17. Amartya Sen points out that a common mistake about identity is to assume it rests on an individual's "singular affiliation" to just one community (Sen 2006, 45).
18. See note 17.
19. Wolterstorff makes the further and more serious objection that to require of religious citizens "that they not base their decisions and discussions concerning political issues on their religion, is to infringe inequitably on the free exercise of their religion" (Audi and Wolterstorff 1996, 105). But that argument, too, is dubious because, as Philip L. Quinn points out, a *moral* duty cannot violate the free exercise of anyone's religion where that freedom is protected by legitimate laws: "We do not violate the religious freedom of fellow citizens and thus fail to honor their freedom and equality when we adhere to a principle according to which some legally permissible exercises of that freedom are contrary to moral duty, and so we are not morally required not to adhere to such a principle in order to honor their freedom and equality" (Quinn 2001, 120–21). The most that can be said is that the moral principle of restraint may give rise to cognitive dissonance in the minds of religious citizens, between the demands of morality and religion, and between the prohibitions of morality and the permission of legitimate laws, and that, in this, religious citizens are made to bear an unfair burden.

20. I'm taking moral obligations and virtue as equivalent for the purpose of this analogy. One might also argue, as Tim Carter pointed out to me, that it is one thing to say that morality unfairly burdens one group over another, and it is another to say that, because of that unfairness, the unfairly burdened group has less of an obligation (or no obligation) to be moral.
21. Those who hold the opposite view, which I believe is mistaken, include Lafont (2007, 241), Boettcher (2009, 238), Loobuyck and Rummens (2011, 241), and Sikka (2012, 95).
22. In a discussion with Charles Taylor, Habermas makes clear that he does not use "secular" in its original religious sense to mean the incursion of religion into ordinary life from its monastic and clerical confines. Rather, he means language as a repository of reasons "shared not only by different religious communities but by believers and nonbelievers alike" (PRPS, 66).
23. Compare with Rawls's duty of civility, which is moral, not legal, and has no concrete institutional basis.
24. See also ND II, 110. Of course, the validity of this point depends on how much conflict a given political reality can bear.
25. See chapter 1, section 1.2.2.
26. For more on this, see Finlayson 2016, 172–73.
27. As we saw in note 22, Habermas has a very rich understanding of "secular" reasons as reasons that can be shared by citizens of different religious faiths and by nonbelievers. Now it is obviously one thing to say that public reasons should be formulated in "generally accessible" (and hence intelligible) language and another thing to say that public reasons are valid in the sense of being acceptable to all (see Skorupski 2017, 188). Thus it is open, for example, for Israeli settlers in the West Bank to justify their actions on the grounds that either the Bible states that God promised them the land (Genesis 13:15) or that it is justified by military necessity. Both reasons are "generally accessible" in that they are intelligible; whether they are acceptable to all (as good reasons) is another question.
28. This position is implied by two passages (BNR 5, 122). In the first, Habermas claims that one must formulate "all laws . . . in a public language that is equally accessible to all citizens, and . . . in addition . . . open to justification in secular terms."
29. Jeremy Gaines's translation of "Religion in the Public Sphere" renders the passage thus: "They should therefore be allowed to express and justify their convictions in a religious language if they cannot find secular 'translations' for them" (RPS, 9–10). However, this is not what Habermas means. In the German original, he states not "if" but "even when": "Sie sollten deshalb ihre Überzeugunungen *auch dann* in religiöser Sprache ehe ausdrücken und begründen dürfen, *wenn* sie dafür keine säklaren 'Übersetzungen' finden" (ZNR, 136). Ciaran Cronin's translation renders Habermas's thought accurately (BNR, 130).
30. This development in Habermas's view of modernization and secularization corresponds to a change in his response to Böckenförde's thesis, namely that "the liberal secularized state is nourished by presuppositions it cannot itself guarantee." Habermas's response up to about 2001 was to deny this and to point to the integrating function of

communication, discourse, and legitimate law. He now sees the question of whether the liberal democratic state can secure the conditions of its own stability as an open empirical question (DS, 21–47, esp. 38).

31. In what follows, I call this openness to the possible truth of religion "political agnosticism." The label is mine, but is faithful to Habermas's claim that "the secular counterpart to religious thinking is an agnostic, but nonreductionist form of post-metaphysical thinking" (BNR, 140).
32. For more on this, see BFN, 96–98, and JA, 1–15.
33. The required translation, according to Habermas, involves two separate processes "formulating all laws, all judicial decisions, and all decrees and directives . . . in a public language that is equally accessible to all citizens, and . . . in addition . . . open to justification in secular terms" (BNR, 5). See also BNR, 122, in which he appears to treat both processes as equivalent.
34. See BNR, 6, 140, 144–50.
35. See also DS, 51. Habermas conceives of "secularists" as those who base their atheistic world view on scientism or reductionist naturalism. Habermas advances various criticisms to expose what he sees as the inadequacy of scientism and reductionist naturalism as a world view (FHN, 106–107; ZNR, 155–87). That said, the particular world view underlying "secularism" is not the issue here.
36. See his claim in BNR, 130.
37. I have argued that, insofar as the question needs answering, a slightly fuller version of the institutional component of his theory will do the job.
38. He also claims that it is "reasonable to expect . . . an ethics of citizenship of all citizens equally, only if it is supported by these complementary learning processes (BNR, 140).
39. Lafont, Yates, and Gordon assume that Habermas's considered answer is that the cognitive burdens are shared equally (Lafont 2007, 247; Yates 2007, 887; Gordon 2016, 470). J. M. Bernstein also thinks this his view but rejects the "thesis of the equality of burdens as patently false" (HR, 159).
40. See Wolterstorff in HR, 102, and Yates 2007, 880.
41. On Habermas's method, see Pedersen 2008 and Rees 2018, 58–68.
42. This mistaken conception of Habermas's theory is common in the literature, particularly among those who think that his theory is similar to Rawls's. For instance: "Habermas defends a symmetrical account of civic obligations by *imposing* somewhat surprising requirements on nonreligious citizens" (Yates 2007, 887, my emphasis); "Habermas's political argument for his particular demands on the secular side" (Holst and Molander 2015, 556); "*As a remedy* for this unfair requirement Habermas has *proposed* that the cognitive burden of public discourse be shared by secular and religious citizens alike" (Gordon 2016, 470, my emphasis).
43. Rawls criticizes Habermas's theory as being "comprehensive while mine is an account of the political and is limited to that" (RH, 47).
44. Lafont makes this point clearly in the conclusion of her article (Lafont 2007, 254). However, she also criticizes Habermas for imposing unfair and asymmetrical cognitive burdens on secularists, since religious citizens are unconditionally free to express their

religious convictions, whereas secularists have to "exercise restraint concerning their secularist attitudes" (Lafont 2007, 247).

45. See BNR, 304, and Reply 3, 385.
46. Recall that "ethics" and "ethical" are technical terms, having to do with subjectivistic conceptions of the good. See BFN, 96–98, and JA, 1–15.
47. BFN, 80, 89; see also Finlayson 2016.
48. See Chapter 3, note 9. Hence the title of Habermas's essay "Pre-political Foundations of the Constitutional State?" ends in a question mark. For more on this, see Gordon 2013.
49. See also Holst and Molander 2015.
50. See the rules of discourse 3.2a: "Everyone is allowed to question any assertion whatever"; and 3.2b: "Everyone is allowed to introduce any assertion whatever into the discourse"' (MCCA, 89).
51. For a critique of the ethical harmonization requirement in BFN, see Finlayson 2016.
52. See note 32.
53. See the excellent discussion in Rees 2018, 143–65. He points out that Habermas bases his theory on a single example of—in his view, successful—sacred-to-secular translation. See also Harrington 2007, 552; Lafont 2007, 245; and Cooke 2011, 485.
54. Lafont also contends that Habermas's requirement for secular citizens to take religious views seriously has a "political rather than a cognitive meaning," though it is unclear to me why she thinks it cannot be both.
55. Habermas himself claims that "rule 3.2 guarantees all participants equal opportunity to contribute to the argumentation and to put forth their own arguments" (MCCA, 89).
56. The least likely element to be modified is the one most resistant to change (Festinger 1985, 28).
57. To reduce dissonance by similar means, religious citizens living in contemporary liberal democratic states would have to withdraw from civil society, for what gives rise to the dissonance are, as Habermas says, "modern conditions of life to which there are no alternatives" (BNR, 138).
58. "Everyone is allowed to introduce any assertion whatever into the discourse" (MCCA, 89).
59. For evidence that King used both religious and political arguments, see King's "'For All . . . A Non-segregated Society,' A Message for Race Relations Sunday," dated February 10, 1957, which he begins with a citation from Paul's Letters to the Galatians 3:28: ". . . ye are all one in Christ Jesus." Then compare the following passage from his "I Have a Dream" speech of August 28, 1963: "When the architects of our republic wrote the magnificent words of the Constitution and the Declaration of Independence, they were signing a promissory note to which every American was to fall heir. This note was a promise that all men would be guaranteed the inalienable rights of life, liberty, and the pursuit of happiness. It is obvious today that America has defaulted on this promissory note insofar as her citizens of color are concerned." For the view that King's politics were ultimately exclusively religious, see Lischer 1995, 220.
60. Rawls gave up the absolute moral prohibition on religious arguments, the "exclusive view" to which he initially inclined, according to which "reasons given explicitly in terms of comprehensive doctrines are never to be introduced into public reason"

(PL, 247), because he felt that King's speeches showed it to be too restrictive. I don't think they do, however, because King's arguments were not exclusively religiously based. Rawls's "inclusive view" was more permissive to the extent that it allowed exclusively and explicitly religious arguments to be made, provided they were made "in ways that strengthen the ideal of public reason" (PL, 247). And the "proviso" was more permissive still.

CONCLUSION

1. See chapter 3, section 3.1, and chapter 6, section 6.3.4.
2. See chapter 5, section 5.3.3; chapter 6, section 6.3.2; and chapter 7, section 7.2.
3. Hrabal 1965, xi.
4. The house to which Hrabal refers is one he loved but no longer wants to live in. That does not apply here. The house in which the family of Rawls and Habermas live is one that, although never quite finished, like several I have known, neither they nor we should be too anxious to leave.

BIBLIOGRAPHY

Adams, N. 2006. *Habermas and Theology.* Cambridge: Cambridge University Press.

Alexy, Robert. 1983. *Theorie der juristischen Argumentation.* Frankfurt: Suhrkamp.

——. 1994. "Basic Rights and Democracy in Jürgen Habermas's Procedural Paradigm of the Law." *Ratio Juris* 7: 227–38.

Arato, Andrew, and Michel Rosenfeld. 1998. *Habermas on Law and Democracy: Critical Exchanges.* Berkeley: University of California Press.

Audi Robert. 1989. "The Separation of Church and State and the Obligations of Citizenship." *Philosophy and Public Affairs* 18 (3): 259–96.

——. 1993. "The Place of Religious Argument in a Free and Democratic Society." *San Diego Law Review* Fall: 677–702.

——. 2005. "Moral Foundations of Liberal Democracy, Secular Reasons, and Liberal Neutrality Toward the Good." *Notre Dame Journal of Law, Ethics, and Public Policy* 19: 197–218.

Audi, Robert, and Nicholas Wolterstorff. 1996. *Religion in the Public Square: The Place of Religious Convictions in Political Debate.* New York: Rowman & Littlefield.

Ayer, Alfred J. 1936. *Language, Truth and Logic.* London: Victor Gollancz.

Baier, Kurt. 1954. "The Point of View of Morality." Australasian *Journal of Philosophy* 32 (2): 104–35.

——. 1989. "Justice and the Aims of Political Philosophy." *Ethics* 99 (4): 771–90.

Baldwin, Thomas. 2008. "Rawls and Moral Psychology." In *Oxford Studies in Metaethics*, ed. Russ Shafer-Landau. Oxford: Oxford University Press.

Bankovsky, Miriam. 2012. *Perfecting Justice in Rawls, Habermas and Honneth: A Deconstructive Perspective.* New York: Continuum.

Baxter, Hugh. 2011. *Habermas: The Discourse Theory of Law and Democracy.* Stanford, Calif.: Stanford Law Books.

Baynes, Kenneth. 1989. "Rational Reconstruction and Social Criticism: Habermas's Model of Interpretive Social Science." *Philosophical Forum* 21: 122–45.

——. 1992. *The Normative Grounds of Social Criticism*. New York: State University of New York Press.

——. 1995. "Democracy and the *Rechtsstaat*: Habermas's *Faktizität und Geltung*." In *The Cambridge Companion to Habermas*, ed. Stephen K. White, 201–232. Cambridge: Cambridge University Press.

——. 2002. "Deliberative Democracy and the Limits of Liberalism." In *Discourse and Democracy: Essays on Habermas's Between Facts and Norms*, ed. René von Schomberg and Kenneth Baynes, 15–31. Albany: State University of New York Press.

——. 2004. "The Transcendental Turn: Habermas's 'Kantian Pragmatism.'" In *The Cambridge Companion to Critical Theory*, ed. Fred Rush. Cambridge: Cambridge University Press.

——. 2014. "Critical Theory and Habermas." In *A Companion to Rawls*, ed. Jon Mandle and David A. Reidy, 487–503. Oxford: Wiley-Blackwell.

——. 2016. *Habermas*. London: Routledge.

Baynes, Kenneth, and René von Schomberg, eds. 2002. *Discourse and Democracy: Essays on Habermas's Between Facts and Norms*. Albany: State University of New York Press.

Beitz, Charles R. 1989. *Political Equality: An Essay in Democratic Theory*. Princeton, N.J.: Princeton University Press.

Benhabib, Seyla. 1986. "The Generalized and the Concrete Other: The Kohlberg–Gilligan Controversy and Feminist Theory." *Praxis International* 5 (1): 402–24.

——. 1987. "The Generalized and the Concrete Other: The Kohlberg–Gilligan Controversy and Feminist Theory." In *Feminism as Critique: Essays on the Politics of Gender in Late-Capitalist Societies*, ed. Seyla Benhabib and Drucilla Cornell, 77–95. London: Polity.

——. 1992. *Situating the Self: Gender, Community and Postmodernism in Contemporary Ethics*. London: Routledge.

——. 1994. "Deliberative Democracy and Models of Democratic Legitimacy." *Constellations* 1 (1): 26–52.

Benhabib, Seyla, and Drucilla Cornell, eds. 1987. *Feminism as Critique: Essays on the Politics of Gender in Late-Capitalist Societies*. London: Polity.

Benhabib, Seyla, and Fred Reinhard Dallmayr. 1995. *The Communicative Ethics Controversy*. Cambridge, Mass.: MIT Press.

Bernstein, J. M. 2013. "Forgetting Isaac: Faith and the Philosophical Impossibility of a Postsecular Society." In *Habermas and Religion*, ed. Craig Calhoun, Eduardo Mendieta, and Jonathan VanAntwerpen, 154–78. Cambridge: Polity.

Bernstein, Richard J. 1996. "The Retrieval of the Democratic Ethos." *Cardozo Law Review* 4: 1127–47.

Blackburn, Simon. 1993. *Essays in Quasi-Realism*. Oxford: Oxford University Press.

——. 2001. *Ruling Passions*. Oxford: Oxford University Press.

Böckenförde, Ernst-Wolfgang. 1976. *Staat, Gesellschaft, Freiheit*. Frankfurt: Suhrkamp.

Boettcher, James W. 2009. "Habermas, Religion and the Ethics of Citizenship." *Philosophy and Social Criticism* 35 (1–2): 215–38.

Bohman, James, and William Rehg, eds. 1997. *Deliberative Democracy: Essays on Reason and Politics*. Cambridge, Mass.: MIT Press.

Borman, David A. 2011. *The Idolatry of the Actual: Habermas, Socialization, and the Possibility of Autonomy*. Albany: State University of New York Press.

Calhoun, Craig, Eduardo Mendieta, and Jonathan VanAntwerpen, eds. 2013. *Habermas and Religion*. Cambridge: Polity.

Chambers, Simone. 1996. *Reasonable Democracy, Jürgen Habermas and the Politics of Discourse*. Ithaca, N.Y.: Cornell University Press.

——. 2007. "How Religion Speaks to the Agnostic: Habermas on the Persistent Value of Religion." *Constellations* 14 (2): 210–23.

——. 2010. "Secularism Minus Exclusion: Developing a Religious-Friendly Idea of Public Reason." *The Good Society* 19 (2): 16–21.

Ciszewski, Wojciech. 2016. "Narrow or Broad? Questioning the Scope of Public Reason." *Zeszyty Naukowe Towarzystwa Doktorantów UJ Nauki Humanistyczne* 14 (3): 79–96. https://depot.ceon.pl/handle/123456789/12736.

Cohen, G. A. 2008. *Rescuing Justice and Equality*. Cambridge, Mass.: Harvard University Press.

Cohen, Jean, and Andrew Arato. 1992. *Civil Society and Political Theory*. Cambridge, Mass.: MIT Press.

Cohen, Joshua. 1989. "Deliberation and Democratic Legitimacy." In *The Good Polity: Normative Analysis of the State*, ed. Alan Hamlin and Philip Pettit, 17–34. Oxford: Blackwell.

——. 1997. "Procedure and Substance in Deliberative Democracy." In *Deliberative Democracy: Essays on Reason and Politics*, ed. James Bohman and William Rehg, 407–39. Cambridge, Mass.: MIT Press.

——. 1999. "Reflections on Habermas on Democracy." *Ratio Juris* 12 (4): 385–416.

Coicaud, Jean-Marc. 2002. *Legitimacy and Politics: A Contribution to the Study of Political Right and Political Responsibility*. Cambridge: Cambridge University Press.

Cooke, Maeve. 2006. "Salvaging and Secularizing the Semantic Contents of Religion: The Limitations of Habermas's Postmetaphysical Proposal." *International Journal for Philosophy of Religion* 60 (1–3): 187–207.

——. 2007. "A Secular State for a Postsecular Society? Postmetaphysical Political Theory and the Place of Religion." *Constellations* 14 (2): 224–38.

——. 2011. "Translating Truth." *Philosophy & Social Criticism* 37 (4): 479–91. https://doi.org/10.1177/0191453710398856.

——. 2013. "Violating Neutrality? Religious Validity Claims and Democratic Neutrality." In *Habermas and Religion*, ed. Craig Calhoun, Eduardo Mendieta, and Jonathan VanAntwerpen, 249–76. Cambridge: Polity.

Daniels, Norman. 2003. "Reflective Equilibrium." In *The Stanford Encyclopedia of Philosophy* (Winter 2016 edition), ed. Edward N. Zalta. https://plato.stanford.edu/archives/win2016/entries/reflective-equilibrium/.

Dawkins, Richard. 2006. *The God Delusion*. London: Bantam.

Dreben, Burton. 2003. "On Rawls and Political Liberalism." In *The Cambridge Companion to Rawls*, ed. Samuel Freeman, 316–46. Cambridge: Cambridge University Press.

Durkheim, Émile. 1997. [1893]. *The Division of Labor in Society*. Translated by W. D. Halls. New York: Free Press.

Dworkin, Ronald. 1993. *Life's Dominion: An Argument About Abortion, Euthanasia, and Individual Freedom*. New York: Knopf.

Eberle, Christopher J. 2002. *Religious Conviction in Liberal Politics*. Cambridge: Cambridge University Press.

Enoch, David. 2015. "Against Public Reason." In *Oxford Studies in Political Philosophy*, vol. 1, ed. David Sobel, Peter Vallentyne, and Steven Wall. Oxford: Oxford University Press.

Estlund, David M. 1992. "Review of *The Normative Grounds of Social Criticism: Kant, Rawls, and Habermas* by Kenneth Baynes." *Political Theory* 20 (4): 694–97.

Ferrara, A. 1985. "A Critique of Habermas's Discourse Ethics." *Telos* 65: 45–74.

——. 2001. "Of Boats and Principles: Reflections on Habermas's 'Constitutional Democracy.'" *Political Theory* 29 (6): 782–91.

——. 2009. "The Separation of Religion and Politics in a Post-secular Society." *Philosophy and Social Criticism* 35 (1–2): 77–91.

Festinger, Leon. 1985. [1957]. *A Theory of Cognitive Dissonance*. Stanford, Calif.: Stanford University Press.

Finlayson, James Gordon. 1999. "Does Hegel's Critique of Kant's Moral Theory Apply to Discourse Ethics?" In *Habermas: A Critical Reader*, ed. Peter Dews, 29–52. Oxford: Blackwell.

——. 2000a. "Modernity and Morality in Habermas's Discourse Ethics." *Inquiry* 43 (3): 319–40.

——. 2000b. "What Are Universalizable Interests?" *Journal of Political Philosophy* 8 (4): 446–72.

——. 2005. "Habermas's Moral Cognitivism and the Frege-Geach Challenge." *European Journal of Philosophy* 13 (3): 319–45.

——. 2012. "Women and the Standpoint of Concrete Others: From the Criticism of Discourse Ethics to Feminist Social Criticism." In *Dialogue, Politics and Gender*, ed. Jude Browne, 13–51. Cambridge: Cambridge University Press.

——. 2013. "The Persistence of Normative Questions in Habermas's *Theory of Communicative Action*." *Constellations* 20 (4): 518–32.

——. 2014. "Hegel, Adorno and Immanent Criticism." *British Journal for the History of. Philosophy*, 22 (6): 1142–66.

——. 2016. "Where the Right Gets In: On Rawls's Criticism of Habermas's Conception of Legitimacy." *Kantian Review* 21 (2): 161–83.

——. 2017. "On Kantians and Pragmatists: Kenneth Baynes's Habermas." *European Journal of Philosophy* 25 (3): 875–84. https://doi.org/10.1111/ejop.12290.

——. 2018. "The Habermas–Rawls Debate." In *The Routledge Companion to the Frankfurt School*, ed. Axel Honneth, Peter E. Gordon, Espen Hammer, and Axel Honneth. New York: Routledge.

Finlayson, James Gordon, and Fabian Freyenhagen, eds. 2011. *Habermas and Rawls: Disputing the Political*. New York: Routledge.

Flynn, Jeffrey. 2003. "Habermas on Human Rights: Law, Morality, and Intercultural Dialogue." *Social Theory and Practice*, 29 (3): 431–57.

——. 2011. "Two Models of Human Rights: Extending the Rawls–Habermas Debate." In *Habermas and Rawls: Disputing the Political*, ed. James Gordon Finlayson and Fabian Freyenhagen, 247–65. New York: Routledge.

Forst, Rainer. 1999. "The Basic Right to Justification: Towards a Constructivist Conception of Human Rights." *Constellations* 6 (1): 35–60.

——. 2002b. *Contexts of Justice*. Translated by John M. Farrell. Berkeley: University of California Press.

——. 2011. "The Justification of Justice: Rawls and Habermas in Dialogue." In *Habermas and Rawls: Disputing the Political*, ed. James Gordon Finlayson and Fabian Freyenhagen, 153–180. New York: Routledge.

——. 2014. *The Right to Justification*. Translated by Jeffrey Flynn. New York: Columbia University Press.

Freeman, Samuel. 1996. "Original Position." In The Stanford Encyclopedia of Philosophy (Winter 2016 edition), ed. Edward N. Zalta. https://plato.stanford.edu/archives/win2016/entries/original-position/.

——. 2000. "Deliberative Democracy: A Sympathetic Comment." *Philosophy and Public Affairs* 29 (4): 371–418.

——, ed. 2003. *The Cambridge Companion to Rawls*. Cambridge: Cambridge University Press.

——. 2007. *Rawls*. New York: Routledge.

——. 2009. *Justice and the Social Contract: Essays on Rawlsian Political Philosophy*. Oxford: Oxford University Press.

Fuller, Lon L. 1965. *The Morality of Law*. Revised edition. New Haven, Conn.: Yale University Press.

Fultner Barbara, ed. 2011. *Jürgen Habermas: Key Concepts*. Durham, UK: Acumen.

Gaus, Daniel. 2013. "Rational Reconstruction as a Method of Political Theory Between Social Critique and Empirical Political Science." *Constellations* 20 (4): 553–70.

Gaus, Gerald F. 2003. *Contemporary Theories of Liberalism: Public Reason as a Post-Enlightenment Project*. London: Sage.

——. 2013. "On the Appropriate Mode of Justifying a Public Moral Constitution." *Harvard Review of Philosophy* 19: 4–22.

Gauthier, David. 1986. *Morals by Agreement*. Oxford: Oxford University Press.

Geuss, Raymond. 2008. *Philosophy and Real Politics*. Princeton, N.J.: Princeton University Press.

Gibbard, Allan. 1990. *Wise Choices, Apt Feelings: A Theory of Normative Judgment*. Oxford: Oxford University Press.

Gilabert, Pablo. 2005. "A Substantivist Construal of Discourse Ethics." *International Journal of Philosophical Studies* 13 (3): 405–37.

Gilligan, Carol. 1982. *In a Different Voice: Psychological Theory and Women's Development*. Cambridge, Mass.: Harvard University Press.

Gledhill, James. 2011. "Procedure in Substance and Substance in Procedure. Reframing the Rawls–Habermas Debate." In *Habermas and Rawls: Disputing the Political*, ed. James Gordon Finlayson and Fabian Freyenhagen, 181–99. New York: Routledge.

——. 2012. "Rawls and Realism." Social Theory and Practice 38 (1): 55–82.

Gordon, Peter E. 2013. "Between Christian Democracy and Critical Theory: Habermas, Böckenförde, and the Dialectics of Secularization in Postwar Germany." *Social Research: An International Quarterly* 80 (1): 173–202.

——. 2016. "Critical Theory Between the Sacred and the Profane." *Constellations* 23 (4): 466–81.

Greenawalt, Kent. 1994. "On Public Reason." Chicago-Kent Law Review 69 (3): 669–89.

Grodnick, Stephen. 2005. "Rediscovering Radical Democracy in Habermas's *Between Facts and Norms*." *Constellations* 12 (3): 392–408.

Gunnarsson, Logi. 2000. *Making Moral Sense: Beyond Habermas and Gauthier*. Cambridge: Cambridge University Press.

Gutmann, Amy, and Dennis Thompson. 1996. *Democracy and Disagreement*. Cambridge, Mass.: Harvard University Press.

Habermas, Jürgen. 1979. *Communication and the Evolution of Society*. Translated by Thomas McCarthy. Boston: Beacon.

——. 1981. *Theorie des kommunikativen Handelns*. 2 vols. Frankfurt: Suhrkamp.

——. 1984. *Vorstudien und Ergänzungen zur Theorie des kommunikativen Handelns*. Frankfurt: Suhrkamp.

——. 1985. *Der philosophische Diskurs der Moderne: Zwölf Vorlesungen*. Frankfurt: Suhrkamp.

——. 1985. *The Theory of Communicative Action*. 2 vols. Translated by Thomas McCarthy. Boston: Beacon.

——. 1987. *The Philosophical Discourse of Modernity: Twelve Lectures*. Translated by Frederick G. Lawrence. Cambridge, Mass.: MIT Press.

——. 1988. *Nachmetaphysisches Denken II: Aufsätze und Repliken*. Frankfurt: Suhrkamp.

——. 1989. "Justice and Solidarity: On the Discussion Concerning 'Stage 6.'" *Philosophical Forum* 21 (1): 32–52.

——. 1989. "Towards a Communication-Concept of Rational Collective Will-Formation: A Thought-Experiment." *Ratio Juris* 2 (2): 144–54. https://doi.org/10.1111/j.1467-9337.1989.tb00033.x.

——. 1990. *Moral Consciousness and Communicative Action*. Translated by Christian Lenhardt and Shierry Weber Nicholsen. Cambridge, Mass.: MIT Press.

——. 1992. *Autonomy and Solidarity: Interviews with Jürgen Habermas*. 2nd ed., ed. Peter Dews. London: Verso.

——. 1992. *Faktizität und Geltung*. Frankfurt: Suhrkamp.

——. 1992. *Postmetaphysical Thinking: Philosophical Essays*. Translated by William Mark Hohengarten. Cambridge, Mass.: MIT Press.

——. 1993. *Justification and Application: Remarks on Discourse Ethics*. Cambridge, Mass.: MIT Press.

——. 1994. *The Past as Future*. Trans. and ed. Max Pensky. Lincoln: University of Nebraska Press.

——. 1995. "Reconciliation Through the Public Use of Reason: Remarks on John Rawls's Political Liberalism." *Journal of Philosophy* 92 (3): 109–31. https://doi.org/10.2307/2940842.

——. 1996. *Between Facts and Norms: Contributions to a Discourse Theory of Law and Democracy*. Translated by William Rehg. Cambridge: Polity.

——. 1996. *Die Einbeziehung des Anderen: Studien zur politischen Theorie*. Frankfurt: Suhrkamp.

——. 1996. "Reply to Symposium Participants, Benjamin N. Cardozo School of Law." Cardozo Law Review 17 (4–5): 1477–1557.

——. 1996. "Sprechakttheoretische Erläuterungen zum Begriff der kommunikativen Rationalität." *Zeitschrift für philosophische Forschung* 50 (1–2): 65–91.

——. 1998. *The Inclusion of the Other: Studies in Political Theory*, ed. Ciaran Cronin and Pablo De Greiff. Translated by Ciaran Cronin. Cambridge: Polity.

——. 1998. "'Reasonable' Versus 'True,' or the Morality of Worldviews." In *The Inclusion of the Other: Studies in Political Theory*, ed. Ciaran P. Cronin and Pablo De Greiff, 75–105.

——. 1998. "Richtigkeit vs. Wahrheit." *Deutsche Zeitschrift der Philosophie* 46 (2): 179–208.

——. 1999. *Wahrheit und Rechtfertigung*. Frankfurt: Suhrkamp.

——. 2000. "Werte und Normen: Ein Kommentar zu Hilary Putnams kantischen Pragmatismus." *Deutsche Zeitschrift für Philosophie* 48 (4): 547–64.

——. 2001. *Die Zukunft der menschlichen Natur: Auf dem Weg zu einer liberalen Eugenik?* Frankfurt: Suhrkamp.

——. 2002. *Religion and Rationality: Essays on Reason, God, and Modernity*. Cambridge, Mass.: MIT Press.

——. 2003. *The Future of Human Nature*. Translated by Hella Beister, William Rehg, and Max Pensky. Cambridge: Polity.

——. 2003. *Truth and Justification*. Translated by Barbara Fultner. Cambridge, Mass.: MIT Press.

——. 2004. "The Moral and the Ethical: A Reconsideration of the Issue of the Priority of the Right Over the Good." In *Pragmatism, Critique, Judgment: Essays for Richard J. Bernstein*, ed. Seyla Benhabib and Nancy Fraser, 29–43. Cambridge, Mass.: MIT Press.

——. 2005. "Religion in der Öffentlichkeit. Kognitive Voraussetzungen für den "öffentlichen Vernunftgebrauch" religiöser und säkularer Bürger." In *Zwischen Naturalismus und Religion: Philosophische Aufsätze*. Frankfurt: Suhrkamp.

——. 2005. *Zwischen Naturalismus und Religion: Philosophische Aufsätze*. Frankfurt: Suhrkamp.

——. 2006. "Religion in the Public Sphere." *European Journal of Philosophy* 14 (1): 1–25.

——. 2008. *Between Naturalism and Religion*. Cambridge, Mass.: MIT Press.

——. 2009. Europe: The Faltering Project. Translated by Ciaran Cronin. Cambridge: Polity.

——. 2010. *An Awareness of What Is Missing: Faith and Reason in a Post-secular Age*. Cambridge: Polity.

——. 2010. "The Concept of Human Dignity and the Realistic Utopia of Human Rights." *Metaphilosophy* 41 (4): 464–80.

——. 2010. "The 'Good Life'—A 'Detestable Phrase': The Significance of the Young Rawls's Religious Ethics for His Political Theory." *European Journal of Philosophy* 18 (3): 443–53.

——. 2011. "'The Political': The Rational Meaning of a Questionable Inheritance of Political Theology." In *The Power of Religion in the Public Sphere*, ed. Eduardo Mendieta and Jonathan VanAntwerpen, 15–33. New York: Columbia University Press.

——. 2011. "Reply to My Critics." In *Habermas and Rawls: Disputing the Political*, ed. James Gordon Finlayson and Fabian Freyenhagen, 283–304. New York: Routledge.

——. 2013. "Reply to My Critics." In *Habermas and Religion*, ed. Craig Calhoun, Eduardo Mendieta, and Jonathan VanAntwerpen, 347–90. Chapter translated by Ciaran Cronin. Cambridge: Polity.

Habermas, Jürgen, and Joseph Ratzinger. 2006. *The Dialectics of Secularization: On Reason and Religion*. Translated by Brian McNeil. San Francisco: Ignatius.

Hampton, Jean. 1989. "Should Political Philosophy Be Done Without Metaphysics?" *Ethics* 99 (4): 791–814.

Harrington, Austin. 2007. "Habermas and the 'Post-Secular Society.' "*European Journal of Social Theory* 10 (4): 543–60.

Hart, H. L. A. 1973. "Rawls on Liberty and Its Priority." *University of Chicago Law Review* 40 (3): 551–55.

Haysom, Keith. 2011. "Civil Society and Social Movements." In *Jürgen Habermas: Key Concepts*, ed. Barbara Fultner, 177–95. Durham, UK: Acumen.

Heath, Joseph. 2011a. "Justice: Transcendental Not Metaphysical." In *Habermas and Rawls: Disputing the Political*, ed. James Gordon Finlayson and Fabian Freyenhagen, 117–35. New York: Routledge.

——. 2011b. "System and Lifeworld." In *Jürgen Habermas: Key Concepts*, ed. Barbara Fultner, 74–90. Durham, UK: Acumen.

——. 2014. "Rebooting Discourse Ethics." *Philosophy and Social Criticism* 40 (9): 829–66. https://doi:10.1177/0191453714545340.

Hedrick, Todd. 2010. *Rawls and Habermas*. Stanford, Calif.: Stanford University Press.

Hegel, Georg Wilhelm Friedrich. 1993. [1888]. *Introductory Lectures on Aesthetics*, ed. Michael Inwood. Translated by Bernard Bosanquet. London: Penguin.

Heller, Agnes. 1985. "The Discourse Ethics of Habermas: Critique and Appraisal." *Thesis Eleven* 10/11 (1): 5–17.

Hennig, Anja. 2015. "Habermas's Translation Proviso and Conservative Religious Actors in the Public Sphere." In *Religious Pluralism: A Resource Book*, ed. Aurélia Bardon, Maria Birnbaum, Lois Lee, and Kristina Stoeckl, 95–102. Florence: European University Institute.

Höffe, Otfried 1984. "Is Rawls' Theory of Justice Really Kantian?" *Ratio* 26: 103–24.

Holst, Cathrine, and Anders Molander. 2015. "Jürgen Habermas on Public Reason and Religion: Do Religious Citizens Suffer an Asymmetrical Cognitive Burden, and Should They Be Compensated?" *Critical Review of International Social and Political Philosophy* 18 (5): 547–63.

Hrabal, Bohumil. 2015. [1965]. *Mr. Kafka and Other Tales from the Time of the Cult*. Translated by Paul Wilson. London: Vintage.

Ingram, David. 2010. *Habermas: Introduction and Analysis*. Ithaca, N.Y.: Cornell University Press.

Kant, Immanuel. 2011. *Groundwork of the Metaphysics of Morals*. Translated by Mary Gregor. Cambridge: Cambridge University Press.

Kelly, Terrence. 2001. "Sociological Not Political: Rawls and the Reconstructive Social Sciences." *Philosophy and the Social Sciences* 31 (1): 3–19.

Kettner, Mathias. 2002. "The Disappearance of Discourse Ethics in Habermas's *Between Facts and Norms*." In *Discourse and Democracy*, ed. René von Schomberg and Kenneth Baynes, 201–19. Albany: State University of New York Press.

Kohlberg, Lawrence. 1973. "The Claim to Moral Adequacy of a Highest Stage of Moral Judgment." *Journal of Philosophy* 70 (18): 630–46. https://doi:10.2307/2025030.

——. 1981. *The Philosophy of Moral Development: Moral Stages and the Idea of Justice*. Vol. 1 of *Essays on Moral Development*. San Francisco: Harper & Row.

——. 1986. "A Current Statement on Some Theoretical Issues." In *Lawrence Kohlberg: Consensus and Controversy*, ed. Sohan Modgil and Celia Modgil. Philadelphia: Falmer.

Kukathas, Chandran, and Philip Pettit. 1990. *Rawls:* A Theory of Justice *and Its Critics*. Stanford, Calif.: Stanford University Press.

Kuper, Andrew. 2006. *Democracy Beyond Borders: Justice and Representation in Global Institutions*. Oxford: Oxford University Press.

Laden, Anthony Simon. 2003. "The House That Jack Built: Thirty Years of Reading Rawls." *Ethics* 113 (2): 367–90.

——. 2011. "The Justice of Justification." In *Habermas and Rawls: Disputing the Political*, ed. James Gordon Finlayson and Fabian Freyenhagen, 135–52. New York: Routledge.

Lafont, Cristina. 2007. "Religion in the Public Sphere: Remarks on Habermas's Conception of Public Deliberation in Postsecular Societies." *Constellations* 14 (2): 239–59.

——. 2009. "Religion and the Public Sphere: What Are the Deliberative Obligations of Democratic Citizenship?" *Philosophy and Social Criticism* 35 (1–2): 127–50.

Langvatn, Silje Aambø. 2013. "The Idea and the Ideal of Public Reason." PhD diss., University of Bergen.

Larmore, Charles. 1995. "The Foundations of Modern Democracy: Reflections on Jürgen Habermas." *European Journal of Philosophy* 3 (1): 55–68.

——. 1996. *The Morals of Modernity*. New York: Cambridge University Press.

——. 1999. "The Moral Basis of Political Liberalism." *Journal of Philosophy* 96 (12): 599–625.

Lischer, Richard. 1995. *The Preacher King: Martin Luther King Jr. and the Word that Moved America*. New York: Oxford University Press.

Lister, Andrew. 2007. "Public Reason and Moral Compromise." *Canadian Journal of Philosophy* 37 (1): 1–34.

Loobuyck, Patrick, and Stefan Rummens. 2011. "Religious Arguments in the Public Sphere: Comparing Rawls with Habermas." In *Religion in the Public Sphere: Proceedings of the 2010 Conference of the European Society for Philosophy of Religion*, ed. Niek Brunsveld and Roger Trigg, 237–50. Utrecht: Ars Disputandi.

Luhmann, Niklas. 2001. [1969]. *Legitimation durch Verfahren*. Frankfurt: Suhrkamp.

Lumer, Christoph. 1997. "Habermas' Diskursethik." *Zeitschrift für philosophische Forschung* 51 (1): 42–64.

Mahoney, John. 2001. "Rights Without Dignity? Some Critical Reflections on Habermas's Procedural Model of Law and Democracy." *Philosophy and Social Criticism* 27 (3): 21–40.

Maihofer, Andrea. 1998. "Care." Translated by Christian Hunold. In *A Companion to Feminist Philosophy*, ed. Alison M. Jaggar and Iris Marion Young, 383–93. Oxford: Blackwell.

Marshall, T. H. 1987. [1950]. *Citizenship and Social Class*, ed. Tom Bottomore. London: Pluto.

Maus, Ingeborg. 1996. "Popular Sovereignty and Liberal Rights." Cardozo Law Review 17 (4–5): 825–82.

——. 2002. "Popular Sovereignty and Liberal Rights." In *Discourse and Democracy*, ed. René von Schomberg and Kenneth Baynes, 89–129. Albany: State University of New York Press.

Mautner, Menny. 2013. "Religion in Politics: Rawls and Habermas on Deliberation and Justification." *Tel Aviv University Law Faculty Papers*. Working Paper 167. http://law.bepress.com/taulwps/art167.

McCarthy, Thomas. 1978. *The Critical Theory of Jürgen Habermas*. Cambridge, Mass.: MIT Press.

——. 1993. *Ideals and Illusions: On Reconstruction and Deconstruction in Contemporary Critical Theory*. Cambridge, Mass.: MIT Press.

——. 1993. "Practical Discourse: On the Relation of Morality to Politics." In *Ideals and Illusions: On Reconstruction and Deconstruction in Contemporary Critical Theory*, 181–99. Cambridge, Mass.: MIT Press.

——. 1994. "Kantian Constructivism and Reconstructivism: Rawls and Habermas in Dialogue." *Ethics* 105 (1): 44–63. https://doi:10.1086/293678.

——. 1996. "Legitimacy and Diversity: Dialectical Reflections on Analytic Distinctions." In *Habermas on Law and Democracy: Critical Exchanges*, 115–56. Berkeley: University of California Press.

McLellan, David, ed. 2000. *Karl Marx: Selected Writings*. Revised edition. Oxford: Oxford University Press.

McMahon, Christopher. 2000. "Discourse and Morality." *Ethics* 110 (3): 514–36. https://doi:10.1086/233322.

——. 2002. "Why There Is No Issue Between Habermas and Rawls." *Journal of Philosophy* 99 (2): 111–29.

——. 2011. "Habermas, Rawls and Moral Impartiality." In *Habermas and Rawls: Disputing the Political*, ed. James Gordon Finlayson and Fabian Freyenhagen, 200–223. New York: Routledge.

Mead, George Herbert. 1967. *Mind, Self, and Society: From the Standpoint of a Social Behaviorist*. Vol. 1 of *The Works of George Herbert Mead*, ed. Charles W. Morris. Chicago: University of Chicago Press.

Meehan, Johanna. 2000. "Feminism and Habermas's Discourse Ethics." *Philosophy and Social Criticism* 26 (3): 39–52.

Mendieta, Eduardo. 2011. "Rationalization, Modernity, and Secularization." In *Jürgen Habermas: Key Concepts*, ed. Barbara Fultner, 222–38. Durham, UK: Acumen.

Mendieta, Eduardo, and Jonathan VanAntwerpen. 2011. *The Power of Religion in the Public Sphere*. New York: Columbia University Press.

Michelman, Frank I. 1996. "Family Quarrel." In *Habermas on Law and Democracy: Critical Exchanges*, 309–23. Berkeley: University of California Press.

——. 1996. "Review of Habermas's *Between Facts and Norms*." *Journal of Philosophy* 93: 307–15.

——. 1997. "How Can the People Ever Make the Laws?" In *Deliberative Democracy: Essays on Reason and Politics*, ed. James Bohman and William Rehg, 145–71. Cambridge, Mass.: MIT Press.

——. 2002. "Rawls on Constitutionalism and Constitutional Law." In *The Cambridge Companion to Rawls*, 394–425, ed. Samuel Freeman. Cambridge: Cambridge University Press.

Moon, J. Donald. 1995. "Practical Discourse and Communicative Ethics." In *The Cambridge Companion to Habermas*, 143–66, ed. Stephen K. White. Cambridge: Cambridge University Press.

Mulhall, Stephen, and Adam Swift. 1992. *Liberals and Communitarians*. Oxford: Blackwell.

Müller-Doohm, Stefan. 2016. Habermas: A Biography. Translated by Daniel Steuer. Cambridge: Polity.

Munoz-Dardé, Veronique. 1998. "Rawls, Justice in the Family and Justice of the Family." *The Philosophical Quarterly* 48 (192): 335–52.

Nussbaum, Martha. 2003. "Rawls and Feminism." In *The Cambridge Companion to Rawls*, ed. Samuel Freeman, 488–521. Cambridge: Cambridge University Press.

Okin, Susan Moller. 1989a. *Justice, Gender, and the Family*. New York: Basic Books.

——. 1989b. "Reason and Feeling in Thinking About Justice." *Ethics* 99 (2): 229–49. https://doi:10.1086/293064.

Olson, Kevin. 2003. "Do Rights Have a Formal Basis? Habermas's Legal Theory and the Normative Foundations of the Law." *Journal of Political Philosophy* 11: 273–94.

——. 2007. "Paradoxes of Constitutional Democracy." *American Journal of Political Science* 51 (2): 330–43.

——. 2011. "Deliberative Democracy." In *Jürgen Habermas: Key Concepts*, ed. Barbara Fultner, 140–55. Durham, UK: Acumen.

O'Neill, Onora. 2015. *Constructing Authorities*. Cambridge: Cambridge University Press.

Ott, Konrad. 1996. "Wie begründet man ein Diskursprinzip der Moral? Ein neuer Versuch zu >U< und >D< ." In *Vom Begründen zum Handeln. Aufsätze zur angewandten Ethik*, 12–50. Tübingen: Attempto Verlag.

Pedersen, Jørgen. 2008. "Habermas's Method: Rational Reconstruction." *Philosophy of the Social Sciences* 38 (4): 457–85.

——. 2011. "Justification and Application: The Revival of the Rawls–Habermas Debate." *Philosophy of the Social Sciences* 42 (3): 399–432.

Pensky, Max. 2008. *The Ends of Solidarity*. Ithaca: State University of New York Press.

Perry, Michael John. 1988. *Morality, Politics and Law: A Bicentennial Essay*. New York: Oxford University Press.

Peters, Bernard. 1994. "On Reconstructive Legal and Political Theory." *Philosophy and Social Criticism* 20 (4): 101–34.

Pettit, Philip. 2005. "Rawls's Political Ontology." *Politics, Philosophy & Economics* 4 (2): 157–74.

Pogge, Thomas. 2007. *John Rawls: His Life and Theory of Justice*. Translated by Michelle Kosch. Oxford: Oxford University Press.

Puntel, Lorenz B. 2012. "Habermas' Postmetaphysical Thinking: A Critique." *Ludwig Maximilians Universität München Fakultät für Philosophie, Wissenschaftstheorie und Religionswissenschaft*. Accessed January 2015. www.philosophie.unimuenchen.de/lehreinheiten/philosophie_1/personen/puntel/download/2013_habermas.pdf.

Putnam, Hilary. 2002. *The Collapse of the Fact Value Distinction and Other Essays*. Cambridge Mass.: Harvard University Press.

Quine, Willard van Orman. 1952. *Methods of Logic*. London: Routledge.

Quinn, Philip L. 1995. "Political Liberalisms and Their Exclusion of the Religious." *Proceedings and Addresses of the American Philosophical Association* 69 (2): 35–56.

——. 2001. "Religious Citizens Within the Limits of Public Reasons." In Quinn, Philip L. 2006. *Essays in the Philosophy of Religion*, ed. Christian B. Miller, 165–87. Oxford: Oxford University Press.

Quong, Jonathan. 2004. "The Scope of Public Reason." *Political Studies* 52 (2): 233–50.

——. 2011. *Liberalism Without Perfection*. Oxford: Oxford University Press.

——. 2013. "On the Idea of Public Reason." In *A Companion to Rawls*, ed. Jon Mandle and David A. Reidy, 265–80. Oxford: Wiley-Blackwell.

Rawls, John. 1972. *A Theory of Justice*. Cambridge, Mass.: Belknap.

——. 1980. "Kantian Constructivism in Moral Theory." *Journal of Philosophy* 77 (9): 515–72. https://doi.org/10.2307/2025790.

——. 1993 [2005]. "The Idea of Public Reason Revisited." In *Political Liberalism*, Expanded Edition (New York: Columbia University Press, 2005), 440–91.

——. 1995. "Political Liberalism: Reply to Habermas." *Journal of Philosophy* 92 (3): 132–80. https://doi.org/10.2307/2940843. Reprinted in *Political Liberalism* (New York: Columbia University Press, 1996); and in *Habermas and Rawls: Disputing the Political*, ed. James Gordon Finlayson and Fabian Freyenhagen (New York: Routledge, 2011).

——. 2001. *Collected Papers*, ed. Samuel Freeman. Cambridge, Mass.: Harvard University Press.

——. 2001. *Justice as Fairness: A Restatement*, ed. Erin Kelly. Cambridge, Mass.: President and Fellows of Harvard College.

——. 2005. *Political Liberalism*. Expanded edition. New York: Columbia University Press.

Raz, Joseph. 1990. "Facing Diversity: The Case of Epistemic Abstinence." *Philosophy & Public Affairs*" 19 (1): 3–46.

Rees, Huw Dafydd. 2018. *The Postsecular Political Philosophy of Jurgen Habermas: Translating the Sacred*. Cardiff: University of Wales Press.

Reese-Schäfer, Walter. 1994. "Sind Hoffnungen auf eine kommunikative Rationalität berechtigt?" In *Vernunft Angesichts der Umweltzerstörung*, ed. Wolfgang Zierhöfer and Dieter Steiner, 69–88. Opladen: VS Verlag für Sozialwissenschaften.

Rehg, W. 1991. "Discourse and the Moral Point of View: Deriving a Dialogical Principle of Universalization." *Inquiry: An Interdisciplinary Journal of Philosophy* 34 (1): 27–48.

——. 1994. *Insight and Solidarity*. Berkeley: University of California Press.

——. 2003. "Grasping the Force of the Better Argument: McMahon Versus Discourse Ethics." *Inquiry* 46 (1): 113–33.

Ron, Amit. 2006. "Rawls as a Critical Theorist: Reflective Equilibrium After the 'Deliberative Turn.'" *Philosophy and Social Criticism* 32 (2): 173–91.

Rosenfeld, Michael, and Andrew Arato, eds. 1996. *Habermas on Law and Democracy: Critical Exchanges*. Berkeley: University of California Press.

Rousseau, Jean-Jacques. 1964. *Oeuvres Complètes de Jean-Jacques Rousseau*. Vol. 3. Bibliothèque de la Pléiade. Paris: Gallimard.

Rummens, Stefan. 2006. "Debate: The Co-originality of Private and Public Autonomy in Deliberative Democracy." *Journal of Political Philosophy* 14 (4): 469–81.

Sandel, Michael J. 1982. *Liberalism and the Limits of Justice*. Cambridge: Cambridge University Press.

——. 1984. "The Procedural Republic and the Unencumbered Self." *Political Theory* 12 (1): 81–96. https://doi:10.1177/0090591784012001005.

Scanlon, T. M. 2003. "Rawls on Justification." In *The Cambridge Companion to Rawls*, ed. Samuel Freeman, 139–67. Cambridge: Cambridge University Press.

Scheuerman, William E. 1999. "Between Radicalism and Resignation: Democratic Theory in Habermas's *Between Facts and Norms*." In *Habermas: A Critical Reader*, ed. Peter Dews, 153–77. Oxford: Blackwell.

Sen, Amartya. 2006. *Identity and Violence: The Illusion of Destiny*. London: Allen Lane.

Sikka, Sonia. 2016. "On Translating Religious Reasons: Rawls, Habermas, and the Quest for a Neutral Public Sphere." *Review of Politics* 78 (1): 91–116.

Skinner, Quentin, Partha Dasgupta, Raymond Geuss, Melissa Lane, Peter Laslett, Onora O'Neill, W. G. Runciman, and Andrew Kuper. 2002. "Political Philosophy: The View from Cambridge." *Journal of Political Philosophy* 10 (1): 1–19. https://doi.org/10.1111/1467-9760.00140.

Skorupski, John. 2017. "Rawls, Liberalism, and Democracy." *Ethics* 128 (1): 173–98.

Specter, Matthew G. 2010. *Habermas: An Intellectual Biography*. Cambridge: Cambridge University Press.

Steinhoff, Uwe. 2009. *The Philosophy of Jürgen Habermas*. Oxford: Oxford University Press.

Stevenson, Charles L. 1979. [1944]. *Ethics and Language*. New York: AMS.

Talisse, Robert B. 2001. *On Rawls: A Liberal Theory of Justice and Justification*. Belmont, Calif.: Wadsworth/Thomson Learning.

——. 2017. "Deweyan Democracy and the Rawlsian Problematic." *Transactions of the Charles S. Peirce Society* 53 (4): 579–83.

——. 2018. "John Rawls and American Pragmatisms." In *Pragmatism, Pluralism, and the Nature of Philosophy*, ed. Scott Aikin and Robert Talisse,. New York: Routledge.

Taylor, Charles. 1982. "The Diversity of Goods." In *Utilitarianism and Beyond*, ed. Amartya Sen and Bernard Williams, 129–35. Cambridge: Cambridge University Press.

——. 1985. "Atomism." In *Philosophy and the Human Sciences*, 187–210. Vol. 2 of *Philosophical Papers*. Cambridge: Cambridge University Press.

——. 1992. *Sources of the Self*. Cambridge, Mass.: Harvard University Press.

Thompson, Janna. 1998. *Discourse and Knowledge: Defence of a Collectivist Ethics*. London: Routledge.

Usturali, Adil. 2017. "Religion in Habermas's Two-Track Political Theory." *European Legacy* 22 (50): 566–82.

Vallier, Kevin. 2011. "Against Public Reason Liberalism's Accessibility Requirement." *Journal of Moral Philosophy* 8 (3): 366–89.

Volkmer, Ingrid. 2014. *The Global Public Sphere: Public Communication in the Age of Reflective Interdependence*. Cambridge: Polity.

von Wright, Georg Henrik. 1963. *The Varieties of Goodness*. New York: Humanities.

Waldron, Jeremy. 2010. "Two-Way Translation. The Ethics of Engaging with Religious Contributions in Public Deliberation." *Mercer Law Review* 63: 845–68.

Weber, Max. 1978. *Economy and Society*, ed. Guenther Roth and Claus Wittich. Berkeley: University of California Press.

Weithman, Paul. 2002. *Religion and the Obligations of Citizenship*. Cambridge: Cambridge University Press.

——. 2010. *Why Political Liberalism? On John Rawls's Political Turn*. Oxford: Oxford University Press.

Wellmer, Albrecht. 1986. *Ethik und Dialog: Elemente des moralischen Urteils bei Kant und in der Diskursethik*. Frankfurt: Suhrkamp.

——. 1991. "Ethics and Dialogue: Elements of Moral Judgment in Kant and Discourse Ethics." In *The Persistence of Modernity: Essays on Aesthetics, Ethics and Postmodernism*, 113–231. Cambridge: Polity.

——. 1991. *The Persistence of Modernity: Essays on Aesthetics, Ethics and Postmodernism*. Cambridge: Polity.

Wolff, Jonathan. 2008. "In Front of the Curtain." *Times Literary Supplement*, March 7. http://tls.timesonline.co.uk/article/0,,25366-2650912_3,00.html.

Williams, Bernard. 2005. *In the Beginning Was the Deed: Realism and Moralism in Political Argument*, ed. Geoffrey Hawthorn. Princeton, N.J.: Princeton University Press.

Wolterstorff, Nicholas. 2013. "An Engagement with Jürgen Habermas on Postmetaphysical Philosophy, Religion, and Political Dialogue." In *Habermas and Religion*, ed. Craig Calhoun, Eduardo Mendieta, and Jonathan VanAntwerpen, 92–114. Cambridge: Polity.

Yates, Melissa. 2007. "Rawls and Habermas on Religion in the Public Sphere." *Philosophy and Social Criticism* 33 (7): 880–91.

——. 2011. "Postmetaphysical Thinking." In *Jürgen Habermas: Key Concepts*, ed. Barbara Fultner, 35–53. Durham, UK: Acumen.

Young, Iris Marion. 1987. "Impartiality and the Civic Republic." *In Feminism as Critique. Essays on the Politics of Gender in Late-Capitalist Societies*, ed. Seyla Behnabib and Drucilla Cornell. London: Polity Press.

Zurn, Christopher. 2010. "Bootstrapping Paradoxes of Constitutional Democracy." *Legal Theory* 16: 191–227.

——. 2011. "Habermas's Discourse Theory of Law." In *Jürgen Habermas: Key Concepts*, ed. Barbara Fultner, 157–76. Durham, UK: Acumen.

INDEX

Note: Habermas and Rawls are referred to as H and R throughout.

accountability, principle of, 29
abductive inference, 32
abortion, 228
Adorno, Theodor W. and Horkheimer, Max: as influences on H, 4, 250n10. *See also* critical theory
agent-relative vs. agent-neutral reasons, 37
Alexy, Robert, 30
Apel, Karl-Otto, 4, 95
Aristotle, 20
asymmetry objection. *See* public reason: and unfairness/asymmetry objection
Audi, Robert, 214, 218–219, 229
Austin, J. L., 4
Austin, John, 85
autonomy, 65, 190, 197–198; Kantian idea of, 23; moral, 99; of parties in original position, 163, 190; political, 89, 96, 99, 100–108, 167, 262n23; priority of private over public in R, 160, 169–172, 173, 191–196, 209, 265n14; R's argument for, 25. *See also* co-originality: of public and private autonomy
avoidance, R's method of, 158–159, 162, 173, 186–187, 197; H's objection to, 203–205

Baier, Kurt, 72
Baldwin, Thomas, 203–204
basic structure of society, 21, 51, 75–76, 135, 167, 196, 254n26
Baxter, Hugh, 86, 97, 229
Baynes, Kenneth, 92, 94, 97, 128, 165, 166, 182
Beitz, Charles, 165
Benhabib, Seyla, 68–74, 109. *See also* feminists and feminism
Berlin, Isaiah, 3, 193
Between Facts and Norms, 79, 93, 98–99, 155; priority of right over good in, 91; as procedural, 166; and rational reconstruction, 245; solidarity in, 106; structure of, 84–87
Böckenförde, Ernst-Wolfgang, 234–235
Brandom, Robert, 6
burdens of judgment, 114, 187, 196

Cassirer, Ernst, 1
Chambers, Simone, 74–75
Chomsky, Noam, 43
circumstances of justice, the, 19
civility, duty of, 134–135, 137, 179, 214–222, 235, 239, 268n23; as applying to political theorists, 180, 233, 244. *See also* public reason
civil society, H's conception of, 99, 104–107, 167, 224–225; and political participation, 209, 265–266n8; and H's institutional translation proviso, 230; and religious citizens, 237. *See also* public sphere
Clarke, Samuel, 1, 132
cognitive dissonance, 231–232, 238–239, 267n19, 270nn56–57
cognitivism, moral, 34–37, 38, 159, 251n25
Cohen, Joshua, 94, 97–98
communicative action, 26, 28–30, 36, 93, 175–176; meta-goods of, 65
communicative power, 104, 106–107
Communist Manifesto, The, 27
communitarianism and communitarians, 7, 45, 52, 57, 71, 132; criticisms of R, 58–61, 63–65, 67–68, 253n6, 253n14; and discourse ethics, 61–65, 253n14; and feminism, 66, 67–68, 71, 73. *See also* Sandel, Michael; Taylor, Charles
comprehensive doctrines, 111–113, 132, 178–179; as able to be reasonably rejected, 182; as affirmed by citizens, 259n21; exclusive vs. inclusive interpretations of, 118, 125–126, 215–216, 259nn19–20; and H's concept of ethical world view, 159–160, 168; metaphysical/philosophical vs. religious and moral, 179; and nonpublic reasons, 217, 259n14; and overlapping consensus, 118–119; reasonable, 114–115, 118, 122, 125–126, 130, 157–158, 160, 185
conceptions of the good, 18, 22, 92–93, 112, 130
consensus, rationally motivated, 29, 228; and ethical values, 62–63; and H's validity requirement, 37, 109; and overlapping consensus, 156, 158; and perfect procedural justice, 163; and truth, 35–36; and universalizable interests, 33
Constant, Benjamin, 169–170, 193
constructivism: H's position as non-constructivist, 32; R's conception of, 3, 23, 52, 159
co-originality, 98–99; architectonic dimension of, 101–102; historical dimension of, 100–101; of moral and civic autonomy, 99, 257n19; of private and public autonomy, 99, 101–102, 170, 191; in R, 194; socio-political dimension of, 102; of system of rights and principle of democracy, 95, 97, 99, 101
critical theory, 7; and discourse ethics, 53; H's critique of Frankfurt School, 53. *See also* Adorno, Theodor W. and Horkheimer, Max
Cronin, Ciaran, 33–34

Daniels, Norman, 24
Dawkins, Richard, 113, 238
democracy: absence of theory in R, 172, 173, 198, 245; H's principle of, 86, 90–95, 96, 167, 228, 233, 244; H's two-track conception of, 102–108, 224; and proceduralism, 165–168; representative, 99, 103, 105
difference principle, 20–21, 140, 205. *See also* two principles of justice
discourse, 28–30, 71; moral vs. ethical, 45–48, 62, 63, 68, 72–73, 91, 229–230; political, 90–91; principle of, 31, 36, 90, 93–98, 109, 163, 233, 252n29; as reflective form of communication, 29; rules of, 29–30, 31, 35, 93, 164, 194, 226, 236, 239, 251n21, 270n50, 270n55, 270n58; theory of law, 79, 84, 194
discourse ethics, 26–34, 150; and communitarianism, 61; as comprehensive doctrine, 9–10,

154–155, 175–183, 187, 204, 243–244; as descriptive not normative, 205–206, 245; development of, 45–48, 51–53, 61–62, 72–74; feminist critique of, 71–73; and justice as fairness, 49–50, 53, 54, 55; and Kant, 38–39; as normative foundation of critical theory, 53; political reading of, 74–76; as post-metaphysical, 38; as procedural not substantive, 38, 55–56, 82, 161, 163–166, 182, 204–205; and rational reconstruction, 44, 98; and R's conception of public reason, 2; as true not just reasonable, 162
Dreben, Burton, 8, 10
Durkheim, Émile, 4, 27; influence on H, 57
Dworkin, Ronald, 84–85, 95

Eberle, Christopher, 216
emotivism, 176
ethical harmonization requirement, H's, 92–93, 165, 182, 226

familial dispute, dispute between H and R as, 145, 213, 250n8, 260n2
family, 21, 70–71, 73, 254n16, 254n26
feminists and feminism: and discourse ethics, 71–73; and Kohlberg, 66–68; and R, 21, 45, 68–69, 70–71, 254n17; R's response to, 254n26. *See also* Benhabib, Seyla; Gilligan, Carol
Festinger, Leon, 238
First Amendment to the U.S. Constitution, 217–218
Fišerová, Viola, 247
Flynn, Jeffrey, 98, 166
Forst, Rainer, 97, 109, 128, 157–158, 166, 185–186, 201, 208
foundationalism, 44
Fraser, Nancy, 68
freedom of speech, 195
Freeman, Samuel, 22, 129, 188, 207
Freud, Sigmund, 238
friendship, 73, 254n16

Gaus, Gerald, 122
"generalized" vs. "concrete" other. *See* Benhabib, Seyla
Gilligan, Carol, 66–69, 74; H's response to, 68. *See also* feminists and feminism
Gledhill, James, 164, 168
Goodman, Nelson, 6, 124

harm principle, 37
Hart, H. L. A., 3, 85
Heath, Joseph, 9, 10
Hedrick, Todd, 83, 128, 140, 206
Hegel, G. W. F. and Hegelianism, 80, 254n23; and H's theory, 9, 80, 176, 249n7; and R's theory, 249n7
Heidegger, Martin, 1
Hennig, Anja, 228
heteronomy, 23
Hobbes, Thomas and Hobbesianism, 51, 80, 201
Hrabal, Bohumil, 247
Hume, David and Humeanism, 32

ideal theory, 6, 14, 82, 87
"immanent" and "transcendent" criticism, 82, 138
impartiality: and discourse principle, 97–98; in H's theory, 32–33; and ideal role taking, 39, 153; in Kantian theories, 254n19; and moral point of view, 84; moral priority of, 91; not required of reasonable persons, 113–114; and original position, 59, 147–148, 150–151. *See also* moral point of view
intuitionism, 3–4, 19, 52, 132

justice, 21, 150; concept vs. conception of, 123; congruence with the good in R, 25, 60; differences between H's and R's views, 50; global, 21, 76, 260n34; procedural, 162–163; standpoint of justice as blind to women's oppression, 70–71 justice as fairness, 19; as applying domestically not globally, 21; and categorical imperative, 24; and discourse ethics, 49–50, 53, 54, 55; H's "descriptivist" critique of, 83, 140–141, 206, 262n26; H's "external" criticism of, 82, 138–139, 140–141, 168, 189–190, 206, 263n29; H's "natural law" criticism of, 80–82, 137–138; H's "serendipity" criticism of, 82–83, 139, 140–141, 169, 200; Kantian interpretation of, 22–24; moral reading of, 75–76; as paternalistic, 205–207; as substantive not procedural, 55–56

justice-qua-morality, 33–34, 39, 47, 50, 61, 64–65, 74–75, 91; and ethical values, 150; and H's conception of society, 56–57; and H's pragmatic conception of rightness, 36; and moral motivation, 46; and political justice, 200; and solidarity, 48

Kant, Immanuel and Kantianism, 42, 58, 80, 95, 112, 117, 118, 120, 178–179, 201; categorical imperative, 22–24, 38–39, 42, 150; communitarian criticisms of, 61, 63–64, 72; and discourse ethics, 38–39, 164; feminist criticisms of, 68–69, 73, 254n19; H's criticisms of, 48, 55; H's Kantian pragmatism, 7, 40, 244; H's Kantian republicanism, 209; H's Kantian view of morality, 89; H's and R's Kantianism, 5–6; idea of autonomy, 23; interpretation of justice as fairness, 22–24, 52, 129; liberalism of, 100, 124, 132, 257n21; R's Kantian constructivism, 23

Kelsen, Hans, 4

King, Martin Luther, Jr., 239–240, 270n59

Kohlberg, Lawrence, 40, 50, 52–53, 64, 70, 74, 147, 150, 179; and discourse ethics, 40–43, 50; feminist criticisms of, 66–68, 72; H's objections to, 42–43, 48, 53; rational reconstruction in, 42

Kuper, Andrew, 3

Kymlicka, Will, 129

Laden, A. S., 25–26, 134

Lafont, Cristina, 237

Larmore, Charles, 95, 97, 109, 111, 136, 166, 169, 177, 182, 197, 204, 208

law: form of, 88, 93–95, 96, 97–98, 108; in H, 84–95, 96–98, 101–103, 105–107, 183, 198, 208; legitimacy of, 7–8, 85, 89–93, 95–98, 225–226, 256n10; and morality, 74, 89, 90–91, 95; in R, 22; and social integration, 47–48, 81–82, 85, 88–89, 92, 107–108, 235; and tension between facticity and validity, 84–86, 87

legal positivism, 85

legitimacy, 7–8, 51, 250n11, 259n26; and ethical harmonization requirement, 165; and H's account of modernization, 181; H's conception of, 8, 89–98, 224–226, 228, 236; H's conception as political, 109, 166, 177, 208; in R, 80–82, 117, 122–123, 130–134, 215, 218; R's objections to H's account of, 178, 182; and stability, 122–123

Leibniz, Gottfried Wilhelm, 1

Lessing, Gotthold Ephraim, 158

liberalism, 7, 100–101, 191, 209; conception of self, 57–61; conception of society, 58–61, 69; feminist critique of, 68–69

liberty principle and basic liberties, 20–21, 163, 191–196. *See also* two principles of justice

lifeworld, 55, 87, 100, 107, 229

Lister, Andrew, 178–179

Locke, John, 51, 80

Luhmann, Niklas, 4, 90

MacIntyre, Alasdair, 58

Marshall, T. H., 166

Marx, Karl and Marxism, 27, 70, 238, 254n22; Marxist criticisms of H, 7

Maus, Ingeborg, 101–102

McCarthy, Thomas, 1, 14, 38, 62, 87

McMahon, Christopher, 9, 151–155, 186

Mead, G. H., 6, 33, 70; and discourse ethics, 39

Michelman, Frank, 171
Mill, John Stuart and Millianism, 4, 117, 118, 120, 124, 132
modernity and modernization, 27–28, 87–89, 181, 231268–269n30; and fact of reasonable pluralism, 111; and morality, 31–32, 46–48, 49, 64–65, 89, 164, 166; and reflexivity, 87, 230–231; and secularization, 176–177; and social integration, 92
Moral Consciousness and Communicative Action, 54, 161, 249n4
moral motivation, 49, 64, 68, 89, 107
moral permissibility constraint, 91–92, 98, 107–108, 165, 167, 177, 182
moral point of view: and discourse, 32–33; feminist critique of, 67–73; H's conception of, 47, 52–53, 84, 108, 205–206, 208; and original position and principle (U), 22, 38, 147, 200; philosophy's task to construct, 55, 73, 162, 163, 205, 245. *See also* impartiality
moral powers, 18, 20, 21–22, 113, 149, 191, 192; as of equal standing, 20
moral psychology, R's, 203–204
moral rightness: its priority over ethics, 47, 62, 64, 73, 88, 91–92, 150; as specification of generic concept of validity, 35, 37; and truth, 34–37, 46, 47, 156, 159, 252n26
Morgenbesser, Sidney, 2, 4
mutual recognition, 57, 164

naturalism, 176
natural law, 79–80, 95, 100, 132, 166, 167, 177, 191, 265n6
neutrality, 93, 130, 168, 235–236
Newton, Isaac, 1
Nietzsche, Friedrich, 238
Nussbaum, Martha, 151

O'Neill, Onora, 3, 209
original position, 17–20; and categorical imperative, 23, 150; as embodying democratic ideal, 163, 167, 192–193; and four-stage sequence, 22, 150–151, 171–172, 187–188, 189, 192, 194; H's criticisms of, 55–58, 146–155, 170–171, 172–173; as implying atomistic social ontology, 51, 56–61; and Kant's conception of autonomy, 23; and Kohlberg's stage six, 42, 52; as moral point of view, 52, 265n3; mutual disinterestedness of parties, 18, 23, 54, 57, 59, 148; in political liberalism, 126, 156; as pure procedural justice, 163; rationality of choosers in, 19, 57, 59, 114, 148, 149, 190; and reflective equilibrium, 25
overlapping consensus, 82, 118–120, 184, 258n13, 264nn7–8; and consensus in discourse ethics, 156, 158; difference between overlap and consensus, 120–121, 126–128; as failing H's validity requirement, 139, 157–158, 185, 201; H's criticisms of, 83, 155–158, 173; and *modus vivendi*, 121–123, 158

Parsons, Talcott, 4, 85
Peirce, Charles Sanders, 4, 6
perfectionism, 19
performative contradiction, 30
Perry, Michael J., 219
Peters, Bernhard, 4, 103
philosophy and philosophers, H's view of role of, 44–45, 55–56, 161, 180–181, 205, 206–207
Piaget, Jean, 43
political conception of justice, 113, 117–121, 221; as complete, 136, 266n5; as freestanding, 125–127, 133, 156–158, 175, 183–185, 188–189, 261n14; as including ideas of the good, 129–130; justice as fairness one political conception among others, 126, 128; as module, 125, 127, 169, 185, 215–216, 220–221; as moral conception, 122, 124, 133, 141, 157, 169, 200, 205

political, domain of the: H's conception of, 109; H's criticisms of R's conception of, 168–169, 173, 196–198, 246; and overlapping consensus, 124; R's conception of, 133, 179, 183
political liberalism, 2, 6, 10, 110–141; changes from *A Theory of Justice*, 49–50, 75, 113, 115–116, 123–124, 137, 147, 172, 175, 190, 203, 253n6, 258n4; H's critique of, 83–84; as ideal theory, 14; legitimacy in, 8; political not metaphysical, 117, 124, 133, 178; quietism in, 6, 159, 176, 180, 187, 242; as reasonable rather than true, 113, 156–157, 158–159; two-stage justification of, 80, 82–83, 126–128, 137–138, 140–141, 156, 183
popular sovereignty. *See* autonomy: political
post-metaphysical thinking, 38, 43–44, 65, 93, 161, 177, 204, 265n5, 269n31
post-secular society, 229–232, 237. *See also* religion; secular and secularism
pragmatism, 6; H and, 6–7; norm of correctness, 35; R and, 6; theory of meaning in H, 28–30, 35–36; theory of rightness in H, 36; theory of truth in H, 35–36, 178
precipitate judgment, the, 5, 7, 8, 9, 12, 14, 155
Price, Richard, 132
primary goods, 18, 19, 21–22, 149
priority of the right over the good, 62, 64, 73, 88, 91–92; H's and R's differing conceptions of, 129; in political liberalism, 129–130
Pritchard, H. A., 3
proviso: difference between R's and H's, 227–228, 230, 233–234; H's institutional translation proviso, 214, 223, 225–226, 230, 233, 237, 240, 269n33; R's, 214, 217, 239–240, 270–271n60
public reason, 122; content of, 135–136, 195; differences between H's and R's conceptions, 235, 240–242; H's conception of, 224, 227–235, 240–242, 245, 265–266n8, 268n28; R's conception of, 131, 133–134, 167, 173, 180, 190, 195–196, 201–202, 215, 217–218, 239–240; R's failure to establish priority of, 207–208; scope of, 134–135, 169, 173, 179, 196–198, 222, 268n27; and split-identity objection, 219, 220–222, 229, 231–233; and unfairness/asymmetry objection, 214, 219–220, 222–223, 229, 232–233, 235–239, 267–268nn19–20
public sphere, 105; formal vs. informal, 103–104, 224–225. *See also* civil society, H's conception of
Putnam, Hilary, 6, 62

Quine, W. v. O., 6, 120, 124
Quong, Jonathan, 127–128, 136, 156, 179, 184, 195–196, 197

rational reconstruction, 4, 6, 43–44, 237–238, 245, 249n6; advantages of approach, 80–82; H as violating method of, 98; and principle (D), 233; and principle of democracy, 95, 233; and principle (U), 233
realism, moral, 34, 37, 251n24
realism, political (political theory), 133
reasonableness, 113–115, 149, 172, 190, 200, 258nn5–6; dilemma of, 199–202; and distinction between overlap and consensus, 120–121; H's objections to R's conception, 158–160; as moral concept, 113–114; and priority of public reasons, 207–208; and toleration 195–196
reasonable pluralism, fact of, 6, 8, 111–112, 115–117, 132–133, 257n1; in philosophy as well as culture, 123–124. *See also* value pluralism
reflective equilibrium, 6, 24–25, 188, 192, 261n17; H's criticisms of, 54–55; narrow vs. wide, 25, 250n7; and original position, 25
reflexivity, 42, 121, 223; and modernization, 87, 230–231
Rehg, William, 65, 75

religion, 112–113, 178–179; and conceptions of the good, 93; freedom of, 119–120, 195, 226, 236, 267n19; and modernization, 49, 88, 100, 177–178, 181; and public reason, 213–214, 217–242, 268n22; and reasonableness, 115, 117; religious reasons, 216, 229; separation of church and state, 214, 217–218, 225. *See also* post-secular society; secular and secularism
republicanism, 100–101, 104, 166, 209
rights: H's system of, 95–102, 108, 109, 162, 166, 167, 244, 256n16; human; 47, 56, 100, 101, 164, 183, 253n4, 262n19
Rorty, Richard, 6
Ross, W. D., 4, 132
Rousseau, Jean-Jacques, 100, 103, 209, 257nn20–21
Rummens, Stefan, 97, 166

Sandel, Michael, 129, 132; criticisms of Rawls, 58–61, 68, 74. *See also* communitarianism and communitarians
Scanlon, T. M., 24, 196–197
Searle, John, 4
secular and secularism, 268n22; H's theory as depending on secular world view, 177–178, 181; and political agnosticism, 231, 236–239, 241, 269n31, 270n54; principle of secular rationale, 218; secularists, 113, 231, 237–239, 241, 269n35, 269–270n44; secular justifications, 218–220, 222–223, 225–233, 235–242, 266n7, 267n14, 268n27; secularization, 49, 100, 177, 231, 253n10, 256n9, 268n30. *See also* post-secular society; religion
Sidgwick, Henry, 4, 132
sincerity, principle of, 29
skepticism: moral, 32, 164
social bases of self-respect, 21
social contract theories, 26, 40–41, 51, 56–57, 75, 80, 100
social order, problem of, 27, 47–48, 81, 85, 87–88
solidarity, 48–49, 56–57, 61, 73, 91–92, 100; and moral motivation, 49, 164; as source of integration, 106–108
speech acts, 28–29
split-identity objection. *See* public reason: and split-identity objection
stability, 160; as central question of political liberalism, 116–117; and moral psychology, 203–204; in R's two-stage justification, 80, 126–127, 138, 156–157; for the right reasons, 8, 122, 124, 130–132, 180, 185, 203–204, 250n11; and validity, 29

Taylor, Charles, 58, 61–65, 68, 72
Theory of Communicative Action, The, 26, 28, 39, 46, 49, 53, 106, 208
Theory of Justice, A, 52, 54, 80, 123, 133; as depending on comprehensive doctrine, 115–116, 137; main ideas of, 17, 20, 129, 149; as political not moral theory, 21, 50, 52; R's later view of, 49–50, 75, 115–116; "standard blueprint" for interpretation of, 25–26, 61, 138, 147–148, 163, 167, 171, 189; structure of, 57, 59; use of "reasonable" in, 113
toleration, 158, 232
truth: compared with moral rightness, 34–37, 46, 47, 159; as specification of generic concept of validity, 35, 37. *See also* pragmatism: theory of truth in H
two principles of justice, 20–21, 52, 54, 140, 149–150, 171, 187–190, 206; lexical ordering of, 20; as standards of social criticism, 138, 190, 254n26. *See also* difference principle, liberty principle and basic liberties

understanding: action oriented toward, 29, 95; as telos of human speech, 28
unfairness objection. *See* public reason: and unfairness/asymmetry objection
universalizable interests, 33–34, 38–39, 56, 63, 151–153; and overlapping consensus, 83. *See also* universalization (U), principle of

universalization (U), principle of, 30–33, 36, 98; and categorical imperative, 38, 44–45; demandingness of, 47; derivation of, 54–55, 94; as dialogical not monological, 38, 42–43, 45, 151–154, 260n7; and distinction between ethics and morality, 62; as ethnocentric, 62; and H's political theory, 165; as implicit in everyday moral discourse, 44–45, 56, 233; as norm-selection procedure, 38; as not in need of justification, 251n14; and original position, 2, 9, 45, 147, 151–155, 165, 261n9; as sensitive to particularity, 71–72. *See also* universalizable interests

utilitarianism, 42, 52, 61, 112

validity: authenticity as validity claim, 46, 226, 230; claims, 28–29, 34–37, 46; and facticity, 81–82, 84–87, 90, 256n10; generic concept of, 35–36, 37; H's validity requirement, 37, 109, 139, 157–158, 201–202, 256n13, 264n8; and rationally motivated consensus, 37, 156; rightness as validity claim, 36–37, 156, 159; truth as validity claim, 35–36, 156, 159, 162, 230

Vallier, Kevin, 228

value pluralism, 63, 82, 88, 101, 111, 257n2. *See also* reasonable pluralism, fact of

veil of ignorance, 18–19, 54, 59, 70, 148, 149, 252n35, 255n30

Weber, Max, 4, 70, 85, 117, 122–123, 131, 229, 237, 254n22, 259n17, 259n26

Weithman, Paul, 214, 218–219, 230

well-ordered society, 115–116, 258n9

Wolff, Jonathan, 3

Wolterstorff, Nicholas, 204, 214, 218–220, 229, 230, 231–233

Young, Iris Marion, 68

Zurn, Christopher, 108